AI Ethics and Higher Education

Good Practice and Guidance for Educators,

Learners, and Institutions

AI Ethics and Higher Education

Good Practice and Guidance for Educators,

Learners, and Institutions

Erin Green / Divya Singh / Roland Chia (Eds.)

Globethics.net Education Ethics No. 10

Globethics.net Education Ethics Series

Director: Prof. Dr Obiora Ike, Executive Director of Globethics.net in Geneva and Professor of Ethics at the Godfrey Okoye University Enugu/Nigeria.
Series Editors: Prof. Dr Divya Singh, Director of Globethics.net Southern Africa, Chief Academic Officer at Stadio Holdings, South Africa.
Prof. Dr Amélé Ékué, Academic Dean of Globethics.net

Globethics.net Education Ethics 10
Erin Green / Divya Singh / Roland Chia (Eds.), *AI Ethics and Higher Education Good Practice and Guidance for Educators, Learners, and Institutions*
Geneva: Globethics.net, 2022
ISBN 978-2-88931-442-3 (online version)
ISBN 978-2-88931-443-0 (print version)
© 2022 Globethics.net

Managing Editor: Dr Ignace Haaz
Assistant Editor: Jakob W. Bühlmann Quero

Globethics.net International Secretariat
150 route de Ferney
1211 Geneva 2, Switzerland
Website: *www.globethics.net/publications*
Email: *publications@globethics.net*

All web links in this text have been verified as of March 2022.

TABLE OF CONTENTS

ACKNOWLEDGMENTS

We are grateful to the organisation PAX (Netherlands) and its authors for their permission to republish the chapters "Conflicted Intelligence" and "Risky Research" originally published as a complete report *Conflicted Intelligence*. The chapter "AI in Student Recruitment and Selection" was originally published in the *South African Qualifications Authority Bulletin* in 2021 and is republished here with permission of the SAQAB and the authors. A version of "Fear of Using AI in Virtual Proctoring?" is present on the SmarterServices corporate blog and is reproduced here with permission of its author.

Dr Erin Green
Dr Divya Singh
Dr Roland Chia
Editors

PREFACE

Welcome to *AI Ethics and Higher Education*, a collection of essays and collage of responses to one of the most compelling developments in both education and ethics in our lifetimes. We hope that the necessity of this volume is already evident to you, its readers, or at least intriguing enough to savour many of the thoughtful, eclectic, and challenging chapters herein. The book you see now emerges from the desire of the editors to contribute to the ever-growing Globethics.net competencies in ethics education and to broader, global debates about how AI will transform various facets of our lives, not the least of which is higher education.

To describe more fully why and how this volume came to be, we turn to three fundamental questions: Why artificial intelligence? Why ethics? And why higher education?

First, artificial intelligence. It seems that AI will be a defining feature of the *Zeitgeist* of the decade in which we find ourselves. What first was a niche field, a somewhat esoteric but enticing challenge for mathematicians and computer programmers in the 1950s, is now an all-pervasive cultural phenomenon. While AI has always been interdisciplinary in character, the connections between AI and other areas of research and methodologies is shifting. Researchers are increasingly attuned to the interplay between AI and the political, social, and cultural structures that give rise to it, use it, and critique it. It is here in this rich ground for the cross-pollination of technology and society that this volume rests.

We have brought together contributions from researchers who understand well both the technical aspects of AI and related digital technologies, but also draw on their expertise as ethicists, educators, philosophers, lawyers, theologians, and more. Through this diversity of perspectives, the impact of AI on our lives will be much more fully understood. AI is undeniably also about power, with much at stake in terms of political, financial, social, and even military dominance. Both narrowly as a tool and broadly as a technological phenomenon, AI is far too precious a resource to be left to developers alone. We hope that in reading these chapters, you will also be inspired to take up AI in your own research and ethical reflection.

Second, ethics. A parallel phenomenon to the rise AI is the rise of so-called AI ethics discourse. This increasingly diverse community has served an important Greek chorus function, commenting in plain and often critical terms on the developments from within corporate and academic research communities. This big and loosely defined AI ethics community provides necessary analysis of AI along intersectional lines including race, disability, gender, Indigenous rights, sexuality, social and economic class, ecological impact and more. Together, they try to hold technological developers and legislators accountable to the people they are intended to serve, especially those who are most at risk for social exclusion, oppression, and even violence from AI and related technologies.

A difficulty, though, with such discourse is its co-option of ethics without significant appreciation for the traditions and methodologies of ethics itself. There are, of course, exceptions. But the burgeoning of AI ethics has been accompanied with the flourishing of self-proclaimed ethicists with little or no training in ethics at all. In this volume we offer a corrective to this through the appreciation of the traditions of ethics, drawing on ethics as an academic discipline in its own right, and claiming epistemic humility when we are not equipped to make ethical judgements or analysis.

Finally, higher education. Globethics.net publishes resources but is not just a publisher. The heart of the network is to embed ethics in higher education, by connecting, teaching, provided open-access resources, and training. By equipping all learners and teachers with foundational skills in ethics, we can hope for positive social change through the strengthening of our collective ethical reasoning. In imbuing all topics with ethical analysis, we hope to contribute to more sustainable, just, and peaceful societies. Places of higher education are essential spaces for the formation of these skills, which makes access to quality and timely resources all the more imperative. We, therefore, humbly, submit this volume to this network, this global community of ethicists and ethics-driven students, teachers, and researchers. We hope you find it fitting fuel for your own reflection on artificial intelligence and a worthy contribution to global discourse in this area.

Dr Erin Green
Dr Divya Singh
Dr Roland Chia
Editors

PART 1

GUIDELINES AND FOUNDATIONAL THINKING

ETHICAL DILEMMAS
AND THE REGULATION OF AI

Peng Hwa Ang

Introduction

Any technology that promises to be as pervasive in society as artificial intelligence (AI) needs some form of regulation through hard law, soft law, the market, social norm, or architecture.[1] These modes of regulation should not be thought of as merely restrictive. For new technologies particularly, many of the laws in fact will be of an enabling nature so as to create an enabling environment for the technology when it disrupts the status quo.

For new technologies, it is important to let the technology mature a little before regulating. Unless of course there is obvious harm from non-regulation. The case of the Utah Digital Signature Act is a good example of trying to keep pace with technology; within a few years of the passage of the law, it was obvious that the law had been overtaken by new technology.[2]

With new technologies such as AI therefore, there are good reasons to avoid hard law but to use soft law, which includes ethics. As will be

---

[1] Lessig, Lawrence. *Code and Other Laws of Cyberspace*, New York: Basic Books, Second 2006 ed. version 2.0, original ed. 1999; https://lessig.org/product/codev2.

[2] Curry, Stephanie. "Washington's electronic signature act: an anachronism in the new millennium," in: *Washington Law Review*, 88 (2), 2013, 559–590.

argued in this paper, AI does throw up issues for which the more fundamental question is whether the issues should be considered as ethical issues to be deliberated upon. The benefits are immediate and clear; the harms are possible but not clear and often unknown. This leads to the so-called *Collingridge dilemma*, which can be defined as following two sets of conditions also named "double-blind", related to the information and the implementation or control.

The social consequences of a technology cannot be predicted early in the life of the technology, which is an information issue. By the time undesirable consequences are discovered, however, the technology is often so much part of the whole economic and social fabric that its control is extremely difficult. This is the dilemma of control. When change is easy, the need for it cannot be foreseen; when the need for change is apparent, change has become expensive, difficult and time consuming.[3]

The Collingridge dilemma suggests that because of the potential pervasiveness of AI it is essential to introduce ethics and soft law. Otherwise, when changes are necessary, it will be wrenching.

What is AI

AI arises from the use of large datasets to pick out patterns that may be applied to similar situations. These patterns are the rules that form the algorithms. Ethical issues can arise around the collection and use of the datasets or the development and disclosure of the algorithms.

A good algorithm requires a large dataset, which is not trivial to gather. Algorithms that are developed using less than optimal numbers can lead to bias and sometimes just plain wrong results. Where there is bias, often the cause is the lack of data.

---

[3] Collingridge, David. *The Social Control of Technology*, London: Frances Pinter, 1980, 11.

To minimise bias, programmers may use *synthetic data,* which is made up data. Or, as is frequently the case, write the rules for the algorithm instead of allowing the computer to do all the work. The more the rules are created by a human, the easier it is to understand the workings of the algorithm.

But in deep learning, where the computer programme is allowed to generate its own rules, there is the *blackbox phenomenon* of AI. Thus, for example, the champion-beating AlphaGo Zero programme developed novel strategies that Go masters are trying out.[4] The strategies were developed entirely by the computer. How the dataset of previous Go games led the programme to come up with novel strategies is unknown. There is an element of unpredictability in deep learning in AI. This fact of unknown rules dictating human actions poses an ethical issue that many principles on the topic aim to address.

General Ethical Principles in AI

What do general ethical guidelines for AI address?

First, it should be noted there are many ethical guidelines around AI and at different levels of abstraction. It is always possible to agree upon ethical guidelines at a high level of abstraction. Disagreement lies in the details of implementation.

Table 1 below contrasts three ethical guidelines from a regional grouping, a national commission, and an international association. The guidelines were compiled by Köbis and Mehner and rearranged by this author to show commonality.[5] And to be sure, there are many areas of

---

[4] Chan, Dawn. "The AI That Has Nothing to Learn From Humans", *The Atlantic,* 20 October 2017, https://www.theatlantic.com/technology/archive/2017/10/alphago-zero-the-ai-that-taught-itself-go/543450/

[5] Köbis, Laura and Mehner, Caroline. "Ethical questions raised by AI-supported mentoring in higher education", in *Frontiers in Artificial Intelligence.* Vol. 4, 30 April 2021. https://doi.org/10.3389/frai.2021.624050.

commonality. Countering the *blackbox* phenomenon through of values of transparency and accountability is a common aim of AI codes of ethics; privacy and security are also common values in such codes.

Table 1, however, shows less commonality than might be expected. While it may be argued that about half of elements in each of the set of guidelines are shared by another set, no element in all three guidelines is shared across all three.

Table 1: Comparison of Data and AI Ethics[6]

Ethics Guidelines for Trustworthy Artificial Intelligence by the European Commission	German Commission on Data Ethics	IEEE Global Initiative on Ethics of Autonomous and Intelligent Systems
2. Technical Robustness and Safety	4. Security	
3. Privacy and Data Governance	3. Privacy	
4. Transparency		5. Transparency
5. Diversity, non-discrimination and fairness	6. Justice and Solidarity	
6. Societal and environmental wellbeing		2. Wellbeing
7. Accountability		6. Accountability
	1. Human Dignity	1. Human Rights
	2. Self-determination	
	5. Democracy	
	7. Sustainability	
1. Human Agency and Oversight		3. Data Agency
		4. Effectiveness
		7. Awareness of Misuse
		8. Competence

Note: The numbering reflects the rank order in the respective set of guidelines.

---

[6] Sources for table: "The Ethics Guidelines for Trustworthy Artificial Intelligence" by the European Commission (*Ethics guidelines for trustworthy AI*, 2019); report by the German Commission on Data Ethics (German Data Commission, 2019); IEEE publication on "Ethically Aligned Design" (IEEE, 2017). Cited by Köbis & Mehner, 2021.

The lower-than-expected commonality casts a spotlight on the approaches adopted and the so-called problems the codes are expected to solve. The EU guidelines adopt a more political frame, addressing fundamental rights and data and *data governance*, which are rights in many European countries. The German Commission on Data Ethics covers general rights and principles on AI and aligns those principles, especially data processing, in algorithmic systems.[7] The German guidelines include *democracy*, which raises the question as to the possible impact of news then of Russian hacking into US elections.[8] The IEEE Global Initiative on Ethics of Autonomous and Intelligent Systems, updated in 2019, adopts are more practical view covering such aspects as *effectiveness*, *competence*, and *knowledge*. The IEEE approach aligns with its members being engineers who have to implement the AI programmes.

Interestingly, Köbis and Mehner did not cite the EU's more abstract ethical principles in the same 2019 report.[9] These principles are: respect for human autonomy, prevention of harm, fairness, explicability. These are higher levels of abstraction of the ethical principles and could be used to cover many of the more specific elements in guidelines that are more geared towards being implemented. But the closer towards applications a set of ethical guidelines is expected to be, the greater the tension and controversy. To its credit, the EU recognised that even among its four high-level principles, there can be tension and the path to resolution is to look at the specifics of the case that posed the tension.

Conceptually, it should be possible to have large swathes of overlap among ethical guidelines at a high level of abstraction. That there is

---

[7] Ibid.

[8] Mayer, Jane. "How Russia helped swing the election for Trump," *New Yorker*, 24 September 2018. https://www.newyorker.com/magazine/2018/10/01/how-russia-helped-to-swing-the-election-for-trump.

[9] Köbis and Mehner.

much less than one might expect suggests that the so-called problems AI ethical codes are intended to solve are not yet agreed upon. It also suggests divergence in the codes as one comes down to specific areas of implementation of AI.

AI in Higher Education

AI is a fast-moving field. At the time of writing, AI had often been implemented in higher education in three areas:

- institutional support,
- student support, and
- instructional support[10]

By institutional support is meant the marketing of the university to potential students, admission and enrolment, and resource and curricular planning.[11]

Student support refers to guidance of student in such areas as financial aid and early warning of academic failure.[12] Georgia State University is an exemplar of such predictive analytics to identify students who might not graduate. Six years after the effort was rolled out, the university had increased the graduation rate from 48% in 2011 to 55% in 2018. To be sure, there were also offline measures such as locating the student advising office to be more accessible and increasing

---

[10] Zeide, Elana. "Artificial Intelligence in Higher Education: Applications, Promise and Perils, and Ethical Questions," in *EduCause Review*, 26 August 2019. https://er.educause.edu/articles/2019/8/artificial-intelligence-in-higher-education-applications-promise-and-perils-and-ethical-questions

[11] Ibid.

[12] Ibid.

student loans. Nevertheless, AI was recognised one of the critical elements in the mix of efforts that successfully raised graduation rates.[13]

Instructional support refers to such matters as learning analytics, tracking student progress, plagiarism detection.[14] Learning analytics and tracking student progress are good examples of possible use of advance statistics. The most significant ethical issues would be personal and data privacy. In many countries, such personal data would have to be secured and protected under privacy law. The use of laws to protect personal and data privacy means that the ethical imperative was now a legal one.

In the United Kingdom, McGraw Hill, Microsoft Corporation, Nord Anglia Education, and Pearson PLC came together in 2018 to launch the Institute for Ethical AI in Education at the University of Buckingham. In March 2021, after two-and-a-half years of widespread consultation culminating in a global conference of 200 attendees in 2020, an Ethical Framework for AI in Education was rolled out. The framework, tabulated in Table 2 below, was intended to guide educators in using AI teaching tools safely and securely.

Table 2: Ethical Framework for AI in Education[15]

- AI should be used to achieve well-defined educational goals based on strong societal, educational or scientific evidence that is for the benefit of learners.
- AI should be used to assess and recognise a broader range of learners' aptitudes.
- AI should boost institutions' capacity while respecting human relationships.
- AI systems should promote equity between different groups of

---

[13] Hefling, Kimberley. "The 'Moneyball' solution for higher education," *Politico,* 1 June 2019. https://www.politico.com/agenda/story/2019/01/16/tracking-student-data-graduation-000868/

[14] Zeide, op. cit.

[15] Source for table: Institute for Ethical AI in Education, 2021

> learners and not discriminate against any group of learners.
> - AI should be used to increase the control learners have over their learning and development.
> - A balance should be struck between privacy and the legitimate use of data to drive well-defined and desired academic goals
> - Humans are ultimately responsible for educational outcomes and should therefore have an appropriate level of oversight of how AI systems operate.
> - Learners and educators should have a reasonable understanding of AI and its implications.
> - AI resources should be designed by people who understand the impact of these resources

In the final report, these broad guidelines are supplemented with checklists to guide decisions. Such guidelines with checklists work best when the environment is familiar and the outcome can be predictable. But they do not address a fundamental problem: should AI be deployed at all?

That question is being faced by AI researchers who have to be more aware of ethical issues in their research; papers may be rejected at conferences if the AI may be misused or cause social harm. One researcher, Joe Redmon, received more than 25,000 citations for three papers on visual recognition using AI he wrote as a graduate student, has stopped his work in that space. The reason: he was not comfortable that his work was being used for surveillance.[16]

To summarise thus far: the *high-level* guidelines on AI ethics tend to be abstract. Because they come from differing perspectives, they may not even agree on the most important issues to address. Even the sector specific guidelines from the Institute of for Ethical AI in Education may

---

[16] Huston, Matthew. "Who Should Stop Unethical AI?" *New Yorker*, 15 February 2021. https://www.newyorker.com/tech/annals-of-technology/who-should-stop-unethical-ai.

not address some significant issues such as whether it is ethical to deploy AI in a particular application.

How should one ethically approach the question as to whether AI should be deployed for a particular function?

The True Ethical Dilemma

This author suggests using ethical principles to address particular issues, rather than looking to develop a sweeping rule.

To narrow the scope for consideration, this author suggests first considering the following framework of ethical rights and wrongs. Table 3 compares ethical rights and wrongs. Where the options are clearly wrong (1) or clearly (2), one may should decide to avoid the wrong and choose the right. Of course there may be a price to pay for choosing but it just goes to show the cost of being ethical.

When the options are not clear (4), it is most difficult to decide. Therefore, it is best to get to the sweet spot of the true ethical dilemma (3), which is the case of right vs right.

Table 3: Ethical Rights and Wrongs

1.	Clear ethical wrongs	The options are ethically wrong.
2.	Clear ethical answers	There is a clear ethically right answer but it cost more time and effort.
3.	True ethical dilemma	There are two options and they are both right. This is discussed in more detail below
4.	Uncertain ethicality	Whether the options are ethically right is uncertain.

This definition of right vs right being a true ethical dilemma was proposed by ethicist Rushworth Kidder who contrasted it with a moral temptation, which is a case of right versus wrong.[17] In this framing, lying because one is under threat of being fired is a moral temptation, not an ethical dilemma. In the work environment, there are many opportunities and rewards to relabel such moral temptations as ethical dilemmas.

The framing of two rights is critical as it sharpens the focus on the two values that are in conflict. Framing the issue as a true ethical dilemma suggests its own solution: have a hierarchy of values.

Thus the ethics panels in AI conferences would be right to reject submissions of research that have been done unthinkingly such that the output could be used in socially harmful ways.

Ethical Principles for Solutions

Weeding out the cases of moral temptations and scoping down the cases to true ethical dilemmas, what principles should one use in deciding whether a course of action is ethical?

The most obvious ethical principle is utilitarianism—the maximum benefit for the maximum number of people. Utilitarianism is a consequentialist ethical code: it assumes a known outcome. But this is not a good choice when the impact of technology is uncertain.

The Kantian approach of trying to develop a rule for as many situations as possible similarly runs up against the uncertainty in the future with the application of AI.

In this writer's view the most appropriate solution is Aristotle's Golden Mean. Typically, this is misunderstood to be a path of compromise or trade-off, a middle path of bravery between recklessness and cowardice. Aristotle himself recognised that it was not always

---

[17] Kidder, Rushworth, *How Good People Make Tough Choices, Resolving the Dilemmas of Ethical Living*, rev. edition, New York: HarperCollins, 2009.

possible to have a middle-class society; and in a true ethical dilemma, what is a middle path?

A better conception of the Golden Mean is as a creative solution. That is, can one come up with a solution that accommodates both ends of the dilemma as far as possible? The Golden Mean is a mean to the extent that it sits in the middle between the dilemma but satisfies both conflicting goals to a great extent. In an ideal case, it would be possible to come up with a creative and ethical solution that addresses the dilemma without sacrificing either option.

Ethics: At the Application and Social Levels

This means looking at the specifics of each case. In the case of a start-up this author is familiar with, the team had developed an essay-writing application aimed at elementary and secondary school students. The main benefit was to help students generate ideas to write, get organised, and write a more polished piece. The question was whether the submission should be graded. The advantage of a grade is obvious – parents can use that to monitor the progress of students; it was also a way to gamify the application. After much deliberation, however, the team decided not to develop that feature. That is, there would be comments and suggestions for improvements but no grade. The main reason was that the system may be gamed. It would give users a false sense of security. It is a teacher using the application who would award the grade.

What ethical guideline might have helped arrive at that decision?

In that case, the closest would be those mentioning possible harm. But this is not obvious. As this paper was being finished, the Ministry of

Education in Singapore appeared to be heading towards using *automated marking* for *English language assignments*.[18]

With AI, it would appear that one should take a broader sweep of what might be considered ethical. An example is that of possible labour displacement. AI's increasingly sophisticated capabilities means that it can even replace some of the work done by professionals such as in drafting contracts or examining medical scans. Is the displacement of labour an ethical issue?

When this author raised it with students, typically, most of the class would say no. The students' main objection was that defining it as an ethical issue would mean stifling all labour-saving innovation.

But after some discussion, many change their minds.

Defining the displacement of labour as an ethical issue does not mean that allowing displacement is unethical. Rather, the question becomes: how can the possible harm from such displacement be minimised. The aim of ethics is not just to avoid harm but to encourage *eudaimonia*, human flourishing . The goal of ethics is not merely to make a morally right decision. It is to have a wiser and happier life, a life worth living.

At the end of it all then, the problems caused by AI, or any innovation for that matter, should not lead merely to a more productive company. It must make society wiser and happier. When posed in this manner, the response to the issue is unanimous: unemployment caused by AI is most certainly an ethical issue. At the end of the class, when I poll the class again, a number would have switched to consider this to be an ethical issue.

---

[18] Ng, Wei Kai. "Upper primary, secondary students to get instant feedback on English assignments with new AI system," *The Straits Times*, 18 August 2021.

Conclusion

One of the findings of research into training in ethics is that such training does not necessarily make a person or an organisation more ethical. Rather, they sensitise the person or organisation to ethical issues. That is, they become more aware that there are potential pitfalls. This is not just the matter of having more power attracting more responsibilities. Rather it is that it is because AI has the power to transform so much of our lives, we should be more aware to be ethically responsible.

AI GUIDELINES

EXPLORING POINTS OF CONVERGENCE BETWEEN FAITH-BASED AND SECULAR STATEMENTS

Ezekiel Kwetchi Takam

In June 2019, the article "Artificial Intelligence: The Global Landscape of Ethics Guideline" was published.[19] This influential article set out to analyse points of convergence among different ethical guidelines on artificial intelligence (AI) produced over the last five years. To accomplish this, the authors used a database of 84 ethical guidelines published by private companies, government agencies, academic and research institutions, intergovernmental organisations, science foundations, federations of worker unions and political parties. The study showed a global convergence around five ethical principles: transparency, justice and fairness, non-maleficence, responsibility, and privacy. These principles are also found in two faith-based ethical guidelines: *The Rome Call for AI Ethics* (hereafter referred to as the Rome Call), published by The Pontifical Academy of Life, and *Artificial Intelligence: An Evangelical Statement of Principles* (hereafter referred to as the Baptist Statement), published by the Southern Baptist Convention[20].

---

[19] Jobin, Anne, Ienca, Marcello and Vayena, Effy, "Artificial Intelligence: Global Landscape of Ethics Guidelines," *Nature Machine Intelligence*, 1(2019), 389-399. https://arxiv.org/ftp/arxiv/papers/1906/1906.11668.pdf

[20] "Rome Call for AI Ethics," https://www.romecall.org; The Southern Baptist Ethics & Religious Liberty Commission (ERLC), 2019, "Artificial Intelligence:

In this chapter, we will highlight the five convergent principles in these two faith-based ethical guidelines. This exercise is relevant for two reasons. On the one hand, it shows through its comparative approach that there are substantial and unanimous ethical points in the existing ethical guidelines, whatever the nature of the producing entities (confessional or non-confessional). On the other hand, the above-mentioned converging principles, are necessary for the productivity of educational systems in the era of artificial intelligence. Consider the goals of access to education and lifelong learning. Artificial intelligence can indeed meet both objectives as an adaptive learning tool; (which analyzes the learner's traces and abilities, in order to propose personalised and adapted learning). However, in order to adapt to different learners, its design must include different learner profiles, taking into account different parameters of ages, cultures, geographical regions etc. In other words, this AI must be fair (second of the five convergent principles) in the sense of inclusion; Hence the importance of the principle of justice/fairness, alongside the other four converging principles. In our following remarks, we will present the different schools of meaning of these five principles and establish the link with the meanings developed in The Rome Call and the Baptist Statement.

Transparency

The concept of transparency is present in 73 of the 84 documents analysed and is often combined with the notions of explicability and interpretability. Its fields of application include the use of data, algorithmic decisions, and the relationship between humans and AI. The study structures the presentation of this transparency in two points: the

---

An Evangelical Statement of Principles," https://erlc.com/resource-library/statements/artificial-intelligence-an-evangelical-statement-of-principles/.

definition of the concept and the means necessary for its effectiveness (or its instrumental component).

Speaking of the definition, the authors of the study specify that it does vary across guidelines. Three main schools of thought emerge. The first defines transparency as a means of minimising the risks of AI and improving it; the second school emphasises its legal dimension and its role in building trust; the third school links it to the notions of dialogue, participation, and the principles of democracy.[21]

As regards the instrumental component, the study also identifies three schools. The first is that of auditing, which involves the democratisation and availability of information on the development and application of AI systems. According to the guidelines, this information to be democratised varies between lines of code and data typologies, without forgetting the limits of AI, its uses and its intentions. The second school, largely made up of the private sector, recommends a technical solution. This includes coding the algorithms to such an extent that they are transparent. The third school, which is like the first, recommends dialogue between developers and the public during the design process in order to build trust.

Transparency is the first principle of *algorethics*. The approach to this notion, as proposed by the Rome Call, is in line with the third school of non-confessional guidelines in terms of definition (the school of dialogue, citizen participation and principles of democracy) as well as the second and third schools of the instrumental component. The latter encourage technical solutions (second school) and dialogue between developers and citizens (third school) respectively.

The Baptist Statement also deals with the principle of transparency. Article 8 of the declaration, among other recommendations, emphasises the concept of informed consent which must be preceded by a consistently good intention. The Baptist Statement is thus close to the

---

[21]   The Southern Baptist Ethics & Religious Liberty Commission, op. cit., 8.

second school of the non-denominational guidelines in terms of definition (building trust) and to the first school of the instrumental component (making information available for audit).

Responsibility

The principle of responsibility was addressed in 60 of the 84 guides analysed. These are structured into three main schools of thought which focus solely on the means necessary for the effectiveness of this principle (the instrumental component). The first proposes a legal reading of responsibility, which could be deployed at the beginning of the technological creation process through the approach of contracts, or at the end through the approach of recourse. The second school focuses on the process of creation and recommends a particular exploration of the underlying mechanisms that can lead to harmful actions. The third school emphasises the need for whistleblowing and redress in the event of danger and the promotion of diversity and education.

The *responsible* actors vary from AI developers, designers, institutions, and so forth. The study also notes that there is a debate about the possibility of attributing responsibility to AI.

In the Rome Call, responsibility is the third principle of algorethics and it is attributed to developers. The principle states that developers, in their creative process, must be transparent and accountable. Through this reading, the Pontifical guideline fits into the second school of non-denominational guidelines, as does the Baptist Declaration. The latter, in its Article 3, which deals with the relationship between AI and humanity, opposes the possibility of attributing any responsibility to AI. This position is reaffirmed in Article 10, which deals with war.[22]

---

[22] Ibid.

Privacy

Privacy is mentioned in 47 of the 84 guides analysed. In terms of definition, two schools of thought exist. The first associates privacy with the notions of data protection and security, while the second links it to the principles of freedom and trust.

As regards the means necessary for the effectiveness of this privacy, the authors of the study identify three schools. The first is that of technical solutions (privacy by design). The second school encourages more research and awareness-raising to make users aware of the issues at stake. The third school opts for the regulatory approach, which consists of regulating AI by creating specific laws and regulations.

Privacy is the sixth principle of algorethics in the Rome Call. It states that AI systems must operate safely and respect the privacy of users. The Rome Call is thus in the first school of non-confessional guidelines in terms of definition. Concerning the register of means necessary for its effectiveness, the call joins the first and second schools which insist respectively on technical solutions (privacy by design) and on education as a tool for raising awareness of the challenges of AI.

Article 8 of the Baptist Statement is introduced by presenting privacy and private property as inseparable from the rights and choices of each individual.[23] This position is in line with the first school of non-confessional guides in terms of definition and the third school in terms of the means necessary to implement the principle.

Non-maleficence

This principle is recommended by 60 of the 84 guides analysed. It is combined with the notions of security, safety, protection, precaution, prevention, and integrity (physical or mental). These guidelines are

---

[23] Ibid.

opposed to the development and use of AI that would undermine the integrity of humans, their psychological and emotional well-being.

According to the Rome Call "[A]ny AI-based technology must never be used to exploit people in any way, especially those who are most vulnerable."[24]

Article 4 of the Baptist Statement defines non-maleficence as one of the criteria to be met by AI in the service of medicine.[25] Article 11 on war opposes the use of AI for reasons of torture, genocide, and so forth.[26] Article 9 on security also opposes the use of AI that would undermine freedom of expression.[27]

Justice and Fairness

Recommended by 68 of the 84 guides analysed, justice/fairness is associated with the notions of inclusion, equality, non-discrimination, equity, diversity, plurality, and bias. The authors identify three schools of definition. The first is the ethical guidelines that define justice as respect for diversity, inclusion, and equality. The second school defines it as the ability to challenge decisions about artificial intelligence, including the right to object. The third school defines it as common access to AI technologies and services.

The means necessary for the effectiveness of this justice are based on five points: 1) technical solutions (justice by design); 2) transparency and awareness-raising among citizens through the democratisation of information relating to the development and deployment of AI; 3) auditing; 4) the strengthening of legal and judicial mechanisms to

---

24 "Rome Call for AI Ethics," https://www.romecall.org/.

25 Artificial Intelligence: An Evangelical Statement of Principles, op. cit.

26 Ibid.

27 Ibid.

oppose actions that would harm citizens; and 5) the promotion of interdisciplinarity and diversity in the innovation process.

The notion of justice comes close to the second principle of algorethics (Inclusion: the needs of all human beings must be taken into consideration so that everyone can benefit, and all individuals can be offered the best possible conditions to express themselves and develop) and to the fourth principle (Impartiality: do not create or act according to bias, thus safeguarding fairness and human dignity). In this reading, the Rome Call falls within the register of the three definitional schools mentioned above (inclusion; the importance and existence of legal mechanisms to counter unfair decisions and actions; and equal access to the benefits of AI). It is, however, intended to emphasise legal mechanisms for redress (the second school) and equal access to the benefits of AI (the third school).[28] In relation to the means necessary for the effectiveness of justice, the Rome Call is in line with the first, second and third schools of non-confessional guides. These recommend respectively technical solutions, transparency and awareness, and legal devices.

---

[28] In the first paragraph of the chapter on rights, the Rome Appeal argues that the "ethical commitment of all stakeholders involved [in the development of artificial intelligence] is a crucial starting point; in order to make this future a reality, values, principles and, in some cases, legal regulations, are absolutely essential to support, structure and guide this process." The last paragraph of the same chapter states that "new forms of regulation must be encouraged to promote transparency and respect for ethical principles, especially for advanced technologies that present a higher risk of impacting on human rights, such as facial recognition. Speaking of common access to the benefits of AI (the third school of definition). The Rome Appeal supports the primacy of the disadvantaged and marginalised. It states that the "development of AI for the benefit of humanity and the planet must be reflected in regulations and principles that protect people - especially the weak and disadvantaged - and the natural environment."

Article 4 of the Baptist Statement defines justice as one of the main criteria that artificial intelligences in the service of medicine will have to respect.[29] Article 5, which deals with algorithmic biases, insists that non-discrimination must characterise AI: "AI must be designed and used in a way that treats all human beings as having equal value and dignity."[30] These articles are thus close to the first school of non-confessional guides in terms of definition (inclusion and equality). Talking about the means necessary for the effectiveness of this principle of justice, the Baptist Statement is in line with the second school of non-denominational guidelines, through its article 11 which stresses the need to involve citizens in defining the role of the AI.

In the end, these five principles are the most represented in the guidelines analysed, alongside other principles such as trust (present in 28 of the 84 ethical guidelines); solidarity (present in 6 of the 84); sustainability (present in 14 of the 84); dignity (13 of the 84); beneficence (41 of the 84); freedom and autonomy (present in 34 of the 84). While this convergence of principles shows to some extent that religious institutions have a place in the international and interdisciplinary debate on the ethics of AI, it also calls into question the plurality of existing ethical guidelines. If there are converging principles, regardless of the institutions that produce them, would it not be possible and preferable to think of a single ethical guide for AI? Moreover, aware that AI, reinforced by globalisation, is increasingly proving to be a technology with a universal impact, could these five key and converging ethical principles not form the basis of a single and universal ethical declaration of AI, similar to the Universal Declaration of Human Rights?

---

[29] Artificial Intelligence: An Evangelical Statement of Principles, op. cit.

[30] Ibid.

Conclusion

The objective of this work was to propose a brief analyse and comment of two ethical AI guidelines produced by religious institutions in contrast to similar non-confessional efforts. We have thus highlighted the five converging principles that are: transparency, justice and fairness, non-maleficence, responsibility and privacy. At the end of this exercise, important questions remain – questions that deserve further reflection. These include questions related to the definition of the relationship between human and AI, the eco-responsibility approach of AI, and the redefinition of education in the AI context.

The first set of questions, those pertaining to the definition of the relationship between human and AI, brings up two issues: the human responsibility and the possibility of considering AI as an electronic person with rights and duties. According to both the Rome Call and the Baptist Statement, the responsibility of the actions of AI must lie with the human creator. This defense of human responsibility is often associated with the denial of the legal recognition of robots as *electronic persons* with rights and duties. The above analysis shows that the human monopoly of responsibility is not contrary to the legal recognition of the rights and duties of AI. Indeed, the arguments against the legal recognition of AI-robots as *electronic persons* are based on two key notions that would be definitional substances of the *person*: free will and the corporal envelopment. However, several neuroscientific and biological studies have challenged these convictions.[31] They invite us to

---

[31] "Le libre arbitre existe-t-il ?" *Science étonnante,* 5 March 2012, https://scienceetonnante.com/2012/03/05/le-libre-arbitre-existe-t-il/ (accessed 3 September 2020); Campa, Riccardo, Corbally, Christoffer and Rappaport, Margaret. "Electronic Persons. Is it Premature to Grant Personhood to Machines but Never Say Never," https://www.researchgate.net/profile/Riccardo-Campa/publication/348592771_Electronic_persons_It_is_premature_to_grant_p ersonhood_to_machines_but_never_say_never/links/6006bd56299bf14088a64d

redefine the concept of responsibility by dissociating it from the problem of the rights and duties of robots. Responsibility must be attributed to human, not because we have free will or a body that would make us a *person*, but for the simple reason that we are the creator and that it is our neural mechanisms that are transposed and reproduced in AI. It is therefore a part of the human, digitised or algorithmised, that is at work in such AI. In relation to these two questions, several theological avenues (not taken up in the two statements) come to mind, notably the concept of *Imago Dei*. On the one hand, the concept of *Imago Dei* affirms the particularity and dignity of humans who are in the image of God, while at the same time attesting to their freedom and equality. It is therefore, from this perspective, a basic theology for the ethical triptych of AI, which is: the protection of freedom, the guarantee of equality and the central importance of human dignity. On the other hand, this concept defines human creativity as a reflection of divine creativity. In doing so, AI, which is part of human creativity, is a counterpart of the human that helps the latter to better understand ourselves (functionalist understanding) and our relationship to God.[32]

As regard to the second set of questions relating to the eco-responsible approach of AI, the Rome Call insists that the environment and its wellbeing must be a central concern in the research, the development and the application of AI. In relation to this position, one can think of an ecotheological approach to AI as a theological extension. This can be articulated in the light of the concept of holism, which was developed at length by the theologian Thomas Berry. According to holism, the human from birth to adulthood is a being that is required to

---

1f/Electronic-persons-It-is-premature-to-grant-personhood-to-machines-but-never-say-never.pdf

[32] This concept is widely used by theologian Anne Foerst in her article: Foerst, Anne. "Cog, a Humanoid Robot, and the Question of the Image of God". *Zygon®*, 1998, 33: 91-111. https://doi.org/10.1111/0591-2385.1291998129

coexist inextricably with the *other* to survive. This *other* includes both human and non-human entities (plant, animal, and so on). The ecotheological approach therefore consists in sacralising this whole, this relationship, this interdependence, by making the history of humans, the history of God, and the history of the earth *one*.[33] It is in this vein of theological reflection that we can see the importance of the other. It is in this vein of ideas that the ecotheologian Sallie McFague proposes to redefine the human way of understanding God's presence in the world. In response to the ecological crisis, she recommends seeing the world as the body of God.[34] This metaphor allows for the sacredness of natural resources, the connectivity between all forms of earthly life, and more.

This also points to the direct need for a redefinition of the educational system (third set of questions), a core concern taken up in this collection of essays. Education was approached by the Rome Call from two angles. On the one hand, as a field of application of AI in order to guarantee, among other things, the principle of life-long learning; on the other hand, as a tool that makes humans distant and critical towards AI and its issues. On the other hand, one could also consider education as a tool that allows humans to communicate with AI, to learn from them, and thus to keep their critical spirit and freedom of thought. Hence the idea of redefining basic education from reading and writing to reading, writing, and coding. This is an initiative that is already being implemented in several countries, notably Japan, which since 2020 has made programming compulsory.

Such education in AI should also emphasise the particularities of the human, the values that define humanity such as courage, sympathy,

---

[33] For more, see Berry, Thomas, Swimme, Brian. *The Universe Story: From the Primordial Flaring Forth to the Ecozoic Era, a Celebration of the Unfolding of the Cosmos*, San Francisco: Harper, 1992.

[34] See McFague, Sallie. *The Body of God: An Ecological Theology* Minneapolis: Fortress Press, 1993.

benevolence, and, most importantly, the vital importance of peaceful relationship with the environment.

The guidelines studied above represent an important step in understanding how we understand the implicit rules of our common lives with AI. This work, however, is not static and requires ongoing debate and resources from all corners of society. As we converge together on an understanding of AI, the pedagogical, ethical element must not be lost by those who will craft the rules and implement them.

BY WHOSE MORAL COMPASS?
CHARTING AN ETHICAL COURSE
FOR AI IN EDUCATION

Brad Huddleston

The New AI Inspired Classroom

A group of Chinese primary school students enters a classroom eager to learn. Before sitting down to begin their lesson, each student picks up their electronic headband and puts it on. As the students carry out their assignments, each AI-empowered headband will monitor their concentration level and send the information directly to the teacher's computer and their parents. If the light on the band turns red, it means the student is deeply focused. Blue means they are distracted, and white indicates that the student is offline. In addition, some Chinese schools have placed robots in classrooms to monitor students' health and levels of engagement.[35]

This is not the work of a science fiction writer. This is happening now.

In these experimental AI-driven schools, students also wear uniforms with embedded chips to track their location. There are also surveillance cameras that monitor the frequency that students check their phones and yawn during classes. Chinese netizens have expressed their concern by posting comments such as: "That's too scary," "Kids these days suffer too much," "This is worse than being a prisoner." Despite these

---

[35]   How China Is Using Artificial Intelligence in Classrooms, *WSJ*. YouTube, *Wall Street Journal*, 2019. https://youtu.be/JMLsHI8aV0g.

concerns, schools say that it was not hard getting parental consent. One parent said, "If it's for our country's research and development, I don't think it's a problem."[36]

Perhaps it should not be surprising that parents are not raising more ethical concerns, given the extreme level of surveillance already present in China. Time will tell if more objections will be raised as the West catches up to China.

Neuroscientist Theodore Zanto, from the University of California in San Francisco, raised concerns about the use of electroencephalography (EEG) being used on children in the classroom, "EEG is very susceptible to artifacts, and so, if you are itchy or just a little fidgety or the EEG wasn't set up properly, so that the electrodes didn't have a good contact, [that] affects the signal."[37]

Other questions remain. If a child shows to be excessively fidgety, will they be offered an alternative mode of education that better suits their learning style, or will they simply be passed over in favor of more self-controlled children? Is AI able to predict if a child will eventually grow out of their reduced capability to sit still?

After outlining some of the various uses of AI, John Lennox, professor of mathematics at Oxford University writes:

> "The danger is that people are carried away with the 'if it can be done, it should be done' mentality without thinking carefully through potential ethical problems. However, it must be said that ethical issues are now rapidly rising in importance on the agenda of leading players in the AI world. [...]

---

[36] Ibid.

[37] Dr Zanto is Director of Neuroscience Division, Neuroscape's Education Division of the UCSF, "dedicated to supporting the development of healthy young minds", see: https://neuroscape.ucsf.edu/education/#classroom-assessments

The big question to be faced is: How can an ethical dimension be built into an algorithm that is itself devoid of heart, soul, and mind?"[38]

AI Definitions

Before covering some of the topics related to artificial intelligence and its application to education, it will prove helpful to provide a broader context of computing.

The concept of AI is often attributed to Alan Turing, the great British mathematician whose 1948 paper on intelligent machinery established a vision for machines that could mimic human behavior in areas as varied as games, language learning, cryptography, and mathematics.[39]

You may have heard of the Turing test. Simply put, if a computer can fool a human into thinking they are communicating with another human, then the computer has passed the Turing test.

Artificial Intelligence

Artificial Intelligence (AI) "leverages computers and machines to mimic the problem-solving and decision-making capabilities of the human mind."[40]

Algorithm

All areas of computing make use of algorithms, which "is a procedure or formula for solving a problem, based on conducting a

---

[38] Lennox, John Carson. "Chapter 1 - Mapping Out the Territory." In *2084: Artificial Intelligence and the Future of Humanity*, Grand Rapids, MI: Zondervan Reflective, 2020, 24.

[39] Abelson, Harold, Ledeen, Ken, Lewis, Harry, and Seltzer, Wendy. "The Next Frontier." *In Blown to Bits: Your Life, Liberty, and Happiness after the Digital Explosion*, New York: Pearson, 2021, 277.

[40] IBM Cloud Education. "What Is Artificial Intelligence (AI)?" IBM, June 3, 2020. https://www.ibm.com/cloud/learn/what-is-artificial-intelligence.

sequence of specified actions. A computer program can be viewed as an elaborate algorithm."[41]

Ethics are often discussed in the context of algorithms. For example, in a Brooking Institute article entitled, "Fairness in algorithmic decision making," the editor's note has the following:

"This report from The Brookings Institution's Artificial Intelligence and Emerging Technology (AIET) Initiative is part of "AI and Bias," a series that explores ways to mitigate possible biases and create a pathway toward greater fairness in AI and emerging technologies."[42]

The article goes on to explain:

"A significant new challenge with these machine learning systems, however, is ascertaining when and how they could introduce bias into the decision-making process. Several technical features of these systems might produce discriminatory decisions that are artifacts of the models themselves. The input data used to train the systems could underrepresent members of protected classes or be infected by past discriminatory practices. Consequently, the data could inadvertently reproduce or magnify historical patterns of bias."[43]

By whose standard are we to determine who is underrepresented? Which ideology should we use in an algorithm to determine if discrimination is occurring? These are just some of the complex issues

---

[41] TechTarget, "What Is Algorithm? - Definition from Whatis.com." *WhatIs.com. TechTarget*, March 20, 2019. https://whatis.techtarget.com/definition/algorithm.

[42] MacCarthy, Mark. "Fairness in Algorithmic Decision-Making." *The Brookings Institute*. December 11, 2019. https://www.brookings.edu/research/fairness-in-algorithmic-decision-making/.

[43] Ibid.

that many AI programmers are being forced to confront. Unfortunately, achieving agreement on these crucial questions is proving to be complicated.

The term algorithm has become part of the global vocabulary in recent years. Many users are warned, temporarily suspended, and even de-platformed from sites such as Facebook and YouTube for not conforming to what they deem to be community standards. Because there is no possible way for humans to keep track of such a large pool of users, elaborate algorithms are used to flag users for posting what technology conglomerates determine to be fake news. Although AI is the driving force behind these algorithms, it is still humans who choose the definition of fake news. As a result, allegations of censorship and arguments over definitions are ongoing.

Machine Learning

Machine learning (ML) "is an application of artificial intelligence (AI) that provides systems the ability to automatically learn and improve from experience without being explicitly programmed. Machine learning focuses on the development of computer programs that can access data and use it to learn for themselves."[44] Everyday applications of ML include virtual personal assistants, Siri, Alexa, Google Now, Amazon Echo, Google Home, traffic predictions, video surveillance systems, and social media services.[45]

Deep Learning

Deep learning is defined as "a subset of machine learning where artificial neural networks, algorithms inspired by the human brain, learn

---

[44] "What Is the Definition of Machine Learning?" *Expert.ai*, May 26, 2021. https://www.expert.ai/blog/machine-learning-definition/.

[45] Software, Daffodil, "9 Applications of Machine Learning from Day-to-Day Life." *Medium*. App Affairs, November 30, 2017. https://medium.com/app-affairs/9-applications-of-machine-learning-from-day-to-day-life-112a47a429d0.

from large amounts of data. Similarly to how we learn from experience, the deep learning algorithm would perform a task repeatedly, each time tweaking it a little to improve the outcome."[46] Applications of deep learning include fraud detection, autonomous cars, investment modeling, and facial recognition systems.[47]

Neural Networks

According to IBM Cloud Education, "Neural networks, also known as artificial neural networks (ANNs) or simulated neural networks (SNNs), are a subset of machine learning and are at the heart of deep learning algorithms. Their name and structure are inspired by the human brain, mimicking the way that biological neurons signal to one another."[48] Applications of neural networks include eCommerce, finance, healthcare, and logistics.[49]

Artificial General Intelligence

Often portrayed in science fiction movies, Artificial General Intelligence (AGI) does not exist. If AGI ever does exist, it "would be a machine capable of understanding the world as well as any human, and

---

[46] Marr, Bernard. "What Is Deep Learning AI? A Simple Guide with 8 Practical Examples." *Forbes Magazine*, December 12, 2018. https://www.forbes.com/sites/bernardmarr/2018/10/01/what-is-deep-learning-ai-a-simple-guide-with-8-practical-examples/?sh=6f55a9a78d4b.

[47] Thomas, Mike, Nordli, Brian. "14 Deep Learning Applications You Need to Know." *Built In*. Nov. 2021. https://builtin.com/artificial-intelligence/deep-learning-applications.

[48] IBM Cloud Education. "What Are Neural Networks?" IBM. Accessed July 28, 2021. https://www.ibm.com/cloud/learn/neural-networks.

[49] Mach, Patrycja. "10 Business Applications of Neural Network (with Examples!)." Agile Software Development Agency in Europe. Accessed July 28, 2021. https://www.ideamotive.co/blog/business-applications-of-neural-network.

with the same capacity to learn how to carry out a huge range of tasks."[50]

Whose Work Is This?

The following headline should send ethical shivers down the spines of educators: "AI can write a passing college paper in 20 minutes."[51] The article goes on to say:

> "AI can do a lot of things extremely well. One thing that it can do just okay - which, frankly, is still quite extraordinary - is write college term papers.

> That's the finding from EduRef, a resource for students and educators, which ran an experiment to determine if a deep learning language prediction model known as GPT-3 could get passing marks in an anonymised trial."[52]

In the experiment, a panel of professors was hired to create a writing prompt that was given to a group of graduates and undergraduate-level writers that was then fed to GPT-3. The panel graded the anonymous submissions and completed a survey for their thoughts about the writers. The article says, "The results were a surprising demonstration of the natural prowess of AI."[53]

In a real-world case, graduate student Tiago, admitted to Futurism.com that he had been using GPT-2 to write essays for this coursework. Tiago is getting his master's degree in business. He was

---

50 Heath, Nick. "What Is Artificial General Intelligence?" ZDNet. August 22, 2018. https://www.zdnet.com/article/what-is-artificial-general-intelligence/.

51 Nichols, Greg. "AI Can Write a Passing College Paper in 20 Minutes." ZDNet. February 24, 2021. https://www.zdnet.com/article/ai-can-write-a-passing-college-paper-in-20-minutes/.

52 Ibid.

53 Ibid.

willing not only to share his story, but copies of his AI-generated essays so long as Futurism did not share any other information about him.[54]

Tiago was not certain if his AI-generated work was plagiarism. One thing is sure: Not all the work was his own. Just how much did he learn? In this brave new AI-in-education world, how do we now define plagiarism? Where does the GPT-2 algorithm get its information?

Honour codes will need to be updated. In addition, honour code enforcement might require new algorithms to detect AI-written materials. How do we protect businesses that might hire someone like Tiago who has questionable qualifications?

What About AI Grammar and Spelling Checkers?

Whenever new educational technologies have emerged, not all educators have been quick to embrace them. In a 1980 research paper titled "The Impact of Electronic Calculators on Educational Performance," Dennis Roberts writes:

> "Educators have long been skeptical about the influence of innovations which either find their way into schools or catch students' eyes outside of school. Programmed instruction, with all of its teaching machines, is a case in point. Educators have argued that teaching machines would merely reinforce rote memory associations rather than encourage students to solve problems creatively."[55]

---

[54] "This Grad Student Used a Neural Network to Write His Papers." *Futurism.* April 21, 2020. https://futurism.com/grad-student-neural-network-write-papers.

[55] Roberts, Dennis M. "The Impact of Electronic Calculators on Educational Performance." Review of Educational Research 50, no. 1 (1980): 71-98. Accessed July 28, 2021. DOI: 10.2307/1170031. https://www.jstor.org/stable/1170031?read-now=1&seq=2#page_scan_tab_contents

We are a long way from 1980, and the debate continues. One 2018 review found that [calculators] increase pupils' fluency and understanding of maths, yet in 2014, calculators were banned from maths SATs tests for 11-year-olds due to concerns that primary school students can be too reliant on them.[56]

With AI now entering the world of education, history is repeating itself. Numerous commercial algorithms are available to assist with and check spelling, grammar, maths, scriptwriting, copyrighting, you name it. For example, Microsoft Word has a built-in editor, and another top-rated product is Grammarly. According to its website:

> "Grammarly's products are powered by an advanced system that combines rules, patterns, and artificial intelligence techniques like machine learning, deep learning, and natural language processing to improve your writing."[57]

In an article entitled "Is Grammarly Cheating? Helpful Professor Explains," the professor argues that students who use the popular program are not cheating because the algorithm does not get grammar correct every time, it does not automatically make changes to your work, it does tell you what you write about, and it does not have answers to your assignment questions.[58]

---

[56] University College London, "Calculators Can Help Boost Children's Maths Skills, Research Suggests." Institute of Education, September 25, 2020. https://www.ucl.ac.uk/ioe/news/2018/mar/calculators-can-help-boost-childrens-maths-skills-research-suggests

[57] "How We Use AI to Enhance Your Writing: Grammarly Spotlight." Grammarly Spotlight, May 17, 2019. https://www.grammarly.com/blog/how-grammarly-uses-ai/

[58] Drew, Chris. "Is Grammarly Cheating? - Helpful Professor Explains." *Helpful Professor*, April 28, 2021. https://helpfulprofessor.com/grammarly-cheating/

Not everyone agrees with the Helpful Professor. In an online article entitled "The Educational Value of Grammarly and the Question of Academic Dishonesty," the author makes the case that some instructors do not allow private tutors for error correction and concludes:

"I don't think we can deny that the software itself, not the student, increases quality of vocabulary and grammar. The software discovers errors, and presents the solution. This is not an indirect method that requires the student solve the issue; the answer is directly given. In a strict sense, this would be academic dishonesty (cheating) because it is essentially the same as the private tutor example above. Student scores will be higher because of a 3rd party, not their own ability."[59]

From an ethical point of view, it is fair to say that educators, when applicable, should teach students, especially in their younger years, to apply critical thinking strategies to all subjects in the analogue world and then be allowed to take advantage of the assistance that AI (and calculators) offers. After all, how would our learners cope in the real world should they experience an extended power outage?

The Ethics of Many Silicon Valley Employees

A New York Times article entitled, "A Silicon Valley School That Doesn't Compute" has surprised many. It turns out that some who work for eBay, Google, Apple, Yahoo, and Hewlett-Packard send their children to schools that have no screens at all, and technology is also discouraged at home. Educators who endorse this philosophy believe

---

[59] "Grammarly: Its Educational Value & the Question of Academic Dishonesty." *English Current*, July 15, 2020. https://www.englishcurrent.com/teachers/educational-value-of-grammarly-academic-dishonesty/.

that computers "inhibit creative thinking, movement, human interaction and attention spans."[60]

Alan Eagle works in executive communications at Google and earned his computer science degree at Dartmouth College. His daughter attended the analogue Waldorf School of the Peninsula and he said, "I fundamentally reject the notion you need technology aids in grammar school. The idea that an app on an iPad can better teach my kids to read or do arithmetic, that's ridiculous."[61]

Pierre Laurrant is a former employee of Microsoft and Intel and has three children who also attended Waldorf schools. Laurrant made his educational sentiments known about human to machine interactions when he said, "Engagement is about human contact, the contact with the teacher, the contact with their peers."[62]

More evidence of how Silicon Valley tech employees feel about their children using the technology that their industry creates came to light in a *New York Times* article entitled, "A Dark Consensus About Screens and Kids Begins to Emerge in Silicon Valley."[63]

Athena Chavarria works at the Chan Zuckerberg Initiative, Mark Zuckerberg's philanthropic organisation. Chavarria left no question about her parental ethics when she said: "I am convinced the devil lives in our phones and is wreaking havoc on our children."[64]

Chris Anderson is the former editor of *Wired Magazine*, founder of GeekDad.com, and is now the chief executive of a drone and robotics

---

[60] Ritchtel, Matt. "A Silicon Valley School That Doesn't Compute." *The New York Times.* October 22, 2011. https://www.nytimes.com/2011/10/23/technology/at-waldorf-school-in-silicon-valley-technology-can-wait.html.

[61] Ibid.

[62] Ibid.

[63] Bowles, Nellie. "A Dark Consensus about Screens and Kids Begins to Emerge in Silicon Valley." *The New York Times.* October 26, 2018. https://www.nytimes.com/2018/10/26/style/phones-children-silicon-valley.html.

[64] Ibid.

company. He believes those who developed technology and those who wrote about the technology revolution were naïve. Anderson was not shy about how he feels when he said, "On the scale between candy and crack cocaine, it's closer to crack cocaine. We thought we could control it. And this is beyond our power to control. This is going straight to the pleasure centers of the developing brain. This is beyond our capacity as regular parents to understand."[65]

Anderson has plenty of neuroscience to back him up. In his book *Glow Kids: How Screen Addiction is Hijacking Our Kids - and How to Break the Trance*, Dr Nicholas Kardaras writes:

> "Ironically, while we've declared a so-called War on Drugs, we've allowed this virtual drug—which Dr. Peter Whybrow, director of neuroscience at UCLA, calls "electronic cocaine"; which Commander Dr. Andrew Doan, who has an M.D. and Ph.D. in neuroscience and heads addiction research for the U.S. Navy, calls digital "pharmakeia" (Greek for "drug"); and which Chinese researchers call "electronic heroin"—to slip into the homes and classrooms of our youngest and most vulnerable, seemingly oblivious to any negative side effects."[66]

When Nick Bilton, reporter for the *New York Times* asked Steve Jobs, "So, your kids must love the iPad?" Jobs replied, "They haven't used it. We limit how much technology our kids use at home."[67]

What do these tech executives and neuroscientists know that we do not? Apparently, a lot.

---

[65] Ibid.

[66] Kardaras, Nicholas. *Glow Kids: How Screen Addiction Is Hijacking Our Kids - and How to Break the Trance*, St. Martin's Press: Kindle Edition, 4.

[67] Bilton, Nick. "Steve Jobs Was a Low-Tech Parent." *The New York Times*. September 10, 2014. https://www.nytimes.com/2014/09/11/fashion/steve-jobs-apple-was-a-low-tech-parent.html.

Why would those who develop technology be willing to push their inventions on the masses yet not allow those in their own homes to use them? Ancient wisdom might have the answer: The love of money is the root of all kinds of evil.

As the world moves into AI 2.0, parents, educators, medical professionals, psychologists, and so on, must give serious thought to how much, if any, technology young children should be exposed to, even in an education setting.[68]

Knowing the very real potential of harming one's brain, alternative non-digital education models should be mandatory. Parents must decide which is more critical, cognition or being on the cutting-edge of technology. For example, there is ample evidence that learners who use longhand remember more and have a deeper understanding of material when taking notes on paper instead of a laptop.[69] The same is true when it comes to reading on paper versus reading on a screen.[70] Sound strategies exist, based on research, that should be considered when implementing technology both at home in education.[71]

---

[68] Yunhe, Pan. "Heading toward Artificial Intelligence 2.0." Elsevier, February 28, 2017. https://www.sciencedirect.com/science/article/pii/S2095809917300772.

[69] May, Cindi. "A Learning Secret: Don't Take Notes with a Laptop." *Scientific American.* June 3, 2014. https://www.scientificamerican.com/article/a-learning-secret-don-t-take-notes-with-a-laptop/.

[70] Barshay, Jill. "Evidence Increases for Reading on Paper Instead of Screens." *The Hechinger Report*, April 8, 2021. https://hechingerreport.org/evidence-increases-for-reading-on-paper-instead-of-screens/.

[71] Huddleston, Brad. "The Advantages of Distance Learning", In: *Ethics in Higher Education: Values-Driven Leaders for the Future*, Stückelberger, C. and Singh, D. (Eds.), Education Ethics Series No. 1, Geneva: Globethics.net, 2017, 339–48. See also Divya Singh's similar essays in the volume.

Whose Ethics Will We Use?

The inevitable question regarding whose moral compass will be used to decide what is right and wrong will always be debated. Few disagree that it is challenging to separate one's worldview and belief system when decisions must be made that potentially affect others. Finding common ground on moral issues can be difficult, but ethics demands that we never stop trying.

AI development in atheistic communist countries has the potential to yield different results than AI developed in countries where freedom and faith are valued. Even still, there will be different morals and ethics between countries that are religion-based. Although AI is based on machine learning and neural networks, humans with individual values are the ones who set the processes in motion, which can ultimately introduce bias. When sharing AI technologies across borders, good ethics and respect demand that algorithmic transparency be maintained.

Inherent in education has always been a battle to influence the hearts and minds of students, not only with academics but with certain ideologies as well. Some have proved to be good, and some downright evil. Therefore, we cannot be naïve when implementing AI in learning.

Fortunately, there is growing concern about student welfare in relation to technology. For example, in 2018, the United Kingdom created its first Institute for Ethical Artificial Intelligence in Education (IEAIED). Following is one of the organisation's goals:

"The Institute will examine the assumptions about human behaviour that underlie current AI development and how social values are manifested in AI design. It will also look at how ethical frameworks can be grounded in responsible innovation and integrated with our assumptions to transform how AI innovators make decisions when designing for educational AI. The IEAIED will also aim to ensure that AI in education does not prioritise certain aspects of learning at the expense of others, which can distort the process of learning and human development."[72]

The IEAIED will likely find it a challenge to get others on board, but worth the effort to pursue ethical agreement.

It is reasonable that certain civil liberties, regardless of worldview, should be agreed upon and respected for all learners, including applying AI to education.

In 1942, science fiction author Isaac Asimov penned his Three Laws of Robotics:

1. A robot may not injure a human being or, through inaction, allow a human being to come to harm.

2. A robot must obey the orders given to it by human beings, except where such orders would conflict with the First Law.

3. A robot must protect its own existence as long as such protection does not conflict with the First or Second Law.[73]

Another time-tested ethic that should be applied to the use of AI in any context is the promise within the Hippocratic Oath that says, "first, do no harm."[74]

More recommendations:

---

[72] University College London, "IOE Professor Co-Founds the UK's First Institute for Ethical Artificial Intelligence in Education." Institute of Education, September 25, 2020. https://www.ucl.ac.uk/ioe/news/2018/oct/ioe-professor-co-founds-uks-first-institute-ethical-artificial-intelligence-education.

[73] arXiv, Emerging Technology from "Do We Need Asimov's Laws?" *MIT Technology Review*. April 2, 2020. https://www.technologyreview.com/2014/05/16/172841/do-we-need-asimovs-laws/.

[74] Shmerling, Robert H. MD. "First, Do No Harm." *Harvard Health*, June 22, 2020. https://www.health.harvard.edu/blog/first-do-no-harm-201510138421.

- Ongoing third-party research as to how new technologies are affecting users' brains, emotions, cognition, and so on;
- Mandatory ongoing parental education regarding the findings from neuroscience and psychology regarding the use of technology;
- Mandatory parental involvement when implementing new educational technologies;
- Parental consent in all matters;
- Data privacy and transparency;
- Students, especially the young, should be told when they are communicating with a machine and warned of the potential and dangers of bonding emotionally with a machine;
- Alternative non-digital modalities of education should always be offered when parents request them.

A quick internet search on both the Hippocratic Oath and the three Laws of Robotics will reveal that many now feel these ethical principles are outdated due to the complexities of modern life. Life on planet Earth has no doubt become complex, but all humans have inherent worth and value and should be treated with dignity and respect above all else. Educators must always go to great lengths to protect their learners, and sometimes, the simple solutions, such as the Hippocratic Oath and the Three Laws of Robotics, are still the ones that work best. We do not always have to over-think complex issues when it comes to ethics. We must have ongoing research and debate about how our teaching methods affect our learners and put their best interests first.

WHY AI NEEDS INTERDISCIPLINARY?
INTERSECTIONAL REASONING

Erin Green

Introduction

As a theologian, curiosity about my interest in AI often comes with the assumption that people of faith somehow feel that their religious beliefs (and occasionally practices) are under threat by advances in science and technology, that we are always just one *fact* away from the whole house of cards collapsing in a *Dawkinian gotcha*. I have always found this line of questioning a bit reminiscent of embellished 17th century confrontations between the Church and Science. The truth is, theological interest in AI typically has little to do with threats to God - God is fine - and the practice of religion. Rather, theological concern rises from profound awareness of the social, historical, and ecological impact of digital technologies including artificial intelligence. Centuries, if not millennia, of communal reasoning and discernment has sharpened theological instincts for exercising caution in the face of *too good to be true* promises from the rich and powerful, from both the sides of the often-mythic science and religion debate. AI again provides such an opportunity to show how theology, along with numerous other academic traditions, can contribute to the robust moral and ethical critique of technology. At the heart of this concern are people, especially those who are marginalised and made vulnerable, as well as the magnificent and mysterious world that sustains all life. Fundamentally, AI must contribute to the flourishing of all, not the enriching of a few and the pathways to this demand interdisciplinary and intersectional thinking, drawing on the collective strength of the diversity of our contexts, academic communities, and embodied human experiences.

AI as an Amplifier

The complexity of artificial intelligence, both in its sheer scale and it the diversity of its deployment, encourages rich metaphorical thinking. In some ways AI is like a mirror, reflecting the priorities and ambitions of those who guide its development. In looking at the questions we seek to resolve, the problems we believe AI can resolve, one can learn much about the motivations of AI developers and those who drive the research forward. Here, military investment cannot be underestimated. While Big Tech and its captivating prophets often grab headlines, the military-industrial complex pours millions and even billions into funding AI research both in the private sector and in publicly funded institutions of higher education.[75] Perhaps the best-known example of military interest in AI is the development of lethal autonomous weapons systems, or LAWS. While research in this area proliferates, there are counter-efforts to restrict its scope. This includes the coordinated efforts of the Campaign to Stop Killer Robots, instrumental in the global momentum to launch a United Nations treaty process to band LAWS. Powerful nations, with big militaries deeply invested in the development of these technologies actively stall international processes, however, as seen at the 2021 Convention on Certain Conventional Weapons in Geneva.[76]

---

[75] Ben Tsvi, Ron. "DARPA'S Next AI Campaign: $2B in AI Research Grants, Eagle Point Funding, 12 January 2020. https://www.eaglepointfunding.com/post/darpa-s-ai-next-campaign-2b-in-ai-research-grants.

[76] Jones, Isabelle. "Historic Opportunity to Regulate Killer Robots Fails as a Handful of States Block the Majority," Campaign to Stop Killer Robots, 17 December 2020. https://www.stopkillerrobots.org/news/historic-opportunity-to-regulate-killer-robots-fails-as-a-handful-of-states-block-the-majority/.

My inclination is to consider AI as an amplifier. Anything phenomenon that you can see in AI exists already elsewhere in humans, our cultures and societies. AI simply makes it bigger, louder, and with greater impact. For example, algorithmic bias is a new expression of existing systemic racism. AI and related technologies are new ways to exacerbate old problems. Of course, AI could and should have an ameliorating influence, but the field is dominated by people and institutions with little demonstrated interest in a seismic methodological shift. As evidenced by Timnit Gebru's ouster from Google, among other events, Big Tech has little appetite for dismantling its complicity in oppression and destruction.[77]

AI needs disruption, a turn away from the values of militarism and capitalism, toward justice for both people and the planet. While policymakers and corporations talk easily about transparent, trustworthy, and responsible AI, those of us on the margins of this power need to make sure these terms have real substance and real impact. It is heartening to see more and more robust discourse under the umbrella of AI ethics. There are many excellent non-profit organisations, research institutes, and training programs dedicated to understanding AI in interdisciplinary and intersectional ways. These groups understand well that AI is best approached not only from a technical perspective, but from social, cultural, historical, and ecological ones as well. They draw on resources and methods that go well beyond the traditional purview of computer science, engineering, and mathematics. The richness of these efforts infuses AI with the perspective and concerns of those who are most likely to face the adverse effects of these technologies. Institutes of higher education have a golden opportunity here to underscore that AI is not only of concern to those who code, but also to those who have the

---

[77] Gebru, Timnit. "For truly ethical AI, its research must be independent from big tech," *The Guardian* 6 December 2021. https://www.theguardian.com/commentisfree/2021/dec/06/google-silicon-valley-ai-timnit-gebru.

hearts and minds of musicians, historians, anthropologists, surgeons, philosophers, and journalists, and more. AI will touch all our lives, so we must all in some way leave our fingerprints on its methods and character.

Representative, Democratic, and Inclusive AI

The current, global AI landscape represents a concentration of influence in just a handful of companies and countries. While the United States and China seek to be the singular world leader in this area, the European Union wants to both write the rules of the AI regulation game and referee it. Lines of influence between state and non-state actors, especially corporations, blur. This is well evidenced in the Cambridge Analytica scandals and the rise of Facebook and other social media as kingmakers. What is lesser known in the English-speaking world and poorly reported in English media, is that this interference of social media in elections and democracy is typically first tested in already vulnerable countries and fragile democracies. For example, while Cambridge Analytica is best known for its potential role in influencing the Brexit referendum in the United Kingdom and the 2016 presidential elections in the United States, the company was also active in Trinidad and Tobago, Nigeria, and the Philippines.[78] Such concentration of political power and capital leads to an ecosystem yielding unrepresentative, undemocratic, and exclusive development and use AI. Below I will outline just a few ways AI functions in this ecosystem, illustrating the need for interdisciplinary reflection that considers how different forms of exclusion or oppression can interact.

---

[78]   Wylie, Christopher. *Mindf*ck*, Random House, 2019.

Refugees

There are an estimated 82 million forcibly displaced people worldwide, including 35 million children with approximately 300,000 babies born each year as refugees. More than 4 million people in this world are stateless.[79] This represents slightly more than one out of every 100 people on Earth, living in uncertainty and extreme vulnerability, and often danger, trauma, and poverty as well. The link between the rise of AI and its impact on refugees, migrants, internally displaced people, and similarly vulnerable groups receives limited attention by researchers and policymakers. This, however, is deserving of far more attention given the difficulties refugees face in exercising their rights and how poorly they are received by most countries. States and political unions like the EU see AI and related digital technologies as an opportunity for increased border security, management, and surveillance. Facial recognition, drone surveillance, and automated decision making in asylum claims are a few ways that AI and related technologies already directly impact the lives of those who seek refuge from war, persecution, and destruction of homes and territories.[80] These so-called advances in technology often take place in environments that are already politically hostile to refugees and migrants. The implementation of *smart* borders enhances the integrity of international borders, but a parallel improvement in safe and legal pathways for refugees and asylum-seekers rarely materialises. In the end, AI implemented in these scenarios risks becoming a digital barbed-wire fence, with the privileged-by-birth on one side and the world's most vulnerable exiled to the other. The United Nations has clearly cautioned member states

---

[79] UNHCR: The UN Refugee Agency, "Refuge Data Finder," https://www.unhcr.org/refugee-statistics/.

[80] Korkmaz, Emre Eren. "Refugees are at risk from dystopian 'smart border' technology," *The Conversation*, 8 December 2020. https://theconversation.com/refugees-are-at-risk-from-dystopian-smart-border-technology-145500.

against a rush to these border management approaches. A 2021 report notes:

> "Digital borders enhance the scope and precision of the racially discriminatory operation of borders. Governments and non-state actors are developing and deploying emerging digital technologies in ways that are uniquely experimental and dangerous in the border and immigration enforcement context. By so doing, they are subjecting refugees, migrants, stateless persons and others to human rights violations, and extracting large quantities of data from these groups on exploitative terms that strip them of fundamental human agency and dignity."[81]

Indigenous Peoples

AI research often takes place within lingering colonial frameworks, including epistemologies and reasoning, language, and institutions. The values of colonialism form many of the assumptions brought to bear on AI research and its use in the world. Undercurrents of racial inferiority, the superiority of one culture over another, exploitation of people and labour, homogeneity and assimilation, and the imposition of one epistemology and methodology over others are all evidenced within AI and its application. It forms a new battel ground for geopolitical contests, and promotes the exploitation of resources, peoples, and labour. Tech colonialism is also manifest in the recurrent race and gender discrimination and ableism emerging from poor quality data sets and research methods. Patterns of violence, exclusion, and loss are now replicated or exacerbated through AI and other digital technologies. Digital and data colonialism forge new divides between peoples and

---

[81] UN Human Rights Council, "Racial and Xenophobic discrimination and the use of digital technologies in border and immigration enforcement," https://www.ohchr.org/EN/HRBodies/HRC/RegularSessions/Session48/Docume nts/A_HRC_48_76_AdvanceUnEditedVersion.docx

nations where there is already a profound need for reconciliation. To paraphrase Jason Edward Lewis, professor of computation arts at Concordia University and co-director of Aboriginal Territories in Cyberspace, "white supremacy is not a bug, it's a feature."[82]

Indigenous peoples have obviously lost – and continue to lose – much to colonialism and its ripple effects. A significant result of colonial efforts is the obliteration of Indigenous languages and dialects through legislation, forced assimilation, loss of traditional lands and waters, and genocide. The United Nations Permanent Forum on Indigenous Issues writes:

> "Indigenous languages are not only methods of communication, but also extensive and complex systems of knowledge that have developed over millennia. They are central to the identity of indigenous peoples, the preservation of their cultures, worldviews and visions and an expression of self-determination. When indigenous languages are under threat, so too are indigenous peoples themselves."[83]

Advances in AI capabilities in language processing show promise, but also challenge for Indigenous peoples and their efforts to preserve the estimated 4000 Indigenous languages still spoken worldwide. In 2018, a small group of Māori media professionals started recording their spoken language, *te reo* (the language), and building datasets to preserve it and facilitate learning. Such data was *culturally valuable* to Māori who have suffered an accelerated loss of language following

---

[82] McMaster, Geoff. "Creating ethical AI from Indigenous perspectives", Oct. 23, Society and Culture, University of Alberta, https://www.ualberta.ca/folio/2020/10/creating-ethical-ai-from-indigenous-perspectives.html

[83] The United Nations Permanent Forum on Indigenous Issues. See also the UNESCO Follow-up to decisions and resolutions adopted by the Executive Board and the General Conference at their previous session, Doc. 210 EX/5.I.D. https://unesdoc.unesco.org/ark:/48223/pf0000374327.locale=en

World War II. Such data was also *economically valuable* to tech companies who saw an opportunity to monetise these preservation efforts and commodify language through translation tools and other software services.[84] Such situations present an ethical dilemma for Indigenous communities, who often lack financial resources and technological means to use AI for language preservation. Further to this, language transcription and translation is a first step in revitalisation but not the last. Governments must also provide funding and other institutional resources for education (including in the higher education context), training programs, and support the transmission of language from one generation to the next. Accepting so-called *partnerships* with tech companies can become yet another iteration of colonialism, where Indigenous culture is exploited for the profit of others.

The Indigenous Protocol and Artificial Intelligence Working Group is a notable Indigenous contribution to the development of AI and an antidote to the challenges outlined above. The group was launched with workshops in 2019 and brings together scholars, artists, founders, and more to nurture Indigenous approaches to AI.

> "Historically, scholarly traditions that homogenise diverse Indigenous cultural practices have resulted in ontological and epistemological violence, and a flattening of the rich texture and variability of Indigenous thought. Our aim is to articulate a multiplicity of Indigenous knowledge systems and technological practices that can and should be brought to bear on the 'question of AI'".[85]

---

84 https://www.wired.co.uk/article/maori-language-tech

85 Lewis, Jason Edward *et al.* (2020) Indigenous Protocol and Artificial Intelligence Position Paper. Project Report. Indigenous Protocol and Artificial Intelligence Working Group and the Canadian Institute for Advanced Research, Honolulu, HI. The Initiative for Indigenous Futures and the Canadian Institute

Their work, so far, has included topics like Indigenous language preservation, imagining how AI fits with Indigenous creation stories, how to draw on Indigenous ethics in the development of AI.[86] The cultivation of such communities, organised on their own terms, respecting the distinctiveness of contextual methodologies and epistemologies are indispensable within AI ethics and AI as a whole. Only through the vibrant participation of those traditionally side-lined in academic, technological, and political decision making, can we hope for inclusive, democratic, and just AI.

Additional Considerations

The two illustrations above show some ways in which AI research and applications can further marginalise already marginalised people and groups. It illustrative rather than exhaustive. Every context for AI will come with a unique constellation of contextual concerns, linking multiple power structures and highlighting imbalances along the way. These systemic problems demand interdisciplinary attention and communal response, drawing on many forms of expertise from the humanities, social and natural sciences, broader civil society, and policymakers. In this short chapter I have drawn attention to two large and diverse groups – refugees and Indigenous peoples. I have left out many who are urgently deserving of fuller inclusion and consideration in AI ethics and higher education. These include racialised people and racial and ethnic minorities, who are subject to algorithmic bias and other forms of AI oppression.[87] Diversity of gender and sexual

---

for Advanced Research (CIFAR). DOI: 10.11573/spectrum.library.concordia.ca. 00986506.

[86] "Position Paper," Indigenous AI, 2020. https://www.indigenous-ai.net/position-paper/.

[87] Noble, Safiya Umoja. Algorithms of Oppression: How Search Engines Reinforce Racism, New York: NYU Press, 2018.

orientation also remains an important dimension of contextual analysis of AI and AI ethics. Narrow and restrictive categories deny the richness of human experience and force categories of a few cultures and languages on the majority. Women are still enormously underrepresented in tech companies, especially in senior leadership roles. This underrepresentation is compounded when both race and gender are considered. Technology plays a huge role in accessibility and shaping the lives of people with disabilities. Researchers here have made significant contributions relating to universal design and accessibility, which can both democratise and enhance AI and its applications.[88] Beyond this, we should also consider the rights of children, who are often forgotten in AI discourse, and the elderly who suffer from social exclusion in a rapidly digitalising world. These are just a few illustrations of the social categories that inform human experience. In any person or community there will be overlap in how people identify and how people experience power and privilege. Attentiveness not only to diversity, but the complexity of this diversity is critical. Finally, all of these are woven together in a common concern for ecological justice and care for creation. AI is an accelerant, facilitating unsustainable consumption at all levels from resource extraction to consumer culture. To this end, we must remember that the counterpart to *artificial intelligence* is not human intelligence, but all natural intelligences. Ecotheologian Thomas Berry dreamed of a Ecozoic Era, "the period when humans would become a mutually beneficial presence on the Earth" and called us to "understand the universe as composed of subjects to be communed with, not as objects to be exploited."[89]

At each turn we must ask ourselves, and encourage others to do the same, "Who am I forgetting? Who is left out? Who is most at risk?" In

---

[88] See for example the research of Dr Aimi Hamraie. https://www.vanderbilt.edu/mhs/person/aimi-hamraie/

[89] Berry, Thomas. *The Great Work*, New York: Harmony/Bell Tower, 1999, x.

thoughtfully seeking answers, we can find new lenses through which to view AI and hopefully direct its advance toward justice and the flourishing of our communities, societies, and our planet.

The Way Forward

Looking at these challenges from the perspective of higher education, I see a few key areas where significant steps can be taken to improve the diverse, democratic, and just character of AI research and its application.

First, researchers and institutions need to start with a critical examination of the methodologies and epistemologies at work in AI research. There are already rich and ample resources to reflect critically on how AI research is structured, what kind of questions it asks, and what it assumes as normative about the human, human intelligence, embodiment and more. These are often found in the humanities, arts, and social sciences. Drawing them closer to AI, and encouraging interdisciplinary reflection, will facilitate such needed and fascinating discourse. The proliferation of interest in AI has both helped and hindered its interdisciplinary quality. As the area of research diversifies, specialisation reduces the amount of cross pollination among disciplines. However, this expansion of interest in AI has also drawn in researchers from related (and even unrelated!) fields who bring their own expertise to bear on many questions emerging from AI research. These points of convergence provide excellent opportunity for collaborative reasoning and problem solving.

Second, in unpacking the foundational assumptions at work in the methods and means of AI research, encourage movement toward collaborative research design. Many independent research centres offer creative, interdisciplinary, intersectional analysis of AI and its impact on human life. These organisations are an invaluable resource in adapting traditional academic research to the realities demanded by AI and a digitalised world.[90] They also enjoy freedom to critique the funders of AI, deploy ethnographic and other research methodologies, connect with people through art and social media more so than many established institutional structures allow.

Third, as much as possible, higher education should encourage open source, open access, democratic, and unconventional dissemination of research relating to AI. The ability for all those who are interested to learn about AI is critical. The University of Helsinki, for one, has offered a massively popular introductory course to help increase public AI literacy. The course in now available in 30 languages and has over 750,000 participants.[91] Similarly, the Montreal AI Ethics Institute does a fantastic job of publishing research summaries, which are short and easy to read, along with an extensive *living* dictionary of AI terms to help people navigate this broad field.[92] These but a few ways in which researchers transcend and subvert traditional academic structures to bring an understanding of AI to everyone. Such initiatives should be encouraged and well-resourced both within the academy and beyond it. Quality open access publishing is also critical for those without an institutional affiliation and for institutions without resources for costly subscriptions to for-profit publications. Not unlike Big Tech, academic publishing represents an undemocratic consolidation of wealth, authority, and power. "The academic publishing industry has a large financial turnover. Its sales amount to more than USD 19 billion . . . the market is largely dominated by five large publishing houses . . . which

---

[90] See for example Data & Society, The Ada Lovelace Institute, and the Distributed Artificial Intelligence Research Institute.

[91] University of Helsinki, "Elements of AI," https://www.elementsofai.com/.

[92] Montreal AI Ethics Institute, "AI Ethics Living Dictionary," https://montrealethics.ai/dictionary/.

control more than 50% of the market between them."[93] Where we house our intellectual labours, our wisdom, and our communal discernment requires much more scrutiny, especially given the broad social, ecological, and historical impact of AI.

Conclusion

Extensive study of AI reveals that it despite its transcendent ambitions it is, in fact, a very human phenomena representing all the beauty, chaos, and shortcomings that come with this. A realistic view of AI is a balanced one. Certainly, the influence of military investment, Big Tech, and the interests of the world's wealthiest countries may seem insurmountable, but there is reason to look hopefully forward. As interest in AI grows, so too does the number of people and organisations dedicated to its constructive, peaceful, and democratic development and use. As connections are made, lines drawn from vertex to vertex, a new interdisciplinary web is emerging. This is a growing movement, one that is ultimately capable of upsetting power balances, launching treaty processes, and subverting traditional pedagogy. The heart of this movement are the people too often made vulnerable by the powerful few. Their robust ethical critique, grounded in their contexts, methods, and epistemology, is indispensable in pointing AI in right and good directions.

---

[93] Hagve, Martin. "The money behind academic publishing," *Tidsskriftet* 17 August 2020, https://tidsskriftet.no/en/2020/08/kronikk/money-behind-academic-publishing.

ETHICAL CONSIDERATIONS REGARDING BIASES IN ALGORITHMS

José Luis Fernández Fernández

The Ethical Ambivalence of Digitalisation

If there is something that should be becoming clearer every day, with differing levels of enthusiasm and scepticism, is that we are moving towards a circumstance where Artificial Intelligence (AI) and digitalisation are acquiring an increasingly decisive role in the configuration of life.[94] All spheres of reality, from the most intimate and personal to the most universal, and all aspects of social, economic, and cultural dynamics are being affected by this situation. This is happening to such an extent that in the words of former United States Deputy Defense Secretary, Patrick Shanahan, it could be said that in terms of cyber-security "we're in a new world."[95]

Naturally, one of the areas where the impact is already felt in a marked way is in the field of education. Taking into consideration, for instance, the new sources and tools that the Internet makes available to any self-learner, it will be necessary to rethink not only methodology,

---

[94] Haenlein, M., & Kaplan, A. "A Brief History of Artificial Intelligence: On the Past, Present and Future of Artificial Intelligence." *California Management Review*, 2019, 61 (4), 5-14.

[95] Sweeney, B. E. "The Nexus Between Cyber and Ethics". *National Defense Mag.*, WA, Arlington: November 2018, 38.

but also content, and above all the objectives for formal, regulated education.

The conditions that made it possible and from which the process will continue to evolve in the future can be synthesised into the following four: first, the increase in computing power; second, the growing expansion of storage capacity; third, the proliferation of data, namely Big Data; and, finally, as a condition of possibility for the analysis and identification of behavioural patterns, we must note as a complementary feature, the progress in the development of algorithms.

The fact is that in the midst of the Fourth Industrial Revolution,[96] with the extraordinary development of AI, Deep learning, cloud computing, 3D technology, robotics, the Internet of Things – and even the Internet of Everything – the prospects for the future do not cease to present themselves with a tone of ambiguity. There are many possibilities open to us across varied contexts, including in the improvement of medicine, increase in development and wellbeing, and in education the use of Big Data in educational processes for the improvement of student performance. Risks and threats also loom over us, derived from the very technological dynamics of digitalisation. These are no less significant than the opportunities before us.

The Antidote to the Not-so-unrealistic Possibility of Cybernetic Dystopia

Let us mention a few examples, without trying to be exhaustive. In the first place, there is the most serious one, which in my opinion represents a formidable claim: the transhumanist revolution, which is expressly betting on a supposed improvement of the human race through

---

[96] Schwab, K. *The Fourth Industrial Revolution*. New York: Crown Business, 2017.

human enhancement, if not on the creation of a new species.[97] The technical possibilities seem to be within reach, through the convergence of the fields known as NBIC: Nanotechnology, Biotechnology, Information Technology, and Cognitive Sciences.

However, there are so many challenges and such profound ethical implications of this transhumanist possibility that, to face its foreseeable risks and potential dangers with a good antidote, a global debate should be held. Not only scientists and technologists, but also jurists, politicians and other representatives of professional bodies and associations, and even private citizens, should be able to participate in this debate. This dialogue should involve not only companies, lobbies, and representatives of economic power, but also various members of *civil society*. Of course, the educational world should also take part in this debate. An education is not only about learning new tools and techniques that facilitate a more complete adaptation to the technological environment in which we will have to develop. It is also, on the one hand, the way to learn to develop and flourish as persons in this new context, and, on the other hand, with the design and implementation of strategies for living together and coexisting in a democratic, peaceful, and sustainable way.

Naturally, in this dialogical process, the voice of ethics and the different cultural and religious traditions of humanity should be included as an essential element.[98] In this regard, the contribution of institutions such as Globethics.net and other think-tanks or similar research centers will be particularly relevant.[99]

---

[97] Cf. Bostrom, N., & Savulescu. J. *Human Enhancement.* Oxford: Oxford University Press, 2009.

[98] Buchanan, A. *Better than Human. The Promise and Perils of Enhancing Ourselves.* Oxford: Oxford University Press, 2011.

[99] Stückelberger, C., & Duggal, P. *Cyber Ethics 4.0 Serving Humanity with Values.* Global Series no. 17, Geneva: Globethics.net, 2018.

So much is at stake, including the dignity of people, the exacerbation of unjust differences between individuals, peoples, and cultures and more. Given this, the threat of a dystopia of such magnitude should make us bear in mind two moral maxims of pure common sense: not everything that is ethically desirable is technically possible at a given historical moment; but, above all, not everything that is technically possible is worthwhile and ethically desirable.[100]

In any case, without having to reach such dangerous dystopian extremes as those that can be intuited in the bid for Singularity, for the *mort de la mort*[101] and for what transhumanism represents, it is possible to find other elements that, without a doubt, also raise disturbing considerations from the moral point of view. Thus, for example, along with the already mentioned cyber-security,[102] there is the risk of increased energy footprint in a digital culture, the displacement of democratic processes by technological solutionism, the loss of social confidence and along with it increased polarisation and fanaticism. This could be due, among other things, to the proliferation of hoaxes and fake news, as well as to the so-called economy of attention, by virtue of which people are constantly being bombarded, not only with more or less subliminal commercial information, but also with other types of messages and manipulations that are contrary to peaceful coexistence. Once again, perhaps one of the most efficient ways to face the situation is through an education capable of expressly stimulating critical thinking, the ability to try to think on one's own, to be open to doubt and not to be afraid, when necessary, to allow heterodoxy and to think

---

[100] Fernández Fernández, J. L. "La Economía como oportunidad y reto de la Ética Profesional", in: J. L. Fernández Fernández, & A. Hortal Alonso, *Ética de las Profesiones*, Madrid: Universidad Pontificia Comillas, 1994, 83-107.

[101] Alexandre, L. *La Mort de la mort. Comment la techno médecine va bouleverser l'humanité.* J. C. Lattès, 2011.

[102] Hurlburt, G. "Toward Applied Cyberethics". *Computer*, September, 2018, 80-84.

against the grain, without falling into the always dangerous self-censorship.

In addition to what is indicated, among the challenges that this cyberspace presents us with, it is worth mentioning the real possibility of ending up living in a new Leviathan, in an excessively controlled and controlling society. For example, the impact of robotisation on production chains, with the appearance of a new digital Taylorism and the redundancy of many jobs. This could happen even in contexts traditionally attended to in a personal and qualitative manner, such as university selection processes and support services, today they are increasingly left to chatbots and other forms of AI, seeking improvement and greater quantitative efficiency. This will have a social and personal impact, relating to the growing autonomy of machines and the corresponding dilution of responsibility on the part of human subjects, exacerbated by the concentration of power in a few hands, otherwise wrapped up in a context of growing opacity. The problems continue with possibility of cybercrimes and bad practices, loss of privacy, unfair use of algorithms that contribute to hide, give legitimacy to, or perpetuate unfair biases and unacceptable processes of discrimination. On this last aspect in particular, I will expand my considerations below. But before that, let us give some indications on how we are trying to conjure up those ethical challenges to which we have just referred.

Multiple Initiatives in the Area of Cyber Ethics

It is worth highlighting the fact that, precisely in response to such serious threats as those we have just listed, there is unanimous recognition of the need to take into account the ethical dimension of the process by which cyber society is taking shape, through digitalisation and the deployment of all related technologies.

In this sense, it could be said that there are many initiatives underway with reference to the proposal of ethical guidelines to channel from the best technical practices and meet the ethical requirements of AI from criteria, principles, and moral values[103]. In fact, in the last five years, a wide range of guides and documents of different tone and tenor have been deployed,[104] both from private companies that report good practices,[105] and from the point of view of IT professionals, system developers, or software companies. This wave of guidelines and best practices of course includes approaches at the administrative level[106] and, above all, political, where there is an explicit commitment to openly propose the need to place technology, AI and algorithms at the service of people, their rights and the most genuinely human values. The voice of academia, as it could not have been otherwise, has also been felt throughout this process of drafting and proposing guidelines and ethical codes for the digital world. The participation of university professors and researchers as AI experts provides a multidisciplinary and systematic perspective, which contributes to enriching the ethical debate and the subsequent ethical proposals.

As an illustrative example, alongside documents of high political significance, such as those produced by the European Union,[107] we can

---

[103] Jobin, A., Ienca, M., & Vayena, E. "The global landscape of AI ethics guidelines". *Natura Machine Intelligence*, 1 (9), 2019, 389-399.

[104] Larsson, S. "On the Governance of Artificial Intelligence through Ethics Guidelines". *Asian Journal of Law and Society*, 2020, 1-15.

[105] Wang, Y., Xiong, M., & Olya, H. G. Toward an Understanding of Responsible Artificial Intelligence Practices (HICSS 2020). *Proceedings of the 53rd Hawaii International Conference on System Sciences*, Maui (Hawaii), 2020, 4962-4971.

[106] Cerillo i Martínez, A. "How can we open the black box of public administration? Transparency and accountability in the use of algorithms." *Revista Catalana de Dret Públic*, n° 58, 2019, 13-28.

[107] European Commission, & Independent High Level Expert Group on AI. 20 December 2018. Ethics Guidelines for Trustworthy AI. Source: https://ec.europa.eu/digital-single-market/en/news/ethics-guidelines-trustworthy-ai European Commission. 20 December 2020. White Paper. On Artificial

also refer to two other recent reports. These two are in line with what has been said, and emphasise the ethical dimension of technology and digitalisation in cyber society. On the one hand, the ENIA report of the Spanish government deserves to be highlighted, where the National Strategy of Artificial Intelligence is addressed. España Digital 2025, and in which strategic axis six is explicitly dedicated to "Establishing an ethical and normative framework that reinforces the protection of individual and collective rights, to guarantee social inclusion and well-being."[108] On the other hand, a recent OECD report on smart-mobility, taking distance from any technocentric approach, expressly advocates in its title the construction of human-centric smart-cities.[109]

This commitment to cyber ethics has, of course, also been translated into the academic world. Call it Technological Ethics,[110] Digital Ethics, Data Ethics,[111] Ethics of Artificial Intelligence,[112] Ethics of

---

Intelligence - A European approach to excellence and trust. Got from: https://ec.europa.eu/info/sites/info/files/commission-white-paper-artificial-intelligence-feb2020_en.pdf

[108] Castejón, Pedro Sánchez, Gobierno de España, ENIA. Estrategia Nacional de Inteligencia Artificial, November 2020, 64-70, https://portal.mineco.gob.es/RecursosNoticia/mineco/prensa/noticias/2020/201202_np_ENIAv.pdf

[109] OECD, & Forum, I. T. Leveraging digital technology and data for human-centric smart cities. The case of smart mobility. Report for the G20 Digital Economy Task Force. OECD, 2020.

[110] Martin, K., Shilton, K., & Smith, J. Business and the Ethical Implications of Technology: Introduction to the Symposium. Journal of Business Ethics, 160, 2019, 307-317.

[111] Floridi, L., & Taddeo, M. "What is Data Ethics?" *Philosophical Transactions of the Royal Society A.*, 374: 20160360, 2016, 1-5. https://doi.org/10.1098/rsta.2016.0360

[112] Kaplan, A., & Haenlein, M. "Rulers of the world unite! The challenges and opportunities of artificial intelligence". *Business Horizons*, 63, 2020, 37-50. Baker-Brunnbauer, J. "Management perspective of ethics in artificial intelligence". *AI and Ethics*, 1:173–181, 2021. https://rdcu.be/ccrpr

Algorithms...[113] or any other variation on the same theme, the academy advances in the necessary reflection and in the proposals regarding how to take advantage of the circumstances and the possibilities that digitalisation is putting in the hands of humanity today.

Because it is clear that we are at a historic moment in which, with political will and the help of technology, we could make very decisive progress in building a fairer, more sustainable and, above all, more fully humane world for everyone. A world where everyone could find the possibility to flourish and develop as a person.

In a recent paper, Mick Ashby goes so far as to say:

"We are the only generation that has the chance to steer the fate of future generations of humanity towards being collectively ruled, potentially for eternity, by benevolent super-ethical systems that create a stable cyberanthropic utopia for us, effectively and ethically minimizing human suffering and environmental problems. The alternative is to allow hubris, insatiable greed, and super-unethical systems to extinguish our rights and freedoms, and either enslave most of us in a cybermisanthropic dystopia or cause the extinction of our species to become a footnote in Gaia's geologic al record."[114]

From this optimism this author offers a concrete proposal of ethics applied to the design and implementation of what is called *super-ethical systems*, from the known Good Regulator Theorem. Mick Ashby goes so

---

[113] Mittelstadt,, B. D., Allo, P., Taddeo, M., Wachter, S., & Floridi, L. "The ethics of algorithms: Mapping the debate". *Big Data & Society*, 3(2), 2016, 1-21. Monasterio Astobiza, A. "Ética algorítmica: Implicaciones éticas de una sociedad cada vez más gobernada por algoritmos". *Dilemata*, n° 24, 2017, 185-217. Martin, K. "Ethical Implications and Accountability of Algorithms". *Journal of Business Ethics* 160, 2019, 835-850.

[114] Ashby, M. "Ethical Regulators and Super-Ethical Systems", *Systems* 8, 2020, no. 4, 25. https://doi.org/10.3390/systems8040053

far as to say, not only that "the implementation of super-ethical systems is identified as an urgent imperative for humanity to avoid the danger that superintelligent machines might lead to a technological dystopia"[115] but, starting from the Good Regulator Theorem, if one attends to the nine requirements that he presents in his approach to the problem one would be able to put into operation a cybernetic regulator effective and ethical. These nine requirements are: purpose, truth, variety of actions, predictability, intelligence, influence on the system, ethics and prioritised rules, integrity of all subsystems, and transparency.

Towards a Common Ethical Factor: Principles in Guidelines and Reports

In the already mentioned work of the year 2019, Jobin, Ienca and Vayena study in detail a corpus of 84 ethical guides on AI, trying to find a kind of *common ethical factor*. After carrying out the analysis of the documents, codifying their contents and quantifying the number of times they are referred to, they offer the following list of ethical principles. The list is in order of priority according to the number of documents in which they are mentioned.

- *Transparency* and its synonyms (e.g., transparency, explainability, explicability, understandability, interpretability, communication, disclosure) appear in 73 of the 84.
- *Justice and Fairness* (e.g., justice, fairness, consistency, inclusion, equality, equity, (non-)bias, (non-)discrimination, diversity, plurality, accessibility, reversibility, remedy, redress, challenges, access, and distribution) appear in 68 of the 84.
- *Non-maleficence* (e.g., non-maleficence, security, safety, harm, protection, precaution, bodily or mental integrity, non-subversion) are reflected in 60 out of 84 guidelines.

---

[115] Ibid.

- *Responsibility* (e.g., responsibility, accountability, liability, acting with integrity) are also reflected in 60 of the 84 documents analysed.

- *Privacy* (e.g., privacy, personal or private information) appears in 47 of the 84.

- *Beneficence* (e.g., benefits, beneficence, well-being, peace, social good, common good) is mentioned in 41 of the 84.

- *Freedom and Autonomy* (e.g., freedom, autonomy, consent, choice, self-determination, liberty, empowerment) in 34 of the 84.

- *Trust* shows up in 28, *sustainability* and related words in 14, *dignity* in 13, and finally, *solidarity* appears in 6 of the 84 analysed texts.

For its part, the High-Level Expert Group from the European Commission provides four ethical principles as foundational to trustworthy AI – respect for human autonomy, prevention of harm, fairness, and explicability. The go beyond this and also address seven prerequisites for a trustworthy AI system – human agency and oversight, technical robustness and safety, privacy and data governance, transparency, diversity, non-discrimination and fairness, societal and environmental wellbeing, and accountability.

As can be seen, the moral principles, ethical values, laws and regulations to be enacted,[116] even virtues[117] and practices to be developed within the framework of the cyber society seem places where there is significant theoretical convergence. This is recognised by most of the different authors we have referred to in this paper. However, there

---

[116] Duggal, Pavan. "Cyber Law and Cyber Ethics: How the Twins Need Each Other". In: C. Stückelberger, & P. Duggal, *Cyber Ethics 4.0. Serving Humanity with Values*, Global Series 17, Geneva: Globethics.net, 2018, 55-68.

[117] Stückelberger, C. "Cyber Society: Core values and Virtues". In: C. Stückelberger, & P. Duggal. *Cyber Ethics 4.0*, op. cit., 23-53.

is still an interesting path to follow: on the one hand, there is a clear mismatch between technological advances and legislative codification; on the other hand, it seems necessary to continue advancing in studies and provisions that help to support from the beginning the processes in the governance of AI and, thirdly, as Larsson points out, there will be a need to abound in the multidisciplinary needs in the study of contemporary applications of data-dependent AI.[118]

Furthermore, it would be advisable to try to avoid excessively abstract formulations that, taken to certain extremes, would end up proposing modes of management of AI that would be far removed from the properly humane uses of personal interaction. Perhaps this would prevent real progress towards a better but realistic future, and in any case, far from Adamian pretensions of starting from scratch, as if the history of humanity and the diversity of cultures did not constitute the great value they represent as the heritage of the human race as a whole.

To illustrate, I will close with a critical approach to one of the most recurrent formulations in the guides and good practice proposals. Specifically, I will consider whether all biases are always morally indefensible. This will make it possible to specify in concrete terms how the great moral declarations in the framework of AI must be landed with good sense and enough common sense to result in situations that improve the way of life and interaction between people, when the dynamics of cyber society becomes general.

Distinction between Unfair Algorithmic Bias and Legitimate Cultural Options

As I have just anticipated, I return to my core research questions on biases in algorithms: 1. Is absolute moral neutrality possible in the

---

[118] Larsson, S. "On the Governance of Artificial Intelligence through Ethics Guidelines". *Asian Journal of Law and Society*, 2020, 1-15.

design of AI systems and algorithms? 2. Is every choice discriminating in a negative sense? 3. Should certain cultural values and choices be prioritised, without necessarily violating other people's basic rights or different cultural approaches, be seen as unconditionally questionable from an ethical point of view? 4. Is there a moral problem in designing an algorithm that expressly favours certain options over others?

As an example to illustrate the considerations I want to make in line with these questions, I look to the case of the French website *Ton prénom*. It is a tool designed to help parents choosing a name for their children. The following image is taken from the website in question and will be discussed as an example of what I have just pointed out. I accessed it in December 2020 to replicate a previous study presented by Monasterio Astobiza.[119]

---

[119] Astobiza, Aníbal Monasterio. "Ética algorítmica: Implicaciones éticas de una sociedad cada vez más gobernada por algoritmos". *Dilemata*, Ética de datos, sociedad y ciudadanía, No. 24, 2017, 185-217.

Here I observe how, in effect, the characteristics and requirements that this author had identified and that he criticises harshly for what he considers intolerable social discrimination, are maintained. As you can see, the website discriminates in favour of some names. The algorithm assumes by default that you want to avoid a name of Arabic origin or that you want to give priority to a French name.

Is this an intolerable ethical overload or could it even be considered as a realistic option, full of common sense in the French context in which the service is inserted? Answer as you will, one should be careful in judging intentions – that the programmer is a racist – since they are never obvious; and it could well be that we are indeed facing an intolerable moral outrage. But it could also be possible to tone down such a negative assessment.

In any case, as I will indicate below, the realism that the processes of socialisation require us to consider should serve as a counterpoint to an ethical maximalism far removed from the ordinary ways of interacting.

I decided to study this case, as I said, replicating a previous investigation of Monasterio Astobiza, because I was curious to see if, in fact, such a page existed; if it presented the characteristics that the author pointed out; and if, necessarily, one would have to share the negative evaluation that the author made with respect to the case in question from an ethical point of view. This paper illustrated with practical examples the discrimination due to bias in the algorithms including social discrimination, economic discrimination, free access to information, abuse of control (including several cases were adduced as examples of malpractice).

It also refers to a couple of pages that, while maintaining certain stigmatising stereotypes, sometimes contributes to the limiting of possibilities of choice for certain groups and minorities. As a more controversial example, the so-called Chinese social credit system is also offered. This initiative aims to classify Chinese citizens based on personal information online. According to this, those who score below a certain level, would see their possibilities reduced, for example, to travel, to access certain services, and so on.

However, the cases presented are heterogeneous, and each of them offers a different degree of ethical problem-solving. Therefore, in my opinion, rather than putting them all in the same basket and qualifying them as ethically questionable in the same degree and sense, it could lead to understand that although, from a moral point of view, all discrimination should always be avoided, not always every proposal and bet should be qualified as discriminatory, in the negative sense of the term.

In any case, perhaps the appropriate thing would be to qualify, distinguish better, and specify with greater precision the assessment in this type of reality. I am firmly convinced that a more impartial attitude in this regard could contribute more to the cause of cyberethics than an over-generalised and abstract approach. Naturally this excludes those cases where discrimination would be considered unjust at its root, such as the case of China, where the government could be carrying out authoritarian and antidemocratic abuses, using Big Data and algorithms.

When we rightly lament the loss of biodiversity at the ecological level, we should reflect on the connections and derivatives that this could have at the social level and the disappearance of what I will call culture-diversity. We would have to consider, perhaps, as little or not at all desirable the seasoning of a unique human culture. If excessive homogenisation and uniformity were to be established, we would run the risk of annulling and even losing forever cultural aspects, elements of idiosyncratic traditions and social peculiarities that, from their variety, are precisely what enriches the cultural heritage of the human race.

One of the examples given is that of Google Translator. According to the article in question, by translating the phrase *O bir doctor* from Turkish to English in 2017, the algorithm translated it "He's a doctor."

For the author, this was an intolerable discrimination, since, in doing so, he would be attributing the profession of doctor to a man. On the contrary, in the case of the phrase *O bir hemsire*, the English version said, "She is a nurse." Again, the author of the paper assumed that this would imply that the profession of nurse is a woman's… and that this was also discriminatory, sexist, and ethically unacceptable.

It seems that both in the case of *O bir doktor* and *O bir hemsire* in Turkish the phoneme *O* would become a kind of neutral article, which would have to be translated by something close to it or they. I do not know Turkish, and I do not know if that is exactly how it is. Nevertheless, I did replicate the experiment. I accessed the Google Translate and, indeed, the system had made changes. In December 2020, three years after the case had been analysed for the first time, when I typed in *O birt doktor*, the translation read "She is a doctor." When I did the same with *O bir hemsire*, the English version that the machine proposed was the following: "He is a nurse."

As far as we can see, things have changed quite a bit, but one is struck by the critical question: Should this way of translating not be considered, in some way, also discriminatory, unfair and, above all, inappropriate or inaccurate? Because, in any case, as we have known for many years, after an abundant methodological[120] and *semiotic* reflection, beyond the pure and strict grammar of the sentences, there are, on the one hand, the *syntactic* aspects, but the *semantic* dimension should also be considered; and, above all, the *pragmatics* of language should be taken into consideration.

The latter has to do basically with the dynamics of relationships and interactions that are necessarily established between people, within the framework of cultures. The insertion in a certain cultural space is a natural, almost biological requirement; and the socialisation processes, constitute the condition of possibility of human development. Only from

---

[120] Bochenski, J. M. *Die Zeitgenössischen Denkmethoden*, Francke Verl. 1954.

the firm ground of a culture and a concrete tradition do individuals begin to unfold their particular characteristics, to develop their personality, and to configure, as second nature acquired, their own moral character.[121]

Through the process of socialisation, subjects internalise the large, impersonal, and linguistically available command – *one must behave in this way!* – which all stable societies and human groups necessarily demonstrate. This has to be done this way, that is which is considered good, not only among us, but also for everyone and without restriction, such other practices should never be carried out, because they violate basic and non-negotiable values, in line with the dignity of persons... and so on.[122]

The process of *socialisation* accompanies each person throughout life. It begins with *primary socialisation* (family, home, childhood) and continues in *secondary socialisation* (school, groups to which one belongs, media, social networks, work and professional environment). On the contrary, one always contributes something new and does not limit oneself to introjecting the objective reality that society offers. Instead, one is always capable of innovation and of externalising new or unusual ways of living.

There, precisely, lies the capacity for improvement and moral development of groups and societies. And, in any case, there is also room for *metanoia*, more or less radical transformations, conversions and *processes of resocialisation*. By virtue of this, someone could stop making his own the traditions and models in which they began their life by inserting oneself.

If necessary, it is possible to opt for different and alternative models of life. But, in short, we will always find the subjects framed in specific

---

[121] Aristotle. (380 B.C.E). *Nicomachean Ethics*. Crisp, R. (Ed.). Cambridge University Press, 2014.

[122] Berger, P. L., & Luckmann, T. *The Social Construction of Reality: A Treatise in the Sociology of Knowledge*. New York: Penguin UK, 1991.

cultural areas and clearly identifiable traditions. Apart from this, it would be very difficult to develop moral personality and to carry out the ethical task of building one's own moral life.

Conclusion

Technological development and AI have led to the emergence of a cyber society environment. The expectations of the future that are opening up before humanity are ambivalent. If, on the one hand, they are fascinating (with all the positive emotion that the term has in its etymological root), on the other hand, they cannot but appear as formidable (of *formido*, fear, in Latin).

Taking the reins of digitisation and making AI work for people and humanity is in our hands. Moreover, the ethical dimension of technological development appears to be one of the most pressing challenges, perhaps on a par with that of the ecological problem, in the coming years.

The moral principles traditionally associated with bioethics will have to find accommodation in the new scenario. Non-maleficence, beneficence, autonomy and justice, in short, remain non-negotiable moral expectations. Perhaps, as we have seen in the first part of this work, they should be complemented with other ethical criteria: transparency and explicability and accountability, above all.

As we have been suggesting in the previous pages, from kindergarten to the moment after having presented the doctoral thesis, the role of formal and regulated education in this whole process, aimed at humanising digitalisation through ethics, is crucial. And this, moreover, from a triple instance: firstly, from instruction, fundamentally, devoted to transmitting technical knowledge and supplying conceptual tools; secondly, from the always inevitable formative dimension, present in any educational process, from which attitudes are moulded and values (sometimes even anti-values) are developed. Thirdly, from the research task, as the creative moment, and true source of new knowledge.

There is no great need to insist much on the transcendence of the aforementioned triple instance of education – instruction, formation, research – when it comes to helping put AI at the service of the common good and of people. Because, given that it is not guaranteed *a priori* that technocracy will always be used in favour of what is human, it is compulsory to articulate a high-quality education that is committed to the good and contributes to eliminating inveterate injustices, to undone irrational prejudices and to delete unacceptable biases that, in the context of the cyber society, could not only be exacerbated, but even ending up *reified*, becoming then extremely difficult to remove later on. Naturally, this points to, among other things, the unnegotiable need to expressly address the ethical dimension of education and that of the educational management, for a digitalised world... with all the ambivalence that that implies.

In any case, it is convenient to continue to reflect on ethics, because, if the algorithms that animate the systems where AI is applied are never neutral, moral asepsis is not the supreme value either. Quite the opposite is true. If people act ordinarily *sub specie boni*, it is precisely moral reflection and ethical discernment that must discriminate, in a well-founded and reasonable manner, between the good, the bad, and the best.

To close these considerations, I will respond in a comprehensive manner to the five research sub-questions that I listed at the beginning of section five of this paper. Absolute moral neutrality in the design of AI systems and algorithms is not possible, nor even, as stated in the previous paragraph, is it ethically desirable. Consequently, although every choice always implies a choice, leaving aside options and alternatives, this does not mean that this choice should always be judged badly by some values to the detriment of others. In this sense, a sound moral judgment should not necessarily amount to a discriminatory choice, in the negative sense of the term. Moreover, in short, giving priority to certain cultural values and options, without necessarily violating the basic rights of other persons or different cultural approaches, should not necessarily be seen as unconditionally questionable, from an ethical point of view.

Honestly, I think it is worth keeping the distinction between AI – much more powerful, capable of storing data, and carrying out operations and computations impossible for any person – and Natural Intelligence. AI is, in short, a human product that surpasses its producer, but only in one aspect of the equation. It surely can be much more *intelligent*, but it can never be cleverer. This is the exclusive heritage of our sentient intelligence. It is imperfect, fallible, limited and fragile. At the same time, it is also poetic, emotional and open to the Spirit and Transcendence. In this, I hope, there will always be a qualitative distinction that will make the difference between the human and the non-human: whether instrumental, trans-humanistic or post-human.

For my part, I will continue to work for humanism in all the activities and situations that are within my reach.

PART 2

TEACHING, LEARNING, AND THE FUNDAMENTAL PURPOSE OF THE UNIVERSITY

AI ETHICS AND THE FUNDAMENTAL PURPOSE OF THE UNIVERSITY

D. John Methuselah

The Assumptions

Universities are factories of growth churning out employable or industry-ready youth, and generators of wealth, economic prosperity, and enhanced quality of life is a misunderstanding of the purpose of universities[123].

However, in reality, university is supposed to cultivate fecund thinkers, "thus is created a pure and clear atmosphere of thought, which the student also breathes."[124] University of Berlin was founded on three principles: unity of research and teaching, freedom of teaching, and academic self-governance.[125]

---

[123] Boulton, Geoffrey and Lukas Colin. *What Are Universities For?* League of European Research Universities, 2008. https://www.leru.org/files/What-are-Universities-for-Full-paper.pdf.

[124] Newman, John Henry. *The Idea of a University*, 1852, Assumption Press, 2014.

[125] Wilhelm von Humboldt wrote a memorandum, "On the Internal and External Organization of the Higher Scientific Institutions in Berlin," establishing the University of Berlin in 1810.

Figure 1. Fundamental Purpose of a University

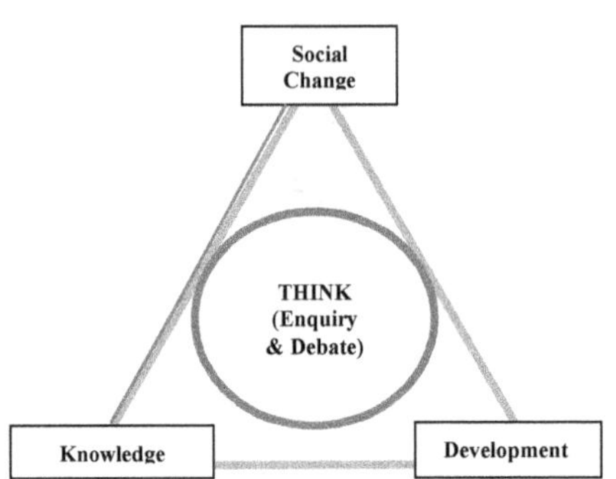

On January 20 2019, Facebook announced $7.5 million over five years' time for research in AI Ethics at the Institute for Ethics in Artificial Intelligence (IEAI), set up in collaboration with the Technical University of Munich (TUM) — one of the top-ranked universities worldwide in the field of artificial intelligence. The research would delve into the fundamental issues, challenges and impact of AI. Other organizations that would join the research are the Partnership for AI, of which Facebook is a founding member, and the AI4People initiative.

The Conference on Beneficial AI (BAI) was organised by the Future of Life Institute in January 2017, in Asilomar, California. Scientists and luminaries like Elon Musk and Stephen Hawking came up with 23 Principles on the precautions and priorities to be followed in developing AI in the future. The focus was on three areas – research issues, ethics and values, and long-term issues of concern. This conferencing is an example of what universities can do in the future with AI and about AI. It is understood that if humankind has to be safe and benefitting, ethics is the only touchstone. Therefore, a deep and continuous discussion on AI Ethics is an inevitability if the fundamental purpose of a university has to be realised.

The thought of the fundamental purpose of a university brings to mind one of the objectives of a hundred-year-old Student Christian

Movement of India which seeks to prepare students "to think critically and participate creatively in the total life of the university."[126] However, for this to happen democratic rational questioning, and constructive debate must be nurtured by the universities. This would contribute to the advancement of knowledge which would inadvertently bring in desired and ethical changes in the society. Therefore, universities are expected to be powerhouses of debate and reasoning aimed at dissemination of knowledge and emancipation from the social evils; stigmas like, race, caste, class, region, religion, nation, language, gender, sexual orientation and so on.

Professor Eric Thomas, President of Universities UK and Vice-Chancellor of the University of Bristol says:

> "The main functions of higher education and universities are predominantly two-fold. One is as educational establishments and the second as generators of knowledge and technology.
>
> As educational establishments, their function is to provide able, self-directed learners that are independent and confident, and will go out into society and give to society through leadership or through civic duties. As knowledge generators, they are research institutions there to provide new knowledge, to change paradigms, to aid society in its development and in meeting new challenges as they come along."[127]

While there is a pipeline from schools to universities, hitherto, the universities have been functioning as islands of higher education with little connection to the school education. Times have changed and school children are studying on the research mode using gadgets

---

[126] Student Christian Movement of India, https://communicationscmi.wordpress.com/2012/08/.

[127] Eric Thomas quoted in "The role of the Universities," https://www.epigeum.com/downloads/ulm_accessible/uk/01_intro/html/course_files/in_2_10.html.

programmed using AI. Picking the baton of AI from the schools is demanding the universities to adapt to new technology.

Universities need to contemplate on the ethical dilemmas in the use of AI. Now that the AI products have become highly commercialised, once again the question of affordability and availability shows its ugly head up. There is every possibility that equal opportunities may become a casualty. Besides, there is a threat of Algorithmic Bias.

It was observed that Natural Language Processing (NLP) - an AI application - erred on colour, gender, race, accent, disabilities, and more. That means bias creeps into the AI programming by the programmer who may have a bias based on his culture, attitude, or the nature of information fed. "Earlier the impact of the biased decisions made by humans was localised and geographically confined. With the advent of AI, the impact of such decisions is spread on a much wider scale."[128]

Another challenge is the continuous updating of the AI. In such case, the fundamental purpose of a university as envisioned is defeated. If the purpose is defeated, how can it be ethical at all? Recently, Facebook has collaborated with Technical University of Munich (TUM) for research in AI, with a particular focus on algorithmic bias.

The first question is how the integration of AI would affect the fundamental purpose of the university. To know the answer to this question, it is important to understand the functioning of a university.

Use of AI in the university can help in making decisions in all these crucial areas mentioned above. However, the how and why of making such decisions is much more important. After all, AI is nothing but a programme in a machine that executes decisions or helps in making crucial decisions working on the sophisticated algorithms (complex permutations and combinations available within the variables of step-by-

---

[128] Damini, Gupta and T.S. Krishnan. "Algorithmic Bias: Why Bother?" *California Review Management,* 17 November 2020 https://cmr.berkeley.edu/2020/11/algorithmic-bias/.

step instructions to accomplish a task in the programme) fed into it as data by a programmer. Therefore, the data translated into algorithms is fed to the machines and that becomes AI. When the machine gives a rational decision based on the algorithms it is supposed and accepted as the best decision. However, the human or team of humans could be biased and that bias, if it goes into the algorithm, may makes the machine take biased decisions or act with bias. Joy Buolamwini, a researcher at MIT and the founder of Algorithmic Justice League has made a film, Coded Bias, which exposes the racial and gender bias in the facial recognition systems engineered through AI.

If society must benefit from AI, then certainly society becomes an important stakeholder. Development of AI in the absence of the stakeholders renders it unethical, useless, and exploitative. The debate over this has to be housed by none other than the universities, since students and faculty in the university can represent the society and its needs.

One cannot turn a Nelson's Eye to AI. There is no Hamletian dilemma about its usage but for the affordability. AI has come to stay, that is the future. Classes in some top universities, especially medical colleges, are using augmented reality to teach anatomy and surgeries. The world cannot let go of the opportunities emerging from AI. However, three two things happen now; one, it is race to grab the opportunities; two, the vice to create unethical opportunities to amass wealth or destabilise democracy and individual freedom; or three, to manipulate history and science for vested interests.

The hacking of classified information, bank accounts, cell phones etc. is a glaring example of the misuse of AI. The future of warfare depends on the ability to use AI. The iron dome developed by Rafael Advanced Defense Systems and Israel Aerospace Industries is an outcome of AI. The world has witnessed its use in the recent times in the Israel-Gaza conflict.

The EdTech market in US is vigorously promoting AI in Education through 2020 and 2021. Thanks to the Covid-19 pandemic, the EdTech business is spreading all over Europe and Asia given the preference to online learning. AI has now found new markets and universities are fast becoming crucial users rather than developers. AI is found more beneficial in Testing, Evaluation, and Assessment (TEA). However, this is where the question of ethics come in.

Universities are not just supermarkets and financial values must be delinked as they have a deeper, fundamental role to play for the progress of the civilization. However, the fundamental role must be to adapt and respond to the changing values and needs of future generations, and from which the outputs cherished by governments are but secondary derivatives.[129] David Orr proposes an "educational 'perestroika'… beginning with the admission that much of what has gone wrong with the world is the result of education.[130]

AI Ethics in a University

Three important areas of concerns to be discussed in order to justify AI ethics in a university are the availability of technology, the affordability of the students, and the accountability of the EdTech companies or AI vendors and the university (on safety, privacy, fairness and transparency). If the above concerns are not addressed then it is a criminal waste of time, resources and precious learning time if not misguiding the students.

It has been a stark reality that Education, for long, has been around employability. Once the students are employed, they survive on adaptability when there is a rotation of jobs in the public sector and

---

[129] Boulton and Lukas.

[130] Orr, David. *Earth in Mind: On Education, Environment and the Human Prospect*, Washington, DC: Island Press, 1994.

firefighting or trouble shooting in the private sector. Education in the university has not been effective in making the students deployable. Perhaps AI could fill that gap. That said, there is every possibility that AI would become a Frankenstein and education its monster and end up in tragedy if it is not noticed, observed, imbibed, implemented with caution and care in the universities and colleges. The race with AI in the universities without accountability may kill its fundamental purpose of making the students think and be beneficial to the society.

Issues, Concerns and the Course Correction

While affordability of gadgets is an undeniable reality, unavailability of strong network and signals is another challenge. Students in many third world countries are unable to source technology and afford required gadgets.

It is not about the purpose of the university but it is about purposeful education for all. That can happen only if AI can help students realise their career anchors. Can AI help students realise their full potential? Sadly, most universities do not have it as an objective even today. They are in a hurry awarding degrees and churning out graduates and postgraduates. Whatever research is being done focuses on Abraham Maslow in his needs hierarchy talks of five essential needs. Self-realization tops the hierarchy and most people die with that need unfulfilled. Once that need is fulfilled, a person becomes more useful and contributive to society. Can use of AI in the university help in fulfilling this need? Pat comes the argument that it is too early to think of self-realisation. If AI is working very fast, then why not? Since most of the students are studying the wrong courses, looking only for employability, there has been a waste of money, time and talents just because they were not discovered and channelised.

The Bertrandian Bugle

Perhaps, AI can be used to make decisions that are wise. Like Bertrand Russell prophetically writes,

> "With every increase of knowledge and skill, wisdom becomes more necessary, for every such increase augments our capacity of realizing our purposes, and therefore augments our capacity for evil, if our purposes are unwise. The world needs wisdom as it has never needed it before; and if knowledge continues to increase, the world will need wisdom in the future even more than it does now."[131]

If wisdom can be taught, then it can be inculcated into AI as well. Then the programming of wisdom into AI is imperative and a challenge as well. Such AI would save time and error, else why should a student take years of time to research? The pandemic has taught the world that making of a vaccine is an urgency and the challenge of multiple variants has brought in multiple demands which forced governments to break or bend the rules. Availability of appropriate AI would have solved the problem. Students in a university could debate on the functioning of AI on the feedback given by it and recommend a course-correction to be programmed into it. Social, economic, political and ethical issues could be discussed as well through simulated experience possible through AI.

Maslow's Hierarchy of Needs and the Purpose of the University

Maslow talks about the five levels of hierarchy of needs before one achieves one's full potential and reinvents oneself to be more useful. Human resource is perishing goods. Education in Universities is aimed at helping the students acuminate their knowledge, skills and talents besides shaping their attitude towards life to be useful to the society.

---

[131] Russell, Bertrand. "Knowledge and Wisdom 1954", *Last Philosophical Testament: 1943-68*, Ed. J. G. Slater, New York: Routledge, 1997, 454.

Competency Mapping (CM) saves precious time, age, unnecessary rigor of uninteresting and mismatching courses and helps not only in catching talent young but nurturing it in a dynamic yet diligent path to make them realise their self. Once that is reached, the behaviour and the attitude change. Therefore, AI can be used for better and near accurate CM. Education thus becomes more meaningful and purposeful.

Simulators are being used in a maritime university to train students on how to steer different ships in different climates in the rough seas, similarly simulators are used to train pilots and even for driving cars. To teach games like chess computers are being used. AI can be used to simulate life situations and the students can be trained to think. Internet of Things (IoT) is the new technology now. The driverless car is an example of IoT run by AI. However, there is a hesitation to use. Its manufacturers like Elon Musk are still not convinced about its efficiency because it is driven by sensors programmed to react and not senses trained to respond. Programming empathy into a computer is still a dream juxtaposed against an irony that not all humans are empathetic - a response to their conscience.

Therefore, teaching using AI can give required or programmed knowledge and skills. However, the programming has to be done by thinking humans; for what they think, and why they think that way - the purpose matters. However, AI should not substitute thinking or in other words thinking should not be outsourced to AI. Once that is done commercialization of thinking happens and Ethics may get compromised. The purpose of education is to educate, and money is just a by-product.

"[At Facebook we're] developing new tools like Fairness Flow, which can help generate metrics for evaluating whether there are unintended biases in certain models... AI poses complex problems which industry alone cannot answer, and the independent academic contributions of the Institute will play a crucial role in furthering ethical research on these topics."[132]

Institute Overview

Drawing on expertise across academia and industry, the Institute will conduct independent, evidence-based research to provide insight and guidance for society, industry, legislators and decision-makers across the private and public sectors. The Institute will address issues that affect the use and impact of artificial intelligence, such as safety, privacy, fairness and transparency.

Through its work, the Institute will seek to contribute to the broader conversation surrounding ethics and AI, pursuing research that can help provide tangible frameworks, methodologies and algorithmic approaches to advise AI developers and practitioners on ethical best practices to address real world challenges.

To help meet the need for thoughtful and ground-breaking academic research in these areas, Facebook looks forward to supporting the Institute and help offer an industry perspective on academic research proposals, rendering the latter more actionable and impactful.

Dr Christoph Lütge. Professor at TUM says that the purpose of the institute is to explore the issues and challenges of AI and develop guidelines for the responsible use of technology for the good of the society.

"Our evidence-based research will address issues that lie at the interface of technology and human values. Core questions arise around trust, privacy, fairness or inclusion, for example, when

---

[132] Quiñonero Candela, Joaquin. "Facebook and the Technical University of Munich Announce New Independent TUM Institute for Ethics and Artificial Intelligence," *Meta Newsroom*, 20 January 2019. https://about.fb.com/news/2019/01/tum-institute-for-ethics-in-ai/.

people leave data traces on the internet or receive certain information by way of algorithms. We will also deal with transparency and accountability, for example in medical treatment scenarios, or with rights and autonomy in human decision-making in situations of human-AI interaction."[133]

Conclusion

Machine Learning (ML), Natural Language Processing (NLP), and Artificial Intelligence (AI) is the future; it is a movement, and there is no stopping. AI Ethics have been continuously evolving while every ethical dilemma at every innovation and advancement has been posing challenges. Rather than the universities, the primary to high schools are fast becoming users and learners of AI. It is an observed fact that universities are adapting to AI slower than the schools. It is true that the fundamental purpose of universities must be to make the students think critically and respond creatively to the needs of the society. They are expected to utilise their knowledge and contribute to usher in innovative solutions to persisting as well as emerging problems in society. In this process of seeking solutions, use of AI helps a lot.

However, the ethical issues emerging from the use of AI, the ethical programming of AI for ethical behaviour depends on the programme developed and programmer. The ethics and values of the institution, individuals or a group of specialists that has developed it, are important.[134] There is every chance that AI can be used from illegal activities to bringing in the next world war if not handled with wisdom.

According to a study by Damini Gupta and T.S. Krishnan in January 2020, FB was ordered to pay $550 million to settle a class-action lawsuit

---

[133] Ibid.

[134] Schroeder, Pete. "U.S. banking regulators seek input on how firms rely on artificial intelligence", *Reuters Financial Reports*, 29 March 2021.

over its unlawful use of facial recognition technology. Capgemini Research Institute's recent survey reveals that more than 80% Indian companies have faced ethical issues from the use of AI systems.[135]

The importance of universities as think-tanks cannot be discounted because of the use of AI. The evidence is loud and clear in the grilling of the CEOs Mark Zuckerberg, Sundar Pichai and Jack Dorsey by lawmakers of US Congress. It was found that these CEOs did not have an instant, convincing, and transparent answer. Zuckerberg dodged question saying his team will get back to the congress on the questions.

There are two things evident; one, either these CEOs know that their companies which run on AI are deliberately misusing or abusing AI or it may be that they are unable to keep track of what is happening, which is much more dangerous. On the other hand it is important to note that the US Congressmen have asked incisive probing questions on their work and its excess. This insightful questioning is needed in the future and that is possible only through a simulation of discussion in the universities. Like English was used against the English to send them away from India, AI can be used as a force and a counter force as well.

In the words of one of the greatest thinkers of twentieth century, Mahatma Gandhi, AI Ethics has a yard stick:

"I will give you a talisman. Whenever you are in doubt, or when the self becomes too much with you, apply the following test. Recall the face of the poorest and the weakest man whom you may have seen, and ask yourself if the step you contemplate is going to be of any use to him. Will he gain anything by it? Will it restore him to a control over his own life and destiny. In other words, will it lead to swaraj for the hungry and spiritually

---

[135] Gupta and Krishnan.

starving millions Then you will find your doubts and yourself melting away."[136]

AI can help in augmenting the human intellect rather than emerging as an alternative to humans believes IBM. AI must help in social transformation by helping humans take well-informed, rational, and responsible decisions for sustainable and livable world[137] if it has to be ethical.

---

[136] Pyarelal, Nayyar. *Mahatma Gandhi, The Last Phase*, Vol. II, 1958, p.65, https://www.mkgandhi.org/gquots1.htm.

[137] Escrigas, Cristina. "A Higher Calling for Higher Education," Great Transition Initiative: Toward a Transformative Vision and Praxis, June 2016. https://greattransition.org/publication/a-higher-calling-for-higher-education.

ROBO-TEACHERS
IN THE UNIVERSITY CLASSROOM
PEDAGOGY, PRAXIS, AND STUDENT PRIVACY

Divya Singh and Avani Singh

Introduction

Higher education today is a rite of passage servicing both pedagogical and andragogical needs. Phrases such as lifelong learning, twenty-first century skills, workplace readiness, and digital transformation are now commonplace in the argot of higher education. The COVID-19 pandemic further impelled the acceptance of digital learning and online teaching and created wider spaces for the discourse on – and possibilities of – machine learning and artificial intelligence to define the transformation imperatives of higher education. In addition, the continued decrease in teaching budgets, and the demands for more individualised teaching have led to a search for more adaptive technological solutions.[138] Against this backdrop, there is no gainsaying the creep and uptake of technology into the university learning and teaching milieu, ranging from new digital platforms and systems to

---

[138] University of Plymouth, "Robots will never replace teachers but can boost children's education," *Science Daily*, 15 August 2018. www.sciencedaily.com/releases/2018/081/180815141433.htm.

chatbots as virtual tutors, and more limitedly to humanoid robots providing student support and a few pilot studies of robots as teachers.

Discussion

The notion of robot teachers engenders a range of emotions from great excitement at one end of the spectrum to horror and disbelief at the other extreme. In 2012, a European survey of 27 000 respondents reported that only 3% of those surveyed agreed that robots should be used in education, with 34% of the sample population believing that robots should, in fact, be banned from 'human areas' such as education.[139] However, as technology has become more ingrained and users become more used to engaging with digital entities, the presence of robots in the classroom is increasingly probable. A statement like this may cause a tsunami of angry rhetoric from educators stressing the shortcomings of intelligent machines to replace the human teacher: notwithstanding, the strategic questions with which future-focused universities must grapple is not *will it happen?* but rather *can robots help teachers improve classroom teaching and learning?*; and, if so, *how much of a role should robots play?* and *what form should their participation take?*

Robots in the Classroom

Several universities globally are already testing robots as teaching assistants and the literature provides a range of interesting examples of artificial intelligence (AI) and robots in the classroom. The responses to this have vacillated between enthusiasm and skepticism.[140] The

---

[139] Eurobarometer (European Commission) 382, "Public attitudes towards robots: Report," September 2012. https://www.ab.gov.tr/files/ardb/evt/Public_attitudes_toward_robots_2012.pdf.

[140] Organisation for Economic Co-operation and Development (OECD). 2021. OECD Digital Education Outlook 2021: Pushing the frontiers with AI,

following sections look at just two of the various possible options: namely, robots as autonomous educators and robots as teaching assistants.

Robots as Autonomous Educators

There are two possibilities when engaging robo-teachers: the autonomous robot teacher that functions independently in the classroom without external control, and robots presented as if they are autonomous but remotely controlled by a human operator.[141] Sometimes, and especially if the robot is geared to function with people, it may be given humanoid form that imitates human form and behaviour, with some further capability of human-like communication.[142] As noted by Newton and Newton,[143] engineers have made robots which can move around classrooms; ask questions; provide information; note and comment on answers; respond to requests; recognise individual students; and maintain a record of those interactions. While the technology has made unprecedented strides, the reality is that "since the 1920s, educators have looked to 'teaching machines' to provide immediate, individual learning experiences at scale."[144] Indeed, new automated approaches

---

blockchain, and robots: Highlights, 5. Available at: https://www.europarl. europa.eu/RegData/etudes/STUD/2020/641530/EPRS_STU(2020)641530_EN.p df.

[141] Sharkey, A.J.C. "Should we welcome robot teachers?" *Ethics and Information Technology.* 18, 2016, 285. DOI: https://doi.org/10.1007/s10676-016-9387-z.

[142] Newton, D.P. and Newton, L.D. "Humanoid robots as teachers and a proposed Code of Practice". November 5. *Frontiers in Education.* 2019, DOI: https://doi.org/10.3389/feduc.2019.00125.

[143] Newton and Newton, 2019: n.p., op. cit.

[144] Holland, B. "Artificial intelligence". *Getting Smart,* 2020, https://www.gettingsmart.com/2020/01/17/artificial-intelligence-the-new-digital-divide/

have been developed, from eye trackers to the monitoring and analysis of other facial features.[145]

One of the key attractions of the robo-teacher is the potential for totally flexible learning and teaching. In a future fantasy of human teachers being replaced by robot teachers, one of the significant attractions is the possibility for students to learn at any time and from any place. Robo-teachers will not be unionised or have set *working hours* and they will not need to take breaks. Class size is immaterial to a robot teacher, who will respond on an individual basis to each student. AI will power these robots providing them with the capabilities for physical and emotional assessment (albeit limited, as we will see later in the discussion) and concomitant individualised teaching, tailored to whether the student is alert, engaged, tired or simply not able to understand the unit of study. In the last-mentioned instance, the robot teacher can provide a recap lesson in basic concepts that will facilitate better understanding of the more involved concepts or immediately refer the student to remedial resources, which is not always feasible in the human teacher-student-classroom engagement.

Newton and Newton emphasise the further potential for more constructive student engagement in the robot-controlled classroom, arguing that in the traditional student-teacher set-up, the human teacher controls the discussion to which the student responds. However, with a robot, the interaction is more balanced with the student enjoying more opportunities to instigate engagement, as would the case in everyday conversation. Further, they reflect on what they describe as students' *performance emotion* and suggest that talking to a robot could be a much less emotive experience, mitigating the anxiety of being judged and promoting more positive attitudes to learning.[146] According to the

---

[145] OECD, 2020, op. cit. 5.

[146] Newton and Newton, 2019, op. cit. n.p.

OECD,[147] technology also enables students with special needs to participate in education, with AI facilitating the ability of blind, visually impaired, deaf and hard-of-hearing students to participate in traditional education settings and practices; further to this, it is noted that some smart technologies "facilitate the diagnosis and remediation of some special needs (e.g., dysgraphia) and support the socio-emotional learning of students with autism so they can more easily participate in mainstream education."

On the other hand, reports from NCTEFL India[148] are much less enthusiastic about the autonomous robot teacher. They identified only one positive benefit of having a robot teacher which would be to ensure that the syllabus was completed within the set time. However, whether this is truly a constructive advantage for students remains uncertain for, while the robot teacher follows the course programme according to a set schedule, the human teacher may take longer to complete a unit of work realizing that students are experiencing difficulties with understanding which requires repetition, more examples, or a slower pace.

Sharkey also raises an interesting question around the trust with which students would accept the robot's answers.[149] Studies seem to suggest that the outcome may be more positive when the responses relate to factual or technical issues: however, notes Sharkey "[a] robot that is unable to answer children's questions when they stray beyond the featured topic would probably be viewed quite skeptically by the children it is 'teaching'."[150]

---

[147] OECD, 2021, op. cit. 6.

[148] NCTEFL. 2018. "Human teachers vs robot teachers: Who are the best for the changing times?" May, 9. *NCTEFL India*. Available at: https://medium.com/@NcTeflIndia/human-teachers-vs-robot-teachers-who-are-the-best-for-the-changing-times-f9368b5796aa.

[149] Sharkey, 2016, op. cit. n.p.

[150] Sharkey, 2016, 286.

Lastly and perhaps most significantly when considering the automation of education and balancing the wonders of technology, none can gainsay the fact that responsive teaching requires human judgement, common sense, often an appreciation of the larger picture and an understanding of the nuance behind peoples' actions, as well as consideration for the values and anticipation of the direction in which events are unfolding.[151] Some may argue that robots could be pre-programmed for such qualities, but the obvious counter-contention is: *Can anyone know every situation that might arise to successfully pre-programme the machine's response?* Summarising the problem Kwok emphasises the intrinsic inability of machines to conduct open ended dialogues and give feedback to open ended questions, nor can they replicate the facial gestures and expressions of human teachers which contributes to the effectiveness of the learning experience.[152] Simply, concludes Kwok "artificial intelligence computer technology is unable to deal with learners' unexpected problems and respond to learners' questions immediately as human teachers do."[153]

Additionally, educators generally agree that in education – both basic education and higher education – there must be some sort of connection or *relationship* between the participants for there to be an effective learning engagement. As pointed out by Belpaeme *et al* "[s]ocial interaction enhances learning between humans in terms of both

---

[151] See Heyns reflecting on the use of autonomous robots albeit in situations of extrajudicial, summary, or arbitrary executions). Heyns, C. 2013. Extrajudicial, Summary or Arbitrary Executions. GAOR, 80, U.N. Doc. A/HRC/23/47. April 9.

[152] Kwok, V.H.Y. "Robot vs. human teacher: Instruction in the digital age for ESL learners". 8(7) *English Language Teaching.* 2015, 158-160. http://dx.doi.org/10.5539/elt.v8n7p157.

[153] Kwok, 2015, op. cit. 158.

cognitive and affective outcomes,"[154] and artificial intelligence is perhaps just not there yet.[155] Acknowledging the central importance of social interactions and the student-educator relationship in the learning experience, MIT Media Lab has commenced working on *social robots* to gauge their effect on learning on undergraduate students and older adults at MIT.[156] As defined by Gottsegen, social robots are meant to promote interaction between humans and robots.[157] Early positive results were recorded with the MIT project leader reporting that "it is not just young children who respond positively to social robots . . . We are seeing a social-emotional benefit across age groups."[158] Contributing to this body of knowledge, the study from the University of Twente in the Netherlands suggests that the social connection also seems to be much stronger with physical robots rather than *intelligent tutors* which students view on computer screens.[159] Belpaeme et al made similar findings noting that "[r]obots can be more engaging and enjoyable than a virtual agent in cooperative tasks and are often perceived more positively."[160] Kwok however is less enthusiastic arguing that "insufficient teacher training and guidance may cause the robot to become nothing more than a distracting toy in the classroom. High

---

[154] Belpaeme, T., Kennedy, J., Ramachandran, A., Scassellati, B. and Tanaka, F. "Social robots for education: A review", *Science Robotics*, 3(21) 2018, 1. https://doi.org/10.1126/scirobotics.aat5954.

[155] Bushweller, K. "Teachers, the robots are coming. But that's not a bad thing". *Classroom Technology.* January 7 2020, https://www.edweek.org/technology/teachers-the-robots-are-coming-but-thats-not-a-bad-thing/2020/01.

[156] Bushweller, 2020, op. cit. n.p.

[157] Gottsegen, G. "Classroom robots are infiltrating the education industry, but teachers are safe – for now". April 6 2019. *Builtin Beta.* n.p. https://builtin.com/robotics/robotics-in-the-classroom,

[158] Bushweller 2020, n.p.; see also Belpaeme et al 2018: 1, op.cit.

[159] Bushweller 2020, n.p.

[160] Belpaeme et al., 2018, op. cit. 1.

student motivation following the initial introduction of the robot decays rapidly."[161]

Interestingly, a recent UNESCO report observed that while there are some notable exceptions, much AI in education has been designed – whether intentionally or not – to replace some teacher tasks, rather than to assist teachers to teach more effectively. UNESCO suggests that a future possibility is that an AI teaching assistant could help the human teacher with many tasks,[162] including providing specialist expertise or professional development resources, collaborating with colleagues, monitoring the students' performance, and tracking progress over time. However, what and how to teach the students would remain the responsibility and prerogative of the teacher, with the AI's role being limited to making the teacher's job easier and more collegiate.

Robots as teaching assistants and for student support

As opposed to autonomous robot teachers, AI has been positively used to support the learning engagement in the university. *Jill* is an AI teaching assistant, developed to enhance student support at the Georgia Institute of Technology. Its developer, Ashok Goel, explains the reason for Jill: every semester he was receiving more than 10,000 messages from his approximately 300 students, too many for him and his eight teaching assistants to handle. Conscious of the retention crisis in universities and correctly ascribing it to the fact that "one of the main reasons students drop out is because they don't receive enough teaching support," Goel and his team of postgraduate students began to work on Jill.

Interestingly Goel points out that as class size increases, so too does the number of enquiries: however, the number of *different* questions

---

[161] Kwok, 2015, 158.

[162] UNESCO. 2021. *AI and education: Guidance for policy-makers*. UNESCO Publishers: France, 18. https://unesdoc.unesco.org/ark:/48223/pf0000376709.

does not go up. Goel and his team tracked almost 40,000 student questions that had previously come up in the different classes and they then began feeding Jill both the questions and answers. By the end of the project Jill was an effective, efficient ninth teaching assistant on the team, receiving positive reviews from the students. Only one student identified that Jill was possibly not a human because '[she] tended to answer questions much faster than the others.'[163]

In the Big Ideas survey conducted by Bushweller with K-12 teachers, notwithstanding the general antipathy to AI robots in the classroom, 44% of the respondents acknowledged that the robots could be of assistance especially with administrative tasks. With reference to student support, 30% believed robots could assist with grading, and 30% recognised a positive role for AI in "translating/communicating with emerging bilinguals."[164] Although referenced for schools, the last-mentioned recommendation may also be something to further consider in the university environment especially regarding additional support for new university entrants required to learn in English, but with only limited understanding of the language.

There is no gainsaying the potential for AI and robots to supplement teaching and facilitate learning. Already many institutions have implemented supplementary education platforms, which use AI algorithms to learn how students in the class engage with the content and their areas of difficulty. Describing the experience:

"These algorithms learn how the student is engaging with content and which areas they are finding difficult to understand by tracking for example how many times they repeat a video in a given timeframe, how many trials it takes for them to get a practice question correct, and the discussions they have engaged in with other students. Upon learning which parts the students

---

[163] Bushweller, 2020, n.p.

[164] Bushwell, 2020, n.p.

need to revise more, the algorithms direct them to more resources for further studying."[165]

Notwithstanding the recorded successes with robots in the classroom, the caution from Fernandez-Llamas *et al.* (2017/2020: 2) is apposite. Recognising how students' attitudes affected the results obtained, but equally noting that most of the research involved only short experiments while the robot was still cool and a classroom novelty, Fernandez-Llamas *et al.* emphasise the need for more research including students' attitudes where the use of robots is a more permanent fixture in the classroom.[166] This is reiterated by Schwartz based on the data from a study at Northwoods Elementary School of Technology and Innovation in North Caroline. Recording heightened levels of engagement and participation by the children engaging with the robot tutor once or twice a month, and a preparedness to focus until the lesson was understood, the class teacher notes:

> "However, I do not feel like it would be as commanding if it was used on a daily basis as an instructional tool, students may lose interest."[167]

---

[165] Muzamhindo, H. "Can a robot replace a teacher?" July 24. *Investec Education.* 2020. *https://www.investec.com/en_za/focus/innovation/can-a-robot-replace-a-teacher.html.*

[166] Fernández-Llamas, Camino, Miguel Ángel Conde, Francisco J. Rodríguez-Sedano, Francisco J. Rodríguez-Lera, Vicente Matellán-Olivera. "Analysing the Computational Competences Acquired by K-12 Students When Lectured by Robotic and Human Teachers Can a Robot Teach Computational Principles to Pre-university Students?". *Int J of Soc Robotics,* 2020, 12:1009–1019. Note by the Editor: pagination of the released article differs from the quoted text marked as the 2017 version.

[167] Schwartz, K. „Robots in the classroom: What are they good for?" 27 May 2014, *Mind Shift.* https://www.kqed.org/mindshift/35611/robots-in-the-class room-what-are-they-good-for.

Similarly, Newton and Newton state:

"Of course, some learning and motivational effects may be due to the current novelty of the robot in the classroom, and it is not entirely certain whether, with familiarity, such benefits will persist. There are indications that they can decline over time."[168]

While initial indications are that machines in the classroom have the potential to assist teaching and support student learning, the only fact that we have at this stage is that *we just don't know enough*. Thus, for now, and accepting that technology will redefine teaching in the future, a controlled adoption - rather than over-reliance - is the safer way to go.[169]

Ethical Considerations

Coupling the benefits of the human teacher with the advantages of complementary student support provided by an algorithm may, at face value, appear to be a constructive approach to teaching and learning in the future-focused university. However, there are ethical considerations to be resolved before this should be entertained by universities. In this context, the reminder from Hanson is apposite: "In higher education … we face a decade in which institutional integrity and legitimacy is under fire."[170] As higher education institutions become adopters of the perceived benefits of technology and especially AI, the duality of the relationship between ethics and technology must consciously align with the broader higher education commitment to academic authenticity and integrity.[171]

---

[168] Newton, 2019, op. cit. n.p.

[169] Kwok, 2015, op. cit. 162.

[170] Hanson, 2009, op. cit. 1.

[171] Singh, D. and Singh, A. "AI in student recruitment and selection: Artificial intelligence and the need for authenticity and integrity", 20(1) 2021, *The South*

UNESCO identifies some of the key ethical questions that arise as follows: what criteria should be considered in defining and continuously updating the ethical boundaries of the collection and use of learners' data; how might schools, students and teachers opt out from, or challenge, their representation in large data sets; what are the ethical implications of not being able to easily interrogate how AI makes decisions (using multi-level neural networks); what are the ethical obligations of private organizations and public authorities; how does the transient nature of students' interests and emotions, as well as the complexity of the learning process, impact on the interpretation of data and ethics of AI applied in educational contexts; and what pedagogical approaches are ethically warranted?[172]

In a deliberate proactive attempt to protect society against the abuse of AI and new technologies, the European Group on Ethics in Science and New Technologies proposes nine ethical principles and democratic prerequisites when considering a new system: human dignity; autonomy; responsibility; justice, equality and solidarity; democracy; the rule of law and accountability; security, safety, and bodily and mental integrity; data protection and privacy; and sustainability.[173] However, we should also bear in mind the *unknown unknowns*, namely those ethical issues raised by the interaction of AI and education that have yet to be identified.[174]

Some of these standards bear deeper reflection in the context of robo-educators and machines in the classroom.

African Qualifications Framework and the Fourth Industrial Revolution. SAQA: Waterkloof, South Africa, 68. Read the article below in this book as well.

[172] UNESCO, 2021, op. cit. 20.

[173] European Group on Ethics in Science and New Technologies. 2018. *Statement on Artificial Intelligence, Robotics and 'Autonomous' Systems*, 8, http://ec.europa.eu/research/ege/pdf/ege_ai_statement_2018.pdf

[174] UNESCO 2021, ibid.

Student privacy

AI solutions for teaching and learning rely on large amounts of education data, including personal data such as biological markers or facial recognition. Classroom robots will impact student privacy as soon as sensors are used to measure engagement responses and when records are kept.[175] An even greater challenge to privacy is when information gathered is stored by the technology and subsequently accessed by others, or immediately accessed by third parties as part of the further teaching engagement. This must raise an alarm even though the aim may be to provide a better learning experience for the student, especially if the full extent of the third-party access is not made clear to the student at the start of the relationship.

The real-world impact of this concern is illustrated in a report in the Wall Street Journal, which revealed that thousands of Chinese students' data had been exposed on the internet.[176] The cache was connected to a surveillance system labelled 'Safe School Shield' and contained facial identification and location data. As noted in the report, this raises serious questions about school surveillance and cybersecurity measures being taken.

Under South African law for example, the Protection of Personal Information Act 4 of 2013 (POPIA) requires that institutions gathering information on students must ensure, among other things, that (1) the affected students are adequately informed of the intention; and (2) any personal information processed complies with the conditions stated in the Act. Specific to the case of robot teachers is the legislative prescript that personal data may only be processed when, given the purpose, it is relevant, not excessive and there is a valid justification for the

---

[175] Sharkey, 2016, op. cit. 283.

[176] Lin, L. "Thousands of Chinese students' data exposed on internet." *Wall Street Journal*, 2020, n.p. https://www.wsj.com/articles/thousands-of-chinese-students-data-exposed-on-internet-11579283410.

processing. Furthermore, the collection of personal information must be for a specific, explicitly defined, and lawful purpose related to a function or activity of the university.[177]

Data protection tends to be better regulated than AI in most countries, although the interplay between the two is in urgent need of further exploration. For example, the only direct guidance under South African law is currently section 71 of POPIA, which provides that data subjects may not be subject to decisions which result in legal consequences or affect them to a substantial degree, which are based solely on the basis of the automated processing of personal information intended to profile such persons. While there are certain exceptions to this, the reality persists that there is very little guidance from a legal perspective on how this provision is to be interpreted. In a report published by the European Parliament on the impact of the General Data Protection Regulation (GDPR) on AI, it was noted while the GDPR generally provides meaningful indications for data protection relative to AI applications, a number of AI-related data protection issues are also not explicitly answered, which may lead to uncertainties and costs. This concern is not unique to the European context and applies equally to data protection frameworks across the globe.

The question is whether universities employing machines in the classroom as educators or teaching assistants will be able to assure compliance with the relevant legal frameworks on privacy to which they are required to comply, especially managing personal information that is voluntarily shared but not intended for further processing. Aggravating the problem, notes Sharkey is the fact that "the mobility and connectedness of robots provide new challenges," and the legal and ethical ramifications are still being explored and debated.[178]

---

[177] Singh and Singh 2021, op. cit. 78. Read also directly the chapter below "AI in Student Recruitment and Selection".

[178] Sharkey, 2016, 288.

A further concern focused on the contravention of the students' privacy rights is if the student develops a trusted relationship with the robo-teacher and reveals emotions or confides information not actually intended for third parties. In a separate case study, Kanda et al describe how their classroom robot used RFID tags to maintain records of children's interactions and *friendship groups*,[179] begging the question whether the robot cannot become an unintended surveillance system storing information that may be used in the future for other purposes such as identification of delinquent behaviour or even suspicion of criminal conduct. Exacerbating this concern is the fact that the robot had been programmed to assume that people who freely came together as a group could be categorised as friends. However, experience informs us that this is not necessarily true as people come together for many reasons, raising other questions about the programming assumptions and the possibility for incorrect results.

Algorithm bias and inaccuracies

Favouritism in the classroom is an age-old complaint and there is an argument to be made that robo-teachers would eliminate this problem. However, notes Sharkey, robots are not necessarily fair and unbiased.[180] Because robots are developed and programmed by humans, they can display the conscious or unconscious social and cultural biases of their programmers. The project leader of the MIT study (referred to above) confirms algorithm bias as a definite downside in the debates on AI in the classroom. She notes:

---

[179] Kanda, T., Sato, R., Saiwaki, N. and Ishiguro, H. "A two-month field trial in an elementary school for long-term human-robot interaction", 23(5), 2007. *IEEE Transactions on Robotics*. 963.

[180] Sharkey, 2016, 292.

"For starters, the AI field right now is not diverse or inclusive and that could affect the kinds of technologies being developed and fuel potential biases in the software."[181]

The University of Plymouth and Belpaeme *et al* also identified specific limitations with robots in the classroom with speech recognition, especially where the accents were different to that with which they had been programmed.[182] Identifying one of the key underlying concerns with AI currently namely *algorithmic fairness*, Kuhlman, Jackson, and Chunara point out that the root cause stems from structural social inequalities that are then carried through to the data used to train predictive models and in their ultimate functions.[183] Where there is underrepresentation of particular social groupings such as ethnic and cultural minorities, or gender imbalances in the development sample, an unintended result may be the presentation of structural biases in the AI programme. This is exacerbated when the scientists are equally unaware of or unconscious to the issue and do not specifically accommodate for the vulnerabilities in the model. Such examples militate against one of the fundamental missions of higher education in the twenty-first century namely adaptive teaching to achieve equity in the learning experience. In such cases, while the robot teacher may be able to provide individualised teaching, the learning may be counter-intuitive to the students' needs.

---

[181] Bushweller, 2020, n.p.

[182] The University of Plymouth. "Robots will never replace teachers but can boost children's education". 15 Aug. 2018. https://www.plymouth.ac.uk/news/robots-will-never-replace-teachers-but-can-boost-childrens-education, see also Belpaeme et al., 2018, op. cit. 2.

[183] Kuhlman, C., Jackson, L. and Chunara, R. "No computation without representation: Avoiding data and algorithm biases through diversity". Feb. 2020, Preprint, https://www.researchgate.net/publication/339550954_No_computation_without_representation_Avoiding_data_and_algorithm_biases_through_diversity.

Burt also highlights other internal and external sources of "algorithmic misbehavior" which would be critical detractors were such machines to be introduced as teaching alternatives.[184] These include such instances as when the data on which the machine was trained "differs too widely from data in the real world" (a so-called internal cause), or if the algorithm is manipulated through an external attack aimed at altering the programmed algorithm (described as an external cause). A further critical concern is the acknowledgement that bias may not be programmed or result through a hack attack, at all but learned by the machines acting on their own. For example, Amazon's experimental recruitment engine – designed to automate the search for "top talent" – displayed a distinct gender bias towards male applicants when it came to technical positions. It transpired that the computer models had been trained on resumes drawn over the previous ten-year period, a time when the industry was overwhelmingly male dominated. Consequently, the machine learned to penalise resumes that included the word *woman*.[185] In another project, the machines were unambiguously trained to reject candidates with poor English language skills, and, over time, the algorithm taught itself to equate English sounding names generally with acceptable qualifications for the job.[186]

---

[184] Burt, A. "The liabilities of artificial intelligence are increasing". 15 June 2020, *Legaltech News*, 4, https://www.law.com/legaltechnews/2020/06/15/the-liabilities-of-artificial-intelligence-are-increasing/?slreturn=20210922140653.

[185] Dastin, J. 2018. "Amazon scraps secret AI recruiting tool that showed bias against women." 10 October 2018. *Reuters*. https://www.reuters.com/article/us-amazon-com-jobs-automation-insight/amazon-scraps-secret-ai-recruiting-tool-that-showed-bias-against-women-idUSKCN1MK08G, Kim, Y., Soyatu, T. and Behnagh, R.F. "Towards emotionally aware AI smart classroom: current issues and directions for engineering and education". *IEEE Access*, 2018. 6. 5308-5331 [online]. Available at: https://doi.org/10.1109/ACCESS.2018.2791861.

[186] www.harver.com/blog/machine-learning-in-recruitment/.

Reacting to the long-term consequences of algorithm bias, Yu points out:

"While the existence of algorithmic bias alone is bad enough, the problem can be exacerbated by the fact that machines learn themselves by feeding the newly generated data back into the algorithms. Because these data will become the new training and feedback data for machine-learning purposes, algorithms that are improperly designed or that use problematic data could amplify real-world biases by creating self-reinforced feedback loops. As time passes, the biases generated through these loops will become much worse than the biases found in the original algorithmic designs or the initial training data."[187]

Accordingly, stresses Remian:

"Authenticating the knowledge and predictions of AI becomes more important when AI is used for education since the further spread of inaccurate or outdated content could defy educational goals and further reinforce false information."[188]

However, UNESCO notes:

"AI is not biased in itself. Instead, if its data are biased or analysed with inappropriate algorithms, the original and perhaps unidentified biases can become more noticeable and have a greater impact. Making these biases noticeable is probably helpful, because it can lead to corrections, but allowing the biases

---

[187] Yu, 2019, op. cit. 17.

[188] Remian, D. Augmenting education: Ethical considerations for incorporating artificial intelligence in education, 20 November 2019, 24. Scholar Works at UMass Boston, https://scholarworks.umb.edu/cgi/viewcontent.cgi?article=1054 andcontext=instruction_capstone.

to have a greater impact can lead to prejudicial outcomes and so should be carefully mitigated."[189]

It appears to be clear that many smart technologies and AI-based solutions are not fully mature yet. For example, while some early warning systems now approach good predictive power, most rely on predictors that are no better than a random guess; furthermore, in the areas of student engagement, there has been seen to be a concerning level of inaccuracy in many of the measures used in the field of learning engagement.[190] It is therefore a challenge to ensure that the developed technology solutions perform their tasks with accuracy, taking into account that the current level of imperfection may not necessarily be more imperfect than humans. It must therefore be noted that institutions adopting AI may be creating concrete liabilities in the process. The research illuminates the need for universities considering AI systems to properly understand how and why the robot was trained and who programmed it. Underscoring the need for institutions to proceed with caution, Popenici and Kerr state:

"With the rise of AI solutions, it is increasingly important for educational institutions to stay alert and see if the power of control over hidden algorithms that run them is not monopolised by the tech-lords… Those who control algorithms that run AI solutions have now unprecedented influence over people and every sector of contemporary society."[191]

---

189 UNESCO, 2021, 25.

190 OECD, 2021, 19.

191 Popenici, S.A.D. and Kerr, S. "Exploring the impact of artificial intelligence on teaching and learning in higher education". *Research and Practice in Technology Enhanced Learning*, 12(22) 2017, 4. https://doi.org/10.1186/s41039-017-0062-8.

Equity and the digital divide

A further consideration to flag is the impact of the digital divide, which remains a prevalent concern globally (and particularly in the global south, as well as in rural and peri-urban areas). It has been noted:

"On the one hand, [smart technologies] clearly do or could help reduce inequity both by increasing access to learning opportunities for all and improving learning effectiveness for those who need it the most. On the other hand, without a widespread and equitable availability of smart technologies, inequity could also rise. They may also leave achievement gaps unchanged or even widened, depending on their differential impact on learners."[192]

For those students who have never encountered such technology – either in the classroom or in their personal lives – the sudden exposure and requisite trust that they will be asked to place in the robot teacher may be startling, uncomfortable and invidious to the student's learning experience. According to Holland:

"Over the past few decades, artificial intelligence (AI) has created a state of disequilibrium not only in society but also in education. Currently, AI can be found driving search engines; powering adaptive learning platforms and intelligent tutoring systems; enabling text-to-speech, dictation, and translation; and monitoring school security. However, these technologies have flooded education faster than research and policy can keep up. As a result, despite all of its promises, there could be very real and significant consequences – particularly when it comes to digital equity.

---

[192] OECD, 2021, 16.

Educators and policymakers have warned of the effects of the digital divide since the 1990s. Initially, this deficit referred to lack of access with computers and the internet. By 2016, the National Education Technology Plan warned of another issue, an emerging digital use divide, as some students learned to use technology for active construction of knowledge and understanding while others remained passive consumers of digital content. With the continued rise of AI, another chasm may emerge as a result of varying experiences with, and exposure to, this innovation."[193]

In this regard, it should be borne in mind that the elements of trust and acceptability that a robot may have will be more prevalent amongst those students who have been exposed to technology from a young age, with the opposite presenting a risk of exclusion. It therefore cannot be ignored that there is a difference in access to devices and connectivity by students from different groups, notably students from lower socio-economic backgrounds; as such, account must be had to the possibility that these students may not have the devices, the connectivity or the resources that allow accessing and using smart technologies either at the learning institution or at home.[194] It also cannot be ignored that high-quality systems are necessary for the robot teacher to function properly, with basic amenities – such as electricity outages or dropped internet connections – either hindering their ability to teach or rendering it a nullity.

Deception, detachment, and loss of human contact

Continued engagement with social robots can shape social behaviours. As Belapeme *et al.* confirm, social robots have been shown to be quite effective at increasing both cognitive and affective outcomes

---

[193] Holland, 2020, op. cit. n.p.

[194] OECD, 2021, op. cit. 16.

because of their physical presence, appearance, and perceived ability to engage.[195] Sharkey discusses the deception factor when social robots are designed to appear as if they understand human behaviour.[196] In such instances, she notes, "[t]he deceptive appearance of robots as real social entities could lead people to form attachments to them, or to imagine that they were capable of or worthy of attachment."[197] When such attachments begin to inform the social development of (perhaps impressionable) students, there is the potential for in tandem antisocial behaviours to be modelled, or in a worst-case scenario a narcissist may be borne. Examples of social dysfunctionality that may develop include students starting to mimic the robot's communication behaviours without learning the normal reciprocity of give and take that attaches to human-human engagement. Other negative behaviours emerge when people become used to the robots acting on their requests without demur and believe that it is accepted social practice to demand and receive, giving rise to a more selfish, self-centred, inconsiderate, and controlling personality type. Thirdly, students interacting with social robots will quickly grasp that they can speak to and/or treat the robot with disregard, disrespect, or even physical abuse with no associated repercussions for their belligerent conduct. Finally, where robots inspire strong emotional attachment from the human participant, the fact that it is not reciprocated can lead to self-doubt and emotional distress, or a belief that emotional artifice is acceptable and 'faking it is ok'.

---

[195] Belapeme et al. 2018, 1, 4-5.

[196] Sharkey, 2016, op. cit. 283. See also Serholt, S., Barendregt, W., and Vasalou, A. "The case of classroom robots: Teachers' deliberations on the ethical tensions", 32(4), 2017, *AI and Society*. 613-31. https://doi.org/10.1007/s00146-016-0667-2.

[197] Sharkey, 2016, 288.

Belpaeme *et al.* point out that:

"Although advanced sensing technologies for reading gesture, posture, and gaze have found their way into tutoring robots, most social robot tutors continue to be limited by the degree to which they can accurately interpret the learner's social behaviour."[198]

Muddled signals can create confusion in the student's mind, and if such behaviours become learned, could lead to demonstrations of social dysfunctionality.

The negative psycho-social effects of human-machine attachment must be investigated further before robots can be introduced as a more permanent fixture in the learning journey. That said, there is also another school of thought. Gottsegen, for instance, notes, "The robots can't actually sense their [human] affection, of course. But they're built to *seem* receptive to it. And for now, that's good enough."[199]

Considering deception to the teaching project, Sharkey describes programmed humanoid robots that measure students' levels of arousal and then adapt their behaviour to enhance engagement. This, too raises a concern pushing teaching "towards a form of 'edutainment' in which any difficult and potentially boring topics were avoided".[200] Belpaeme *et al.* (2018: 7) also consider the possibility of a more impoverished learning experience, which prioritises what is technologically identified over what is actually needed by the learner.

---

[198] Belpaeme *et al.*, 2018, op. cit. 2.
[199] Gottsegen, G. 2019, op. cit.
[200] Sharkey, "Should we welcome robot teachers?", 2016, 288.

Conclusion: Will Robots Replace Teachers in the Classroom?

In 2019, UNESCO published the Beijing Consensus on Artificial Intelligence and Education, which called for AI to empower teaching and teachers.[201] The Report underscores the point that:

> "while AI provides opportunities to support teachers in their educational and pedagogical responsibilities, human interaction and collaboration between teachers and learners must remain at the core of education."

The idea of machines replacing people in the workplace is neither novel nor a simple straightforward response. Several studies are available analysing jobs that are susceptible to automation and the reasons why other job are more protected. Citing statistics from the website *Will robots take my job*, Kupferman notes that teachers are deemed 'totally safe' with a 1% suggestion of complete automation. Similarly, the study by Elliott which discusses the role of AI and technology in replacing human engagement in the workplace, without any reference to the schools, universities, and the teaching profession.[202] In contemplating proclivity to automation, the different studies highlight the following levers as being key to a lower propensity for automation: managing and developing people, applying expertise to decision-making, planning and creative tasks, interface/engagement with stakeholders, and working (physical activities or operating machinery) in an unpredictable environment. On the other hand, notes McKinsey, jobs characterised by "predictable environments" and data collection and processing lend themselves to automation.[203] Applying this lens,

---

[201] UNESCO, 2019, 5.

[202] Elliott, 2018.

[203] McKinsey Global Institute. A future that works: Automation, employment, and productivity, Executive Summary, 2017. 6. https://www.mckinsey.com/~/

they highlight the significantly lower potential of education to automation (27%), even lower than job sectors such as arts, entertainment, and recreation (41% automation potential), information (36% automation potential), and management (35% automation potential).[204] Bakshi and Windsor, and Frey and Osborne have also advanced the view that straightforward repetitive tasks will always be more susceptible to autonomous control, whereas robots "will struggle when tasks are highly interpretative, geared at products whose final form is not fully specified in advance, and when work task environments are complex."[205] Emphasising the factors of deeper learning, Frey and Osborne highlight that:

> "...while sophisticated algorithms and developments in MR, building upon with big data, now allow many non-routine tasks to be automated, occupations that involve complex perception and manipulation tasks, creative intelligence tasks, and social intelligence tasks are unlikely to be substituted by computer capital over the next decade or two."[206]

In advancing her view on why robots cannot replace teachers, Middleditch focusses on the crucial development of the critical twenty-first century skills of problem-solving, flexibility, empathy,

---

media/mckinsey/featured%20insights/Digital%20Disruption/Harnessing%20aut omation%20for%20a%20future%20that%20works/MGI-A-future-that-works-Executive-summary.ashx.

[204] McKinsey Global Institute, 2017, 7-8.

[205] Bakshi, H and Windsor, G. *The creative economy and the future of employment.* 21 April 2015. Nesta, 3-4. Available at: https://www.nesta.org.uk/ report/the-creative-economy-and-the-future-of-employment/.

[206] Frey, C.B. and Osborne, M. The future of employment: How susceptible are jobs to computerisation?, 1 September 2013. *Oxford Martin Programme on Technology and Employment.* London, 26-7. https://www.oxford martin.ox.ac.uk/publications/the-future-of-employment/.

collaboration and teamwork, reflexivity, and creativity.[207] Serholt *et al* raise a concern that classroom robots that the students perceived as 'too credible' – as a source that knows everything – might result in students becoming over-reliant on the machines and losing their capacity to be critical.[208] Of further concern, Newton and Newton question whether a robot would be able to adequately assess thinking that involves personal values, beliefs, and goals, as in decision-making.[209] The disquiet is markedly higher if the machine is the sole educator as there is the concomitant danger that the robot perspective becomes the complete education. In such instances, all the transformation goals of inculcating twenty-first century skills and deeper learning into the higher education curriculum will be effaced.

For many, university is a rite of passage into adulthood and the workplace. It is the university educators' job to widen horizons, foster curiosity, and prepare students for this new world. Good teaching is undergirded by constant creativity and innovation, and there is no gainsaying the relational psycho-social engagements including empathy and sympathy between the educator and the student. Robotic guidance in this regard would be limited as these responses would have to be artificially programmed. Human teachers on the other hand have the natural ability to read, show and respond to emotions, assisting them to support students to bridge the gap between school and university, and deal with the exigencies of the independent learning environment of the university. As succinctly pointed out by NCTEFL India, human beings display responsive behavioural and psychological reactions that 'define their social skills and interactivity'.[210]

---

[207] Middleditch, K. 5 Reasons why robots can't replace teachers. 25 July 2018, 25. *Open University News*, n.p. https://ounews.co/education-languages-health/education/5-reasons-why-robots-cant-replace-teachers/.

[208] Serholt *et al.*, 2017, op. cit. 626.

[209] Newton and Newton, 2019, op. cit. n.p.

[210] NCTEFL, India, 2018, op. cit. n.p.

Thus, "How much the technical developments are, it surely is difficult for robot teachers to match up to the 'unique' social skills and cognitive ratio exclusively found in humans."[211]

Teachers in the future should have the time and opportunity to stimulate and positively reinforce the identified skills necessary to succeed in the twenty-first century, while perhaps more mundane administrative tasks and limited student support activities may be taken over by machines. At most, it is suggested, robots can be considered as a complementary tool to improve the academic performance of students.[212]

Furthermore, and as explained by the OECD, while there are good reasons to believe that smart technologies, including AI, can contribute to the effectiveness and cost-efficiency of education systems,[213] there is need for a certain measure of caution to keep in mind for any organization seeking to reap those benefits:

- Smart technologies are human-AI hybrid systems, and as such it is key to involve end-users in their design, give control to humans for important decisions, and negotiate their usage with society in a transparent way in order for it to be both useful and socially acceptable.
- Smart technologies support humans in many ways without being perfect. As such, transparency about how accurate they are at measuring, diagnosing, or acting is an important requirement, although their limits should be compared to the limits of humans performing similar tasks.

---

[211] NCTEFL, 2018, n.p.

[212] Sanchez, H., Martinez, L.S. and Gonzalez, J.D. "Educational robotics as a teaching tool in higher education institutions: A bibliographical analysis." *Journal of Physics: Conference Series*, 2019, 1. DOI: https://doi.org/10.1088/1742-6596/1391/1/012128.

[213] OECD, 2021, 6.

- More evidence about effective pedagogical uses of smart technologies in and outside of the classroom, as well as their uses for system management purposes, should be funded without focusing on the technology exclusively.

- The adoption of smart technologies relies on robust data protection and privacy regulation based on risk assessment, but also ethical considerations where regulation does not exist. For example, there is mounting concern about the fairness of algorithms, which could be verified through 'open algorithms' verified by third parties.

- Smart technologies have a cost, and a cost-benefit analysis should guide their adoption, acknowledging that their benefits go beyond pecuniary ones. In many cases, the identification of data patterns allows for better policy design and interventions that are more likely to improve equity and effectiveness. Policy makers should also encourage the development of technologies that are affordable and sustainable thanks to open standards and interoperability.

Absent a crystal ball, none can predict what good higher education teaching will look like in the future and some may argue that the approach of US Supreme Court Justice Potter Stewart (albeit when describing pornography) is appropriate: "I know it when I see it." However, it appears – for now, at least – that robo-teachers will not provide a complete solution in achieving the higher education transformation agenda of education for the common good.[214] Human interaction and a professional trained in pedagogy are key imperatives if we are to successfully achieve these outcomes.[215] Discipline leaders in education describe the science around pedagogy that both ensures constructive alignment of curriculum outcomes and leads to a fruitful

---

[214] UNESCO, 2015.

[215] Aoun, op. cit. 2018.

learning experience. This would need to be carefully pre-programmed through deep integrated engagement between developers and seasoned educators.

Accepting that higher education is a complex learning engagement integrating discipline knowledge and skills with social consciousness and responsibility, robots may not serve this purpose in the classroom. As noted by NEFTL:

> "However unable to really understand various complex standpoints of human beings, the biggest asset of human teachers is they are 'real with their experiences, knowledge and analytical whereabouts' and is not imposed artificially through software or programming."[216]

And, of course, we need to be thinking more deeply around ethics and the ethical journey that needs to be undertaken before AI and robots are introduced into the classroom particularly the question *How far do we want to delegate the education of the next generation to robots?*. Perhaps, therefore, it is premature to discuss educators being replaced by AI but the compendium of challenges because of fiscal constraints in higher education, coupled with larger class sizes and more diverse student groupings, as well as the need to do more with less, drive a real need for increased technological support. In this milieu the more pivotal role that educators could play is to prepare the teaching project for the influence and responsible use and integration of AI. According to the Beijing Consensus (UNESCO 2019: 5), it is necessary to ensure that the rights and working conditions of educators are protected, and to dynamically review and define educators' roles and required competencies in the context of teacher policies; furthermore, attention should be paid to strengthening teacher training institutions, and

---

[216] NEFTL, 2018.

developing appropriate capacity-building programmes to prepare teachers to work effectively in AI-rich education settings.

Succinctly summarizing the educator's role, Bushweller highlights:

"They need to play a big role in the development of the technologies so that whatever is produced is ethical and unbiased, improves student learning, and helps teachers spend more time inspiring students, building strong relationships with them, and focusing on the priorities that matter most. If designed with educator input, these technologies could free up teachers to do what they do best: inspire students to learn and coach them along the way."[217]

Thus, as the allure and complexity of technology increases, institutions adopting AI must make deliberate efforts to balance the introduction of machines with the expanded values and priorities of higher education outlined in the World Declaration on Higher Education for the Twenty-First Century: Vision and Action (UNESCO 1998).

---

[217] Bushweller, 2020, n.p.

FEAR OF USING AI IN VIRTUAL PROCTORING?

YOUR INSTITUTION HAS MORE CONTROL THAN YOU MAY REALISE

Mac Adkins

Introduction

Hollywood has produced several blockbuster films in which artificial intelligence (AI) in some way takes over the world.[218] *The Matrix* is a great example of a film in which superintelligent AI becomes a reality. Even back in 1982 *Blade Runner* was a story about bioengineered replicas of humans powered by AI that lived amongst real humans. And who can forget *The Terminator* in which AI suddenly turns evil? The underlying theme is that the *artificial* intelligence becomes more intelligent than the humans who created it – thus we need to fear AI.

While the fear of AI has been great for the movie industry, we argue that it should not be a factor that limits the acceptance of the use of AI in the exam proctoring industry. For example, at SmarterServices, an American educational assessment services company, we engage in dialogue with faculty and administrators of higher education institutions and are often asked questions about the degree to which schools are in control of the AI utilised in virtual proctoring. We find it most helpful

---

[218] https://towardsdatascience.com/top-20-movies-about-machine-learning-ai-and-data-science-8382d408c8c3

for both institutions of higher education and the learners who are proctored by virtual tools to address common misconceptions and concerns one by one. Here, we hope to *terminate* some of these common misconceptions.

Fears Associated with AI

Some of the fear associated with the use of AI in virtual proctoring comes from a lack of understanding about the actions that the AI is constantly monitoring. Not only are some schools and their faculty concerned about this, but it is a good practice for students to also be informed about their actions that could trigger the AI to flag a potential testing anomaly. To help ease these fears, we argue for a transparent approach for all stakeholders that outlines exactly what virtual proctoring does and does not do.

What AI is Monitoring?

The things that AI is watching for in virtual proctoring can be summed up in three words: face, voice, and screen. The AI within the tools and services that we develop looks for certain visual signals to detect whether the integrity of an exam may be compromised. These signals can either be a point-in-time or be ranged; meaning that they occur for a duration.

AI and Facial Monitoring

First, let us examine more closely the things associated with a face that AI is monitoring. The AI is continuously keeping track of the test taker's face. It is watching for events like the face disappearing or another face (or faces) appearing. This aspect of virtual proctoring relies on proprietary facial tracking technology that uses real-time computer vision, a specialised technology emerging from the field of computer vision, which is "devoted to analyzing, modifying, and high-level understanding of images."[219] This allows our system to achieve maximum accuracy by reducing false positives that can occur based on a single video frame by analysing multiple frames dynamically (i.e., in real-time) based on the webcam's frame rate. Our system is also tuning the colours in the image to provide accuracy of analysis across multiple ethnicities and levels of lighting. The AI is constantly getting smarter based on human acceptance or denial of automatically detected events.

Jason Fill, CEO of SmarterServices gives the following explanation:

"Our algorithm is really good and constantly getting better at cutting down on false   positives by maintaining face tracking even when only parts of the face are visible. For example, if a test taker turns their head to sneeze to the point that only one eye is   visible, we still track and report that as the face being present. Earlier forms of such   software could have flagged that. Our sophisticated approach also allows for a test   taker to be wearing a mask for COVID-19 protection and we are still able to track them."

He further explains that the technology is constantly monitoring for the presence of facial elements such as eyes, nose, and mouth, not changes in these facial elements. For this reason, a person looking away from the screen as they are thinking or moving their lips as they silently read exam content to help them focus are typically not flagged as anomalies. It is possible, however, that if a person looks straight down at their desk or floor to the degree that their face is not visible, this would likely be flagged since no face would be visible.

It is also important to note that our service, SmarterProctoring, does not collect nor store any biometric data. The facial recognition

---

[219] Pulli, Kari, Baksheev, Anatoly *et al.* "Real-Time Computer Vision with OpenCV", *Communications of the ACM*, June 2012, Vol. 55 No. 6, 61-69, DOI 10.1145/2184319.2184337

technology that we use is only making sure that the same face is present throughout the testing session. We are not making a determination during the testing session that the face is the face of any particular person, but just the same face from start to finish of the exam. No record of that facial biometric is stored after the testing session. In regards to the retention of the video stream associated with a testing session that may contain images of a person and their government-issued ID, schools decide on how long that session video content is stored. For example, schools could delete it one week after the testing session or one year later.

AI and Vocal Monitoring

Now let us think about ways that the AI monitors voice. During a testing session, our AI is continuously listening for any speech. This could include speech from the test taker, a television, a nearby person, or a phone. For this reason, it is important that the testing environment control for the presence of external sounds as much as possible. Students can be instructed to not read the exam questions out loud to themselves. When a person has a documented disability for which an accommodation is to allow them to read test questions orally, the audio component of the AI can be turned off as an accommodation for that student. That is just one example of the AI not being in control.

AI and Screen Monitoring

Finally, screen monitoring is a crucial part of online proctoring and can include many different elements. For example, artificial intelligence can monitor for attempts at a number of activities including using another application than the web browser, using more than one monitor, copying and pasting, right clicking, and so on. These activities could be indicators of academic dishonesty.

Staying In Control of AI

The above illustrations should provide an overview and understanding of what AI is monitoring when deployed in virtual proctoring. While the description above only points to a small slice of how we can use AI to enhance online learning and evaluation experiences, it is representative of the opportunities for AI in higher education that lay before us. Of course, such applications need to be developed carefully and improved continuously. Crucially, the question of control emerges as central to the use of AI in higher education. In applications like SmaterProctoring, schools and faculty have a range of options to introduce and modify levels of control as they consider appropriate.[220] Keeping human oversight in the loop is essential for ethical and constructive use of AI in assessment services. This can be done at three levels: enterprise, exam level, and individual student level for accommodations.

Staying In Control of AI at the Enterprise Level

First, let us look at the highest or most all-encompassing level, the enterprise level. This is where schools and other institutions can exercise greatest control over how AI is deployed in virtual proctoring, and other applications of AI in higher education. Even as sophisticated and accurate as facial detection and tracking approaches are, we understand that there are some institutions that are concerned with any use of facial metrics. This is a motivating factor in introducing control over such features at the enterprise level – they can be turned on and off, while still allowing the voice and screen monitoring options described above. At the enterprise level, this is an institution-wide decision, impacting all exams and all virtual proctoring sessions.

---

[220] https://smarterservices.com/smarterproctoring/

Staying In Control of AI at the Exam Level

Configuration can also happen at the exam level, offering again more opportunities to responsibly control face, voice, and screen monitoring. This is the most common level at which AI configurations are made and applies to all students taking the exam. Some exams are more rigorous and have higher stakes than others. Faculty can configure the AI to match the nature of the exam. For example, tighter controls could be set for a final exam than for unit quizzes.

To make the process of exam configuration easier and faster for faculty and instructional designers, we have two pre-set AI configurations: *Strict* and *Lenient*. As is shown in the figures below, the *Strict* pre-set turns on all possible controls. However, the *Lenient* pre-set does not force a full screen, allows other tabs to be opened, does not automatically close any already open tabs, and does not block any other browser extensions.

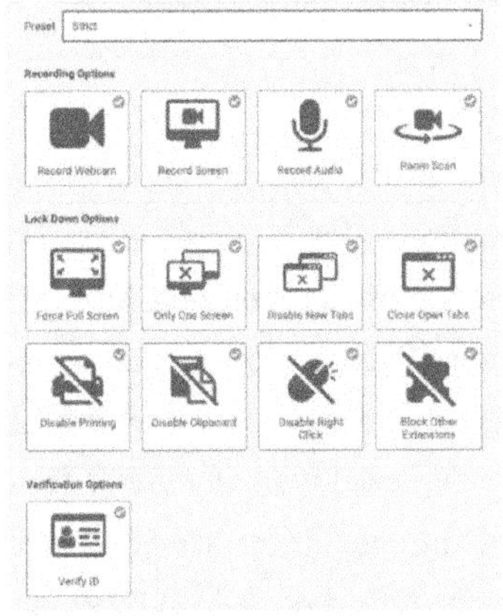
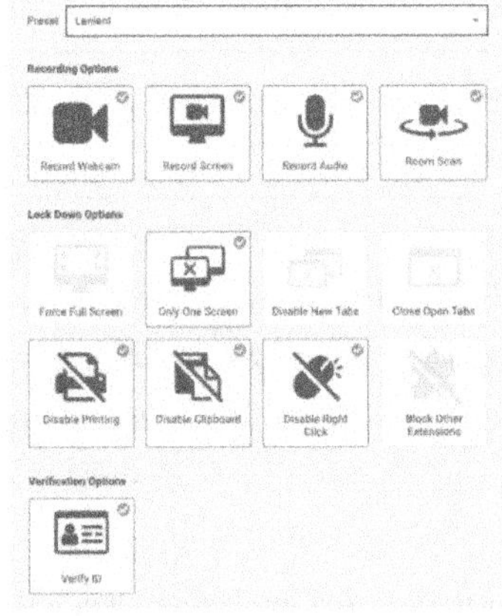

If either of these pre-set levels is not exactly what the instructor has in mind for the exam, any (or all) of the following aspects of an automated session can be turned on or off. These configuration settings include:

- *Recording the Webcam*: Records the test-taker and all activities in view of the webcam during the proctoring session.

- *Recording the Screen*: Records the screen the test-taker selected during the onboarding process. If multiple screens are allowed, only one screen will be recorded.
- *Recording Audio*: Records the audio during the proctoring session.
- *Doing a Room Scan*: Prompts the test-taker to do a 360-degree scan of the room during the onboarding process. Although one cannot guarantee the accuracy of a room scan, we do provide a sample video of a thorough room scan for test-takers to view.
- *Forcing Full Screen*: If enabled, the test-taker is forced into full screen, so the browser is all they can see on their screen. Since our system uses a Chrome extension it is not possible to lock the test-taker into the browser window. However, it will track the test-taker and flag the session if they move off the browser window.
- *Allowing Only One Screen*: The test-taker is asked to disconnect any external monitors and only test with a single screen. Even if the student has multiple monitors, only one screen will be recorded.
- *Disabling New Tabs*: If the test-taker attempts to open a new tab it will be automatically closed.
- *Closing Open Tabs*: Closes other tabs the test-taker has open when starting their proctoring session.
- *Disabling Printing:* If the test-taker attempts to print, the printer dialog will appear on-screen, but a blank page will be printed.
- *Disabling Clipboard*: Clears the current contents of the clipboard and disables the use of all clipboard (copy and paste) functions. Including interaction from the context menu and keyboard shortcuts.
- *Disabling Right Click:* Does not permit right-clicking to open the standard context menu.

- *Blocking Other Extensions*: When the proctoring session is started, known extensions that could compromise the integrity of the examination are disabled. Including password-saving extensions such as LastPass or 1Password.
- *Verifying Identification*: When the test-taker is going through the onboarding process, they are asked to show their government-issued ID to validate their identity.

In addition to the exam level settings in regards to the degree that the AI is controlling and monitoring the testing session, SmartProctoring also allows the faculty member to configure several elements of the testing environment in regards to permitted items. Faculty can toggle on/off each of the following possibly permitted items: notes, open textbook, calculator, earplugs, formula sheets, dictionary, website, and blank paper. For each item that they toggle on they can add notes such as what type of calculator is allowable. Faculty can also toggle whether or not a bio-break is allowable. Some faculty have added an instruction to their exam prompting the students to hold up their allowed items to the camera for visual verification.

Staying In Control of AI at the Student Level

Lastly, users of virtual proctoring can stay in control of the AI at the student level. One of the advantages of SmartProctoring is that any and all of the AI settings that can be configured at the exam level to apply to all test takers can be adjusted for any individual test taker when an accommodation is needed. As an example, for a visually impaired student who needs a screen reader to orally read the screen during the exam and this is achieved through a browser extension, the block other extensions setting could be turned off.

Some students have expressed concern that virtual proctoring software could invade their privacy by accessing their webcam or controlling their software after the exam. We communicate to students that SmartProctoring only works within an exam within their learning management system. There is no way that our software nor any of our employees have any access to or control over their computing device after the exam. To further assure them of this we provide instructions on how they can easily uninstall the SmarterProcotoring browser extension if they so choose.

Institutions are in Control of the AI Used in Virtual Proctoring

The challenges facing the use of AI in virtual proctoring specifically and higher education generally are significant. We believe, however, that the opportunities are still greater. The impetus toward online and remote learning exerted by the global pandemic has shown that virtual learning and assessment can be a positive aspect of the higher education ecosystem. As any other aspect of AI and related technologies, the application of AI in learning assessment depends on feedback, continual testing and improvement, and adaptation to changing contexts. Finally, artificial intelligence used in higher education, including virtual proctoring, is constantly getting *smarter* as the potential anomalies that are identified are either confirmed or rejected by human reviewers. We only monitor and report possible testing anomalies, the AI does not stop the exam. But even though AI is getting smarter, it will never take over the world. In fact, it will not even take over your exam.[221]

---

[221] A version of this article was originally published on the Smarter Services blog and is republished here with permission of its author.

IS ARTIFICIAL INTELLIGENCE
THE MAGIC POTION
THAT WILL LEAD US TO IMPROVE
THE QUALITY OF HIGHER EDUCATION?

Carina Lion

Higher Level Education

Context Features

The breathtaking pace of technological development in recent years (machine learning, artificial intelligence, internet of things, Big Data; 3- and 4D impressions, among others) offers a framework to rethink the relationship with higher-level education, understanding that changes in teaching are slow and not always visible. The augmented humanity concept begins to account for hybridisations between the human and the artificial.[222] Changes in body postures in relation to technology, the progressive generalisation of an *interface body*,[223] the advancements of datafication, digitalisation, artificial intelligence and robotics set out complex challenges in relation to the social control processes and our

---

[222] Sadin, W. *La humanidad aumentada. La administración digital del mundo.* Buenos Aires: Caja Negra, 2017. Baricco, A. *The Game.* Buenos Aires: Anagrama, 2019.

[223] Sadin, Éric. *La inteligencia artificial o el desafío del siglo. Anatomía de un antihumanismo radical,* Buenos Aires: Caja Negra Editora, 2020, 328pp.

levels of autonomy in decision-making.[224] As Sadin points out, "a new anthropology is more widely set up thanks to the emergence of an intelligence of the technique dedicated to extending our understanding skills, as well as to generating historically unedited ways of understanding the world."[225] In this sense, we are experiencing an automation in the name of economic-political processes that enables certain technological evolution which builds a simulation of progress and produces tireless, deep effects in our existence. Understanding which the margins of autonomy in decision making are when teaching is mediated by technologies becomes a highly relevant matter. Some questions that can be formulated in this sense are: Are there differences between human and automated tutoring? What value does higher level teaching add to self-study courses that universities are currently starting to implement? To what extent can AI developments impact the transformation of university education?

We understand AI as the way of simulating the human brain's intelligence skills.[226] AI is a part of computer science, which is in charge of the design of intelligent systems, that is, systems that show the features we associate with intelligence in human behaviours.

Mariño and Primorac go deeper into the matter by stating that AI is conceived as part of computer science, which enables us to provide "a diversity of methods, techniques and tools to model and solve problems simulating the acts of subjective knowers."[227] From another point of

---

[224] Deleuze, G. Posdata de las sociedades de control. In: Ferrer, C. (Comp.) *El lenguaje literario*, T° 2, Transl. Martín Caparrós, Montevideo: Ed. Nordan, 1991.

[225] Sadin, 2017, op. cit. 31.

[226] Badaró, S; Ibañez, L; Agüero, J. "Sistemas Expertos: Fundamentos, Metodologías y Aplicaciones", *Ciencia y tecnología*, No. 13, 2013, Buenos Aires, 349-364. https://dialnet.unirioja.es/servlet/articulo?codigo=4843871

[227] Mariño, S. I., and C. R. Primorac. "Propuesta metodológica Para Desarrollo De Modelos De Redes Neuronales Artificiales Supervisadas". *IJERI:*

view, AI can be understood in the terms presented by Herrera and Muñoz, who conceive it as a science oriented to the search of deep understanding of intelligence, taking into account its delimitation, possibilities, and characterising it as a highly complex challenge.[228] But to go deeper into the context of AI, we should go back to its beginnings, that is, refer to Alan Turing as one of the pioneers in this aspect when designing the famous *Turing machine* which, under the data processing scheme in a binary system was able to process any type of possible calculation. In the last few years of his life, he thought about developing the *Turing machine test*. This imagined situation made it possible for the machine to have the attribution of thought on one condition; that the observer cannot distinguish clearly their behaviour from that of a human being. In other words, something like a mimetic independence; in this way, an implied paradigm is established as the genesis to the great pioneers of this branch of knowledge, such as McCulloch, Turing, von Neumann, Wiener and Pitts, Gardner, among others.[229]

The current AI developments are currently included in a society highly traversed by technologies. The *network society* constitutes the contextual framework within which both the scope of education technology as a field and the reasons for including technologies in

---

International Journal of Educational Research and Innovation, no. 6, May 2016, 232. https://www.upo.es/revistas/index.php/IJERI/article/view/1654.

[228] Hernández, P., Muñoz-Herrera, M., Sánchez, A. "Heterogeneous network games: Conflicting preferences", *Games and Economic Behavior*, Vol. 79, 2013, 56-66, https://doi.org/10.1016/j.geb.2013.01.004.

[229] Ramos Franco, L. "Psicología cognitiva e inteligencia artificial: mitos y verdades". *Avances En Psicología, 22*(1), 2014, 21-27. https://doi.org/10.33539/avpsicol.2014.v22n1.270 ; Ocaña-Fernández, Yolvi. "Artificial Intelligence and its Implications in Higher Education", *Propósitos y Representaciones*, May. - Aug. 2019, Vol. 7, N° 2, 536-568, http://dx.doi.org/10.20511/pyr2019.v7n2.274

education must be reviewed.[230] On the one hand, information and communication technologies are expanding and are part of central activities in society including the economy, research, and social movements. On the other hand, they are starting to support the emergence of a cognitive ecology that questions the literate culture, including not only the forms of specialised knowledge but also the social and cultural trends in which young people have central participation and which demand a review of teaching practices.[231]

To be accurate, today's society is not exclusively a disciplinary society, but rather a society that prioritises performance, expels what is different, and shows itself as a society of freedom when there is actually a full observation of what we say and do through the *digital panopticon*.[232] We assist hyperactivity, extreme performance, low tolerance to tedium and boredom, and to the disappearance of otherness, because in our eagerness to be different, differences are really blurred; because hyper communication makes us more solitary and because relationships are replaced by connections.[233] These are some critical

---

[230] Castells, M., 2001. *La galaxia Internet*. Barcelona: Areté. Castells, M., 2009. *Comunicación y poder*. Madrid: Alianza.

[231] Craig, R. *College Disrupted: the Great Unbundling of Higher Education.* New York: Palgrave Macmillan Trade, 2015. Petit, M. *Nuevos acercamientos a los jóvenes y la lectura*. México: Fondo de Cultura Económica, 1999. Piscitelli, A., *El paréntesis de Gutenberg, La religión digital en la era de las pantallas ubicuas*. Buenos Aires: Santillana, 2011. Cordón García, J. A., López Lucas, J., Gómez Díaz, R. & Alonso Arévalo, J. *Las nuevas fuentes de información. Información y búsqueda documental en el contexto de la web 2.0.* Madrid: Pirámide, 2010. Serres, M. *Pulgarcita*. Buenos Aires: Fondo de Cultura Económica, 2013. Barbero, Martin. *Cultura y nuevas mediaciones tecnológicas*. México: Fondo de Cultura Económica, 2014.

[232] Bul Chun, Han. *La sociedad del cansancio*, translated by Arantzazu Saratxaga Arregi, Buenos Aires: Herder, 2018.

[233] Bul Chun, Han. *La expulsión de lo distinto*, translated by Joaquín Alberto Ciria Cosculluela, Buenos Aires: Herder, 2018.

features that become relevant to understand the context contemporary university life is going through.

In the last few years, many reports have studied trends observed in practices impacted by technology in educational settings, explicitly stating the learning possibilities offered by information and communication technologies in higher education. These reports highlight the extended opportunities for continuous, active, personalised and rhizomatic learning,[234] game-based learning and the culture of doing,[235] story and event-based learning,[236] and dynamic and incidental learning.[237]

As of the impact of the pandemic on the world, technologies, in particular remote education, have had greater visibility. The UNESCO IESALC estimates show that the temporary closure affects approximately 23.4 million higher education students and 1.4 million teachers in Latin America and the Caribbean; this represents approximately more than 98% of the region's population of higher education students and teachers.[238]

According to a survey developed by the OECD about e-learning in higher education in Latin America, before the COVID-19 pandemic face-to-face education was still highly prevalent being the predominant

---

[234] Sharples, M. *et al. Innovating Pedagogy 2012*: Open University Innovation Report 1, Milton Keynes: The Open University, 2012.

[235] Sharples, M. *et al. Innovating Pedagogy 2013*: Open University Innovation Report 2, Milton Keynes: The Open University, 2013.

[236] Sharples, M. *et al. Innovating Pedagogy 2014*: Open University Innovation Report 3, Milton Keynes: The Open University, 2014.

[237] Sharples, M. *et al. Innovating Pedagogy 2015*: Open University Innovation Report 4, Milton Keynes: The Open University, 2015.

[238] IESALC, *COVID-19 and higher education: Impact analysis, policy responses and recommendations.* 2020, http://www.iesalc.unesco.org/en/wp content/uploads/2020/04/COVID-19-EN-090420-2.pdf

model in 65% of the universities, compared to 16% with a predominant hybrid model and 19% centered on e-learning.

In spite of the pandemic and of having migrated classes to virtual environments, this has not necessarily implied a deep change in university education, since the didactic model is a classic one: explanation – application – verification.[239] We have observed that in online lessons this didactic format has been maintained without making deep changes.

The debate about AI underscores the possibility of subverting the most traditional teaching structures. In view of the development of platforms that bet on affective computing and hyper personalisation, to what extent does the deployment of AI compromise the teaching and learning experience?[240] How will graduates be able to learn critical thinking skills as AI advances? Are there margins of autonomy in decision making before the advancement of extreme datafication and digitalisation? How can we create a critical digital citizenship that gives response to the complex challenges of the coming years?

New ways of teaching?

Universities have the purpose of building original and relevant knowledge in its articulation with the demands of society. Among their missions are teaching, research and extension, that is, transfer. University education emphasises on the design of professional profiles that are framed to work and generation of knowledge. Insofar this century, higher university education has tipped over an innovative socio-cognitive paradigm, where the learning process is ongoing and in permanent evolution, in which the content and methodologies must be in agreement with the specific needs of each reality, with the need to

---

[239] Litwin, E. *Las configuraciones didácticas. Una nueva agenda para la enseñanza superior.* Buenos Aires: Paidós, 1997.

[240] Williamson, B. *Big data en educación: el futuro digital del aprendizaje, la política y la práctica.* Madrid: Morata, 2018.

implement metacognitive strategies, logical reasoning based on new communication styles and digital interaction.[241]

Morín explained that two opposed profiles coexist in the university mission: 1) Vital conservation, which is oriented to preserving and safeguarding, in accordance with the development process that feeds the future, grounded on the basis of a preserved past, transmitted under the typical standards of academic cloisters; since, to the best of his knowledge, the future, as such, cannot materialise itself if it is not tightly linked to a safeguarded past. 2) Sterile conservation, an aspect which would not be so negative if, historically referenced, for a long time and due to its origins, university has itself kept under an obsolete and conservative dogma, since in its cloisters, rigidity and ostracism have long been the guiding standard of its existence, as what occurred in the oldest universities known; and that, without taking into account the fierce clerical adoptions that have set the grounds of many of them in the old continent.[242]

In more classical universities, the year 2020 has led to review their education proposals. In the case of University of Buenos Aires and pursuant to a study conducted to over 200 teachers, one prominent trend observed is that before the CRTS, the use of technology tools by teachers ranged from very little to moderate (74% on average in both institutions). As a result of the Preventive and Compulsory Social Isolation (in Spanish, ASPO), they were able to review the strategies and tools used and now consider that technologies enrich their teaching practice. This shows a change in the representation about the value of technology tools for university teaching. It is true that the context forced them to use tools such as synchronous videoconferencing and virtual environments. For this reason, the most commonly used tools were

---

[241] Mariño y Primorac, 2016, op. cit.

[242] Morin, E. *Enseñar a vivir. Manifiesto para cambiar la educación.* Barcelona: Paidós, 2016.

synchronous videoconferencing tools, YouTube videos or videos created by faculty members, and the use of virtual environments to upload materials and various activities.

These results are in complete accordance with those obtained through a survey developed by the International Association of Universities showing that "at almost all HEIs, COVID-19 affected teaching and learning, with two-thirds of them reporting that classroom teaching has been replaced by distance teaching and learning. The shift from face-to-face to distance teaching did not come without challenges, the main ones being: access to technical infrastructure, competences and pedagogies for distance learning and the requirements of specific fields of study. At the same time, the forced move to distance teaching and learning offers important opportunities to propose more flexible learning possibilities, explore blended or hybrid learning and to mix synchronous learning with asynchronous learning.[243]

In view of this context, we believe we are facing an opportunity to transform the university teaching practices. That same survey reveals that the transformation experience towards technology-mediated practices is regarded as a positive experience by 63.5% of the teachers and that 80% of them believe that their new experience with the use of digital tools will affect their pedagogic practice. In addition, they think that this experience has helped them to be prepared for future similar situations (62%). This implies that there is a vision for change in the pedagogic practices for the learning experience, but there are not any certainties that these changes will be reflected in higher education teaching practices in the future. This is something that will have to be

---

[243] Marinoni, G., van't Land, H. & Jensen, T. *The Impact of COVID-19 on Higher Education around the World*, Paris: International Association of Universities, 2020. https://www.iau-aiu.net/IMG/pdf/iau_covid19_and_he_survey_report_final_may_2020.pdf

studied in the coming years, verifying what has been learned and how this will affect future practices.

University practices tend to be classical in their didactic structure and follow a progressive linear sequence of explanation, application, verification.[244] Although we admit pedagogical changes are slow, cultural ways do not wait, let alone in these times in which our everyday rhythm is set by the Internet.[245] In this sense, Martín Barbero offers a strong articulation when he places us in the chaotic scene where the digital reconfigures human beings in relation to vital dimensions, at the time it entails the demolition of the hegemony and challenges the previous certainties.[246] The redesign of university teaching practices process involves the creation or deepening of certain conditions that support the renewed practice. It is not about conditions that must be favorable for the redesign to take place, but rather which are expressed as tension/negotiation processes to the inside of institutions, especially when they question the typically biased practices that have turned into routine. Contemporary cultural scenarios demand creative and original strategies that inspire a different class for people who have changed. To what extent would AI promote or hinder these types of changes in higher education? We will elaborate on this topic in the next section.

The Challenges of Autonomy in the Face of AI

Smart tutorials and adaptive learning

According to Williamson, in recent years there has been a trend towards datafication (transformation into quantifiable information that can be incorporated into databases in order to apply different measurement and calculation techniques), digitisation (understood as the

---

[244] Litwin 2006, op. cit.

[245] Maggio, M. *Reinventar la clase en la universidad.* Buenos Aires: Paidós, 2018.

[246] Barbero, Martin, 2014, op. cit.

translation of the data to software code) and the design of individualised programs through adaptive, personalised and easy-to-use platforms.[247] With the availability of digital data in various areas of public and private life, a new measuring device has spread as well as a series of cultural changes in which measurement is considered highly desirable. In the educational system this translates into personalisation; evidence-based learning; continuous innovation and more efficient information management. We constantly obtain data. The changes caused by the construction of meaning by the emergence of social networks, by which data constantly moves, changes, comes and goes between different actors, and media are carried, patched, altered, designed, pasted, and commented.[248] We have data in different virtual locations. As Cobo points out, as people we are becoming our own data and we accept the conditions that technologies impose on us when we allow access to said information.[249]

Understanding the power of datafication in the contemporary context, we are interested in advancing a line of AI that refers to intelligent tutorials, adaptive learning and affective computing.

Among the broader interests of affective computing is not only identifying human emotions and reacting appropriately but also being able to simulate emotions that can make the emotion in question recognisable to human beings by increasing persuasiveness and deliberately generating an emotional response.[250] In this sense, there are also platform developments for the educational field that include innovations with which the systems can recognise, interpret, and

---

[247] Williamson, 2018, op. cit.

[248] Rose, F. *The Art of Immersion: How the Digital Generation Is Remaking Hollywood, Madison Avenue, and the Way We Tell Stories.* New York: W. W. Norton & Company, 2011.

[249] Cobo, Cristóbal. *Acepto las Condiciones: Usos y abusos de las tecnologías digitales.* Fundación Santillana: Madrid, 2019.

[250] Rose, op. cit.

simulate emotions to account for the emotional dimension in the learning process (what moves us, amuses us, annoys, bores us when we are learning content). That is, they incorporate automatic analysis of emotions into learning analytics measurements to obtain a holistic picture of progress; and to be able to offer more assistance, feedback, and personalised guidance in online courses.[251]

On the other hand, and in a different line to that of affective computing, there are numerous studies that have shown the relevance of students learning from the real world with access to digital resources that they use in their activities and being assisted by their teachers in learning.[252] We are facing changes from the approach of technology-assisted learning in general and that of web-based learning, towards that of mobile learning, and especially towards that of *context-aware ubiquitous learning*, as indicated by Liu and Hwang.[253]

We are facing developments in affective computing and *smart tutorials* in the context of adaptive learning to support students based on their learning status and other personal factors, such as their way of progressing in learning, levels of knowledge previous studies, learning

---

[251] Montero, S. and Suhonen, J. "Emotion analysis meets learning analytics: online learner profiling beyond numerical data", *Koli Calling 14th International Conference on Computing Education Research November 2014*, 165–169, 2014, https://doi.org/10.1145/2674683.2674699

[252] Bomsdorf, B. "Adaptation of Learning Spaces: Supporting Ubiquitous Learning in Higher Distance Education", Dagstuhl Seminar Proceedings 05181, 2005, https://drops.dagstuhl.de/opus/volltexte/2005/371/ Hwang, Gwo-Jen et al. "A concept map approach to developing collaborative Mindtools for context-aware ubiquitous learning." *Br. J. Educ. Technol.* 42, 2011, 778-789.

[253] Liu, G.-Z. and Hwang, G.-J. "A key step to understanding paradigm shifts in e-learning: towards context-aware ubiquitous learning". *British Journal of Educational Technology*, 41: E1-E9. 2010, https://doi.org/10.1111/j.1467-8535.2009.00976.x

styles, cognitive styles and preferences, have been written about extensively.[254]

Ocaña Fernández argues that the application of AI can, in a certain way, be considered as a viable solution, since automated assistance in relation to student help allows a new and attractive perspective for learning.[255] In virtual interaction, regulated by AI parameters, it enables learning to be facilitated, since support mechanisms are available when necessary, regardless of the user's time and space.

In this sense, one of the uses that could be relevant is linked to *adaptive learning*, which gives an account of flexibility in the trajectories; versatile curricula that adapt quickly to the new ways of building knowledge and validation in the present century. It would be an adaptive support in pedagogical help and in the delivery of resources: to carry this out in a sensitive, relevant, and pertinent way with the personal and group learning situation of the students, in response to their demand for knowledge and for the development of their skills.[256]

---

[254] Mampadi, F.; Ghinea, G. and Chen, S. "Design of adaptive hypermedia learning systems: A cognitive style approach". *Computers & Education*, Vol. 56, Issue 4, 2011, 1003-1011, https://doi.org/10.1016/j.compedu.2010.11.018.; Papanikolaou, K.; Grigoriadou, M.; Magoulas, G. and Kornilakis, H. "Towards new forms of knowledge communication: the adaptive dimension of a web-based learning environment", *Computers & Education*, Vol. 39, 4, 2002, 333-360, https://doi.org/10.1016/S0360-1315(02)00067-2. Yang, Xin-She and He, Xingshi. "Bat algorithm: literature review and applications", *International Journal of Bio-Inspired Computation* 2013 5:3, 141-149.

[255] Ocaña-Fernández, 2019, op. cit.

[256] Martens, Alke and Uhrmacher, Adelinde M. "Adaptive Tutoring Processes and Mental Plans". In: *Intelligent Tutoring Systems, 6th International Conference, ITS 2002, Biarritz, France and San Sebastian, Spain, June 2-7, 2002, Proceedings*. Proceedings, 71-80. On what counts as criteria for the evolution of adaptability and contextualization see also: van Seters and others. J.R. van Seters, M.A. Ossevoort, J. Tramper, M.J. Goedhart. "The influence of student characteristics on the use of adaptive e-learning material*", Computers & Education*, Vol. 58, 3, 2012, 942-952, https://doi.org/10.1016/

Smart tutoring systems are based on automated tutors that have been used to teach science, math, languages, and other disciplines; they are based on interactive technologies, in many cases. Human natural language processing systems, especially combined with automated learning and crowdsourcing, have promoted online learning, which had a positive impact on teaching by significantly expanding the dimensions of classic classrooms and, at the same time, addressing the various needs and student learning styles. Online learning data sets have driven rapid growth in analytical learning.

Therefore, we could agree with Hwang and say that intelligent technology allows *intelligent learning environments* that make recommendations, adaptations of help to the individual.[257] For example, it gives guidance (feedback, advice or affordances), and provide adequate support in the place where the need for help occurs, at the right time according to the needs individual students, and in the most efficient way. Further, it coordinates what could be determined by analysing learning behaviors, past and ongoing performance, and student contexts, both online and in the real world.

It is about understanding how to put data analytics together; the automation of certain response processes and the creativity that university teaching continues to demand to generate experiences that do not require mediated responses through *smart* tutorials. Currently

---

j.compedu.2011.11.002. On the concept of adaptive learning system which stands for the fact that developing intelligent tutorial systems is designed to help students learn, and that they do so, with elements that guide the adaptation of learning interfaces and resources, also called "systems for adaptive learning", or "adaptive learning systems" (ALS), see: Adams, WJ, Gray, KL, Garner, M, Graf, EW. "High-level face adaptation without awareness". *Psychol Sci.* 2010 Feb. 21(2), 205-10. doi: 10.1177/09567976609359508. Kinshuk. & Lin, Taiyu. "Application of Learning Styles Adaptivity in Mobile Learning Environments". *ASEE Annual Conference and Exposition. Nashville, Tennessee*, 2003.

[257] Hwang and co-authors, 2008, op. cit.

applications such as apps and many free downloadable programs and online teaching systems such as Carnegie Speech or Duolingo, provide training in foreign languages using Automatic Speech Recognition (ASR) and NLP techniques (programming neurolinguistics) to recognise language errors and help users correct them. All of the above is possible with the new programming tools supported by AI, as well as powerful programming tools based on the same format such as Ruby or Python, whose algorithms allow generating a more effective interface, as well as the cost of verifying and correcting errors.

Cognitive tutors developed for virtual platforms under the AI approach are developed under algorithms based on requirements analysis and object-oriented design, which are the basis of software engineering to achieve imitation of the role of an acceptable human tutor, for example, by providing clues when a student is stuck with a math problem. Based on the clue provided and the response generated, the Smart Tutor will provide context-specific feedback. Intelligent tutoring systems, in a certain way, are not new, since from their modest origins they have provided solicitous assistance on various aspects, such as training in geography, circuits, medical diagnosis, computer science and programming, genetics and chemistry as it is the case of some American schools that have already been using these tools.

Real-time interactivity and fast responses from the AI application can generate timely feedback, but where are teachers left? With the developments in affective computing, what will be the hybridisations between human and computational teaching?

Following the idea of Baricco of a double analogue-and-digital driving force part of our university systems, it would be possible to think of a way of automating low-transfer learning and strengthening deep learning, through teaching strategies that promote unique experiences, not plausible to be automated or regulated via AI? [258]

---

[258] Baricco, 2019, op. cit.

At the University of Buenos Aires, the goal is to generate experiences that are worth living, unique, creative, and original that cannot be algorithmically replicated due to the force of permanent change. We will return to these last points in the discussion item.[259]

The challenge of digital skills

A basic point in such an intricate dilemma of what uses to give to AI and the relationship with autonomy and deep and meaningful learning. It is situated in the field of the new literacy of the university student: digital literacy. These aspects are related to the field of digital competencies based on AI has already been raised some time ago by the European Commission, assuming that digital competence should be understood as one of the key competencies very necessary for continuous learning.[260] This competence is defined as the amalgamation of attitudes, capacities, and knowledge with which an adequate use of critical nature of technology is ensured in the field of information societies, which will be used in various activities ranging from education, work, communication until leisure. Said requirements, according to the aforementioned body, are rooted in basic competencies in matters of information and communication technologies, the use of the computer to obtain, evaluate, store, produce, present and exchange information and communicate, in addition to participating in communities interactive virtual through the internet. Then it could be said that digital competencies tend to be the sum of all the knowledge, attitudes, and skills in technological, informational, and virtual aspects generated in the melting pot of higher education, and based on a new and very complex technological literacy of a functional nature, since it

---

[259] Maggio, 2018, op. cit.

[260] Ibid.

includes the use of tools in a productive way, which would encompass much more than a strictly operational use.[261]

In 1997, the Organization for Economic Cooperation and Development (OECD) began the so-called Definition of Selection and Competency Project (DeSeCo), with the aim of analysing the competencies that are considered necessary for the citizens of the modern world; that is, the psychosocial prerequisites for the proper functioning of society. The anticipated purpose of this project had to do with providing a framework that could guide the development of evaluations of these new competencies in the long term, grouping the key competencies into three groups:

- Interactive use of tools
- Interaction between heterogeneous groups
- Act autonomously

The ability of individuals to think for themselves and take responsibility for their learning and actions were at the center of this framework. The DeSeCo results constitute the theoretical foundations of Pisa, which seeks to monitor the extent to which students on the edge of compulsory education have acquired the knowledge and skills necessary for full participation in society. They focus on the ability of young people to use their knowledge and skills in relation to real-life challenges, rather than their ability to master a specific school curriculum.

DeSeCo had two important characteristics:

- An innovative literacy concept related to the ability of students to apply their knowledge and skills in key disciplinary areas and to analyse, reason, and communicate effectively as they raise, solve, and interpret problems in different situations.

---

[261] Gisbert, M. and Esteve, F. "Digital Learners: la competencia digital de los estudiantes universitarios", *La Cuestión Universitaria*, no. 7, 2011, 48-59.

- An innovative literacy concept related to the ability of students to apply their knowledge and skills in key disciplinary areas and to analyse, reason and communicate effectively as they raise, solve and interpret problems in different situations.

- Its relevance to lifelong learning, which not only limits Pisa to assessing curricular and cross-curricular competencies, but also requires that they report on their own motivation to learn, beliefs about themselves, and their learning strategies.[262]

At the time, they argued that an education in which only memory and mastery of certain skills prevail makes less and less sense in this complex and changing world. We must develop skills and competencies based on the complexity in our students. The poorly structured, polyhedral and interacting knowledge, problem-based teaching, the use of narrative strategies, invite the student to investigate, dialogue, re-construct information, and generate their own relevant and meaningful learning.

The challenge is to generate new types of skills that articulate academics with professional insertion and that account for processes that are now necessary given the advancement of AI.

One of these skills is linked to self-regulation; understanding that knowledge results from an interaction between new information and previous representations, and "learning is building models to interpret the information we receive through [...] our own psychological system."[263] This way of conceiving the construction of knowledge implies an active role of the learning subject based on reflection and awareness, and in which the context (through intersubjective functioning

---

[262] Definition and Selection of Competencies (DeSeCo), https://www.deseco.ch

[263] Monereo i Font, Carles; Pozo Municio, Juan Ignacio. "El alumno en entornos virtuales: condiciones, perfil y competencias", in: *Psicología de la educación virtual* / coord. por César Coll Salvador, Carles Monereo i Font, 2008, 134.

or cultural practices) are inherent to the development and learning itself.[264]

In very general terms, Zimmerman refers to self-regulated learning as "the way in which students become masters of their own learning,"[265] and ensures that it is not a mental ability or a capacity academic, but a self-directed process by which the learner transforms his mental abilities into academic abilities to achieve the goals that he has set.[266] Under this idea of "owning their own learning," a self-regulated student can be described as "an active participant in their personal cognitive, motivational and behavioral learning processes."[267]

We understand that AI developments, especially in relation to adaptive learning and affective computing, are still far from accounting for the complex nature of learning, especially in its metacognitive components; in the active, conscious, and constructive way in which students monitor and regulate their cognition, motivation, and behavior with the intention of achieving the goals they have set for their learning, always based on the changing characteristics of the context.[268]

Discussion and Controversies

As from the deployed development, we can observe the relevance of AI in teaching and learning in the realm of higher education. There are

---

[264] Schunk, D.H. *Motivation and Self-Regulated Learning: Theory, Research, and Application*, Springer, 2012.

[265] Zimmerman, Barry J. "Self-Regulated Learning and Academic Achievement: An Overview", *Educational Psychologist*, 25:1, 4, 1990, DOI: 10.1207/s15326985ep2501_2

[266] Zimmerman, Barry J. "Becoming a Self-Regulated Learner: An Overview", *Theory Into Practice*, 41:2, 2002, 64-70, DOI: 10.1207/s15430421tip4102_2

[267] Zimmerman, Barry J. "Self-Regulated Learning and Academic Achievement: An Overview", ibid.

[268] Lion, C. (Comp.) *Aprendizaje y tecnologías. Habilidades del presente, proyecciones de futuro*. Buenos Aires: Novedades educativas, 144pp. 2020.

theoretical approaches, practices and debates on learning and teaching strategies in line with *intelligent pedagogy* or tutorial accompaniment systems for adaptive learning; highly technological and unique services based on digital environments and mobile apps; the configuration of intelligent innovative classrooms with easy local/remote interaction of students, teachers and centers for the local/remote collaboration among students; design and development of enriched multimedia contents based on the web, with web-based interactive presentations, videoconferences, questionnaires and interactive tests that allow instant and intelligent assessment of knowledge; other affordances and environments managed with intelligent response technology and software that include AI developments.

The rapid progress made by wireless mobile technologies and detection procedures led to the development of u-learning (ubiquitous learning) which is context-sensitive.

With regard to what is intelligent, research has grown considerably all over the globe, both in the field of computer science and teaching engineering. But it will be fundamental to make progress in innovative practices to satisfy the demands of emerging learning and didactic accompaniment models in higher education levels which can gradually spot obstacles in the processes of knowledge architecture, processing interactions in the educational community, and offering recommendations to support and improve academic performance.

We have concluded that an intelligent learning environment meets the following potential criteria: 1) It is sensitive and aware of the context and can elaborate recommendations according to it. That is to say, it perceives the student's situation in the real-world context and is able to offer help to the student accordingly. 2) It is adaptative: it can offer immediate and special support to students through the analysis of their needs in order to organise teaching in the smallest and quickest level and it can do so from different perspectives (for instance from learning performance perspective, taking into consideration the students learning strategies, their working and studying profiles, emotional factors in line with affective computing, as well as their context on line and that of the real world (family, friends, habits, and so on). This characteristic also represents varied and active pedagogic aid, including specific learning guides, commentaries, suggestions and educational affordances suitable to their needs. 3) It can modify during its execution, the user's interface (that is to say, information display) and subjects contents adapting them to personal features (for example, the way in which the user reads and recognises information more efficiently, his learning characteristics and preferences as regards reading and interpreting information) and individual students learning status (for instance, introducing information in the best way and when learning performance is at its best).

The user's interface is not necessarily a conventional computer, it can also be a smartphone or a tablet. Students may interact with the learning system on actual devices, such as smartphones or tablets, new devices as virtual reality glasses, digital watches, or even computing systems integrated into everyday objects (Internet of things, IoT). Research is being made to adapt users' interfaces and respond to specific educational needs within the framework of intelligent learning.

However, this perspective opens a new debate.

On the one hand, we are facing an ethical debate. Those who investigate augmented humanity state that AI is capable of showing autonomous decision making; that means, of carrying out acts without any human validation. It will not only be able to interpret behavior but manipulate the nature and rhythm of certain behaviours. Which will be our real autonomy scope? According to Sadin it implies the underestimation of subjective judgment in favor of algorithmic management, the disregard of what is human mainly made invisible by informatics.[269] How to strengthen decision-making when algorithms tell us what to do?[270] What about what is human and what is robotic? Which are the limits of experimentation? These are not only epistemological but ethical debates.

On the other hand, we encounter the debate about the same platforms; their convergence, their rhizomatic and analytic data connections. We find platforms that are increasingly similar, and which make a profit with their data.[271] As regards environments that are so similar to each other, a few examples come to mind including Blackboard, Moodle, Ed Tex, and Edmodo. How to increase creativity when the environment itself limits your possibilities? These queries are as enlightening as cleavage points to understand that today's mindtools (devices, apps, platforms) can create dilemmas for education that we will have to analyze in the future. Which learning should be promoted, which experiences will be valuable, which knowledge relevant and how will we go on learning when technology is in between?

Ubiquitous resources offer the possibility not only for the student to access learning sources and material as well as knowledge in general, from anywhere, but also for the student to be aided by the system, thanks to the information collected about their habits, styles, and learning methods.

In short, this debate demonstrates that current educational systems face several challenges. Among them, a broader approach and consideration of informal learning (outside school rooms), ongoing access gaps; demand of creativity and flexibility at work, and at the same time, platforms that show uniformity and little variation of

---

[269] Sadin, 2020, op. cit.

[270] Cobo, 2019, op. cit.

[271] Srnicek, Nick. *Platform capitalism,* Malden: Polity Press, 2016; ed. note: the author refers to the German translation of 2018, by U. Schäfer at Hamburger Press.

educational proposals and a lack of correspondence between the careers offered to individuals and those demanded by the working force.

Conclusion

Throughout the article, we have shown the conflicts between AI developments (in intelligent environments or tutorial systems that make adaptive learning stronger, or in objects that are being developed in line with IoT) and the scope of autonomy for the design of strategies that surprise and build support for long-lasting learning with distant transfer along with the demands of contemporary society.

We have emphasised the importance of effective learning strategies, tools, and the support of customised learning in ubiquitous learning systems aware of context; we have discussed what is implied in the inclusion of intelligent tutorials or adaptative learning techniques.[272] On the other hand, we are far from having systems that direct teaching design and the organisation of educational processes in tune with the diversity and heterogeneity of our current university classrooms.

We have acknowledged that in the face of datafication and algorithmisation, which obtain performance results through data interpretation, the challenge lies in environments that invite us *to think outside the box*, that encourage flexibility in decision making, autonomy, and critical thinking as well as the critical ability to empathise in the years to come. We believe that the intelligent systems which are growing in adaptative and contextualised learning environments can work in detection and recommendations, but give little opportunity for creative and critical thinking.

---

[272] Hung, Chun-Ming *et al.* "Effects of digital game-based learning on students' self-efficacy, motivation, anxiety, and achievements in learning mathematics". *J. Comput. Educ.* 1, 2014, 151–166. https://doi.org/10.1007/ s40692-014-0008-8

We are convinced the next questions will be related to learning scenarios immersed in real-world problems, which will imply cognitive activities of a higher order and significant thinking during the learning process. Research conducted by Sherman and Craig determines that immersive learning environments are fundamental because users can interpret visual, audio, and touch instructions to collect information and simultaneously get involved in the process within a virtual reality environment.[273] Context-aware environments help students understand and organise knowledge, solve problems and make inferences based on what they have learned.[274] Immersive environments can facilitate a way to connect students, engaging them in interpreting, analysing and summarising new ideas from their experiential learning, from discovering or learning by doing.[275] Lukosch evaluates immersive environments as an appropriate tool to improve situated and experiential learning, transferring knowledge to a working situation, connecting theoretical problems with real situations.[276]

In this sense, we believe that intelligent systems cannot be excluded from university management, but their scope and restraints should be determined. Part of their scope is political, and it is related to the

---

[273] Sherman, William R. and Alan B. Craig. *Understanding Virtual Reality: Interface, Application, and Design*, San Francisco, CA: Morgan Kaufmann Publishers, 2003. pp. 429-431, illus.

[274] Chu, H. C., Hwang, G. J. *et al.* "A concept map approach to developing collaborative Mindtools for context-aware ubiquitous learning", *Proceedings of the 17th International Conference on Computers in Education, ICCE* 2009, 559-563.

[275] Toca, Torres, C. and Carrillo Rodríguez, J. "Los entornos de aprendizaje inmersivo y la enseñanza a ciber-generaciones. Immersive learning environments for teaching the cyber generations", *Educação e Pesquisa*, v. 45, 2019, https://doi.org/10.1590/S1678-4634201945187369

[276] Lukosch, H., Kurapati, S., Groen, D., Verbraeck, A. "Microgames for Situated Learning: A Case Study in Interdependent Planning". *Simulation & Gaming*. 47(3), 2016, 346-367. doi:10.1177/1046878116635468

detection of education dropout to foster inclusion, to keep track of different backgrounds and types of learning strategies, and to strengthen them.

Traditionally, universities have provided training for new professional fields, mainly those closely related to science and basic theoretical developments. The debates mentioned before evidence a new role with the aim of giving university graduates the tools to work efficiently with artificially intelligent systems. Consequently, university teachers will have the responsibility to encourage the construction of knowledge for both new and traditional degrees, so that students enter their working places with a real knowledge of the limitations of AI and the ability to keep on learning as AI develops and continues changing the roles and expectations at the working place.

This is a change universities should not miss. AI can help solve great challenges that Higher Level Education has in the Knowledge Society, particularly those posing disruptive innovations. In the strategic field of university policies, AI can offer part of the solutions to great challenges present in decision-making processes in universities. We will have to decide which limits and decisions we will embrace vis-a-vis this *augmented humanity*.

TECH-LOGY: ERROR.CODES.FUTURE
A DEFENCE OF ACADEMIC FREEDOM

Erny Gillen

Errors or Mistakes?

Errors are the daily bread of IT and AI developers and users. When in any computerised system an error code pops up, they know: something went wrong. Luckily *error codes* are sometimes themselves an error. A simple restart of the device magically solves the issue. But if *error codes* persist and the system cannot fix them humans or meta-systems must intervene with their specific degrees of freedom.

Decoding and retracing errors can be a fastidious job. You have to go back into the machinery of algorithms and rules to check why they deviated from their laid-out path or goal. The more complex the bugged systems are, the more difficult the task will be to properly address the *error as technical expression for a failure within the processes.* If, however, the origin of the error resides in the design of the deadlocked process, I will throughout this article consistently refer to it as a *mistake that in the end is related to intentions or objectives of the human designers and their free choices.* It is obvious that errors can be related to mistakes and that it is not an easy task to untangle them analytically.

The title of my essay also suggest that errors code the future. This is true as far as they require a human intervention implementing a change of course for a bugged system. Such meta-interventions are the result of choices and intentions for which humans are responsible and where the semantic field of *mistake* opens. In this article I will focus on moral responsibility and moral accountability but not enter into the juridical aspects. The purpose of my essay is an epistemological one. There are no binding definitions for *error* and *mistake* and both words are usually mixed in discussions and papers; therefore, it seems best to first define what I introduce as distinctive characteristics. The here proposed distinction between *error* and *mistake* shall serve a better understanding of the different roles, functions and responsibilities in the chains of command of AI driven applications.

Humans between Nature and Technology

I am writing this article in the midst of the Corona pandemic, which reminds the human family drastically that it itself is *part of nature* and its lifecycles with their own rules and struggles for existence. Today's way of life in major parts of planet Earth certainly is the result of our relentless efforts to build an own specific and artificial - in contrast to natural - ecosystem for humankind. I will call the driver for our human evolution and emancipation from nature *artificial intelligence,* because of the way we outwitted and still outwit nature and its many expressions notably through the invention of *time as our history* in contrast to the recurrent cycles of renewal in nature.[277] To differentiate AI and IT driven systems as tools in the hands of human artificial intelligence I will consistently use the abbreviations AI and IT in the broadest way and not enter into the many distinctions.

When SARS-CoV 2 was finally recognised as a pandemic humans started first hiding in their homes and later hiding their faces. Back in

---

[277] See: Rovelli, Carlo. *The Order of Time*, Adelphi Edizione SPA:Milano, 2018; *Und wenn es die Zeit nicht gäbe*, Rowohlt Verlag : Reinbeck bei Berlin, 2018. In today's physics time has become a variable. Rovelli argues for more fundamental research and for more critical dialogue. He calls our experienced time the thermodynamical time. J.T. Ismael, How physics makes us free: Oxford University Press, New York, 2016.

our caves we used our accumulated and aggressively filled reservoirs to survive against an invisible and unknown enemy. We stopped our time to let the virus pass by and boosted research to come up with vaccines and medication in record time. With those tools under hand, we then were able again to impose our timeframe step by step on the virus's nature and our old equilibrium among humans with its inequalities and inequities even further deepened during that crisis.

What can we learn from the SARS-CoV 2 crisis for handling AI? Our technical skills as part of human artificial intelligence are still very powerful when it comes to defend our domination within nature. Nature, as we know it, has become a raw material at the service of human civilisations, and the former Gods and Goddesses a myth for those who need more time for the transition into the Anthropocene. Intentions, goals and objectives are reserved to the pure domain of humankind. Nature has its own laws and sub-laws, but no intentions, goals, or objectives. Through our artificial intelligence we are able to decode all elements and put them at service for humanity. Karl Popper coined the term "trial and error" for our way to dominate nature by building our technical interfaces. Dealing with nature and its laws we need phases of testing because our own intentions, goals and plans must first be checked against their feasibility and their capacity to become part of our artificial domain within nature. If our technique works our own habitat and our freedom grow (for those who live on the right side of power). If our trial does not work, we step back and prepare a next one expecting that this time no *error code* will pop up and block the intended path.

Our main tools to dominate planet Earth and already its Lower Orbit are our technical tools obeying to the different laws of physics. Our machines and engineering skills in materials and biology become our second nature with its growing but limited freedom (of movement, communication, healthcare, warfare, and so on). Our technologies are truly disruptive in the sense that they erupt us from our natural habitat and the instinctive and intuitive connections we have with it to confine us into a world of its own governed by our artificial intelligence.

AI technologies now seem to become a turning point in the evolution of our self-created second nature. The disruptions caused by its applications seem to aim for its users. New myths and projections rise. They offer an old narrative now applied to our second nature: AI will have one day its own intentions, objectives and plans and thus govern humans, as humans formerly governed nature and animals. In the worst and dystopian visions AI will sooner or later exploit humans as resources for its own purpose. Theology is replaced by a new kind of Tech-logy. Technics and its priests talk, guide and impose on us their intentions, as formerly God and its theologians told people what to think and do.

One merit of Shoshona Zuboff's surveillance capitalism approach is the early demystification of this projection.[278] Behind AI as technology, there are people and deciders who hide themselves and their selfish intentions as far as possible behind algorithms. According to Zuboff, the authors and owners are about to build a sharp divide between those handled and observed by their AI, and themselves as the true winners of the new divide orchestrated through so-called AI applications.

Regardless of scientific and societal warnings, AI technologies become a new necessity in the political arena imposing its pace and rhythm to humanity.[279] The geopolitical competition further nurtures this sometimes-naïve accelerating.[280] There are even proposals by

---

[278] Zuboff, Shoshona. *The Age of Surveillance Capitalism. The Fight for a Human Future at the New Frontier of Power*, New York: PublicAffairs, 2019.

[279] See for example the calls for a ban on face-surveillance in the European Union: https://epic.org/banfacesurveillance/

[280] See: Shaping Europe's digital future. Strategy for artificial intelligence following as first strand the aim to 'place Europe ahead of technological developments': https://digital-strategy.ec.europa.eu/en/policies/strategy-artificial -intelligence

lawmakers to invest some AI driven applications with an own legal personality[281] and in some EU documents AI is already considered as an agent of its own to be invested with trust by citizens.[282]

Right now, humanity seems to be locked between nature reduced to a limited resource and technology invested with the power to build a future for our species. This paradigm, notably promoted by Yuval Harari, is misleading.[283] It underestimates our human artificial intelligence and leads to a TINA mindset in a world where *there is no alternative* to violent but fruitless debates and manifestations or simply to resignation.

Errors and Mistakes Do not Code *the* End

Fortunately, neither nature nor technology simply determine our future as humans in our specific time as humans. They shape our habitat, condition our choices, and stop us with their *error codes* when we ignore their limits. Taming nature, physics and chemistry works best with our *trial-and-error* methods in labs and controlled experiments, before scaled up for industrial and large field applications.[284] Nature and

---

[281] See proposal 59f of the Motion 2015/2103(INL) passed by the European Parliament: https://www.europarl.europa.eu/doceo/document/A-8-2017-0005_ EN.html

[282] See the Introduction of Ethics Guidelines for trustworthy AI: https://digital-strategy.ec.europa.eu/en/library/ethics-guidelines-trustworthy-ai (accessed 16 August 2021) and my critical reflections about this approach: https://www.moralfactory.com/#blog, summarised in: Erny, Gillen, "Die Ethik-Falle", in: Frankfurter Allgemeine Zeitung, 10 January 2019, 9.

[283] Harari, Yuval Noah. *21 Lessons for the 21st Century*, London: Vintage, 2018. e.a.

[284] During the corona crises billions of inpatient people and thousands of politicians and scientists pressed hard to take shortcuts for quick wins, and thus allowed possibly the greatest large field experiments ever executed. This factual paradigm shift will certainly affect the ways AI applications will be generalised

technology react according to their own paces and cycles. Errors pop up when initiated processes meet the limits of a given system. Even if we forcefully can change nature to a certain extend and build innovative technologies, there are limits to our artificial intelligence and practical freedom. Sometimes those limits popup through technical error codes. But sometimes those limits also come from within the human family or important parts of it. They manifest their opposition and do not agree with the chosen pathways they consider being ethical mistakes. In both cases and in liberal democracies the authors of new ways will stop and look for technical respectively political-ethical alternatives.

Ideally societal deadlocks are solved peacefully and in dialogue. This is part of the *ruse* artificial intelligence also stands for.[285] Many political and ethical decisions are complex and based on accurate information provided by trustworthy researchers.[286] Thus, academic institutions and commercial tech camps become important influencers.

Again, the corona-crisis has shown the heights and the depths of this delicate cooperation. Scientists became norm setters and politicians a kind of science explainers, while both mixed up their roles and functions. Science was understood as firm grounds and able to predict and manage the future. A similar situation is met with climate politics. When talking as politicians or journalists even highly regarded scientists avoid telling their lay audience that their work is based on models and hypotheses while interpreting data. When explaining scientific models and data politicians avoid telling citizens that their work follows *many,*

---

quicker and quicker under the pressure of our linear time where acceleration seems the only way to gain time.

[285] Detienne, Marcel, Vernant, Jean-Pierre. *Les ruses de l'intelligence. La mètis des Grecs*: Flammarion, Paris, 1974. In this article I use the concepts of *mètis* as elaborated by Detienne and Vernant. The specific use of mètis by humans I call, for the reasons of thought provocation, artificial intelligence.

[286] In contrast to trustworthy machines or AI, which I would call in my semantics safe or secure.

told and untold, intentions and objectives while tackling the corona health crisis. In both scenarios scientists and politicians make use of their own artificial intelligence to package and sell their knowledge to the best of their interests. The pandemic was (and is) a brilliant showcase for academic and political manoeuvring. In a nutshell and within a limited timeframe we could (and can) observe the strategies of trial, errors and mistakes. Classic Greek philosophy has labelled this kind of practical intelligence as *mètis*, a kind of ruse or stratagem to achieve one's goals.

Mètis as practical intelligence within the world of the living hides the predators' goal, thus equipping for example a weak hunter with ruse to overpower its prey by deceiving it with a lure and surprise. Those deluding stratagems are present in nature and serve a given species to go beyond its limited constitution. Indeed, in ancient Greece the fox and the octopus were admired for their ruse or *mètis*. I call them artificial intelligence, because they offer some animals a contextual window in the natural struggle for existence to achieve more than their physical boundaries would allow without ruse. The human species is certainly the master of *mètis* within the natural world as well as within inter-human cooperation and disputes.

Mètis deals with errors and mistakes not as the end of a journey, but as starting point for a new attempt to achieve its goals. Among humans, mistakes are therefore an important discussion point because there is no common agreement about what is to be considered a mistake. Here opens the whole field of ethics and politics to discuss and to fix, at least temporarily, what a powerful majority and even a powerful minority considers as mistake. In that moral and political struggle for the *right way* the *mètis* of the ones and the others plays an important role.

Necessity and Tech-logy

Introducing a kind of necessity into ethical or political discussions is a well-known stratagem to try to end them. With that mindset, our continues production of carbon dioxide is for example no longer a matter for human freedom, but an existential threat. Where necessity is proven or accepted the free will ends. The same stratagem works with AI. The thesis that the champion will take it all, states that the race to be the first and ahead of all as a necessity within a world of competition. Necessity seems to be the last resort argument accepted by a vast majority. Therefore, it is an important stratagem within the discourses of politicians and even academics.

In the framework of necessity *error codes* become the anonymous language of power framing and limiting human agency instead of unleashing it. Epistemologically speaking, those real, virtual, or faked *error codes* are coding the future by closing it down for further explorations. Confronted with the many *error codes* produced by the climate of planet Earth humans are told to listen to nature and to change their lifestyles. After centuries of intensive agriculture and industrial technologies nature itself becomes again a hard frontier no longer at the service of humanity and its artificial intelligence.

In this narrative the human project to dominate planet Earth has failed. Our calculations were wrong because they did not take into account the limited resources of nature and our care for the next generations. As we seem blocked in our evolution some invest into their escape to further planets while others are willing to entrust the future of humanity to AI because of its massive calculation power able to include present and potential human activity as data.

In this last scenario, humans risk to become objects of timeless and tireless calculations of AI systems. The former subject of history risks to become an element of nature and technology. For the sake of their endangered existence humans seem willing to accept to be taken care of

- this time - by their *last invention,* as some like to call AI.[287] The promoters of the human family's way ahead enabled by AI are already building their strategies by labelling and promoting their systems of trustworthy[288], good[289] or human centric AI.[290] In those narratives, ethics and politics will in the long run be taken care of by anonymous, neutral and omniscient systems.

But remember the warnings of Shoshona Zuboff: behind any AI we should expect some members of our own species who prefer to share the limited resources with a few observers, while sacrificing the rest of humanity.

Whether we are already lured by any shadow games and fake news or not, there is a need for a global debate about the purpose of humanity. Who are we and where should our journey lead us as one human family? Those questions are existential, and they cannot be delegated to systems without our understanding of time and history, unless we give up our purpose and opt for a life as animals under the governance of a good AI, as Harari ironically puts it.

---

[287] See for example authors like James Barrat, Nick Bostrom (Future of Humanity Institute, Oxford) or Max Tegmark (Future of Life Institute, Massachusetts).

[288] cf. notes 6 and 8.

[289] https://www.goodai.com (accessed 16 August 2021). Others, like Virginia Dignum promote responsible AI: https://ec.europa.eu/jrc/communities/sites/default/files/03_dignum_v.pdf (accessed 16 August 2021).

[290] This term attributing agency and action power to AI as far as it uses its so-called autonomy to leave humans at the center of its intentions and actions seems now largely used and accepted by the European Union. Cf. https://digital-strategy.ec.europa.eu/en/library/communication-building-trust-human-centric-artificial-intelligence (accessed 16 August 2021). The EU Commission herein defines the role of the Union no longer as protector of consumers, but as one of building trust within citizens into so-called human-centric AI.

Civilisation, Freedom, and Equality

In the living world the art of hunting and exploitation has evolved over centuries. Territories and species had to be protected and taken out of the hunter's scope. Only a few centuries ago humans were protected against other humans taken advantage of them: an equal dignity in each and every person was recognised. Hunting or exploiting humans became an important *error code* in our societal systems of legislations and democratic institutions. Our fragile civilisation is built on this self-imposed culture and at stake when *error codes* tell us that human dignity was hurt.

Western societies accepted to use their freedom within self-imposed norms derived from a shared humanity. The boundaries related to this paradigm are even somehow protected by international laws and institutions. But our civilisation is not recognised by all as the universal model as it produces enough *error codes* to disillusion other forms of living together. Wilderness among humans is back on the stage and new hunting and exploitation methods are underway.

Human artificial intelligence focusses more on the domination of other humans, nature and technology than on common achievements. Intentions and objectives are framed to lure counterparts and even partners to take them by surprise. In this sociologically difficult context academic freedom can become a lure itself. It can be bought, conditioned, alienated or mislead. The use of *mètis* among humans can be surprisingly creative to achieve their hidden and multiple intentions.

Responsible academics are alert about the dual and multiple use of their inventions and prototypes, but also depending on the funding of their activities. AI in the technical sense of the word seems to be a huge and complex domain promising a better future for the many. Governmental and commercial sponsors seek to get their part of influence by financing specific projects serving their interest. As long as the critical thinking of the scientific community about the intentions and objectives of their sponsors is not excluded, academic freedom seems *prima facie* safeguarded. But very often the financially strong know more about the natural appetite of their prey, than the researchers would be willing to admit. Lucky slaves are great enemies of freedom and critical thinking often ends with one's own interests.[291]

It is not enough to state or manifest academic freedom. Against the potentially dramatic power of AI technics and the proven artificial intelligence of the mighty it is recommendable to openly debate about this freedom among researchers as such and together with their sponsors. Such debates can help scientists to unmask the lures and discuss at eye level with sponsors and politicians.

Integrating professional ethicists into such processes and honest debates can help both sides to build trust on true grounds. This will take time and cost money. It will slow down the rush but nurture common enthusiasm, thus breaking the artificial divide between citizens who pay and citizens who are paid.

Conclusion

Universities and research facilities should always be open for the unprecedented and thus not serve the mere goal to reproduce the present for the future. Whoever is funding research in AI should foresee ethical reviews on all levels, starting with the strategic governance where ethical questions are all too often relayed to the lower levels.

Researchers, developers, and designers in the waste fields of AI are often much more alert about the inherent and potential risks of their endeavours than those ordering or using their tools. The greater need for ethical awareness, formation and training is seen with those at the top

---

[291] Beckert, Rudi. *Glücklicher Sklave. Eine Justizkarriere in der DDR*: Metropol-Verlag, Berlin, 2010. Beckert was the highest ranking judge in the Eastern Democratic Republic of Germany.

and those at the end of the chain of command. In my experience the scientific community is open and accustomed to productively deal with critical questioning. They are used to productively handle *error codes* and mistakes as teams if not unduly put under threatening economic pressure or constraints of predefined success in the current geopolitical rush to win the race of AI.

Coding the future is a sacred human activity where mistakes are possible. It seems better to exclude potential mistakes from our intentions, objectives and plans, than to meet and address them later in our achievements as *error codes* popping up from a hurt nature, a technical dead end or deceived populations.

All of us can use their human artificial intelligence for the common good and the global commons. These open concepts can make a difference for our own freedom of action while courageously exploring new territories of cooperation and innovation. When freedom of action grows for many, humanity is on the right track: more fields for its inherent artificial intelligence or *mètis* will become accessible and offer new and even better opportunities for an open future.

AI IN STUDENT RECRUITMENT AND SELECTION

ARTIFICIAL INTELLIGENCE AND THE NEED FOR AUTHENTICITY AND INTEGRITY

Divya Singh and Avani Singh

Introduction

There is no gainsaying the changes wrought by technology to regular human engagement.[292] Technology enables connection across geographic borders as well as social and economic boundaries, creating new and still unchartered opportunities for learning and self-development. These changes, with their inherent potential for innovation and development, are recognised in the objectives of the National Qualifications Framework (NQF). Sections 5(1)(b) and (d) of the NQF Act 67 of 2008 are of specific relevance, providing that:

> The objectives of the NQF are … (b) to facilitate access to, and mobility and progression within education, training and career paths; … (d) accelerate the redress of past unfair discrimination in education, training and employment opportunities.

This paper focusses on the critical issue of access to higher education through recruitment and selection processes. The discussions consider the efficacy of technology-enabled selection and recruitment practices in

---

[292] This article was originally published in the *South African Qualifications Authority Bulletin*, 20:1 September 2021, and is republished here with permission.

higher education institutions, and the likelihood of technology optimising the NQF agenda. As institutions become increasingly responsive to the possibilities proffered by the Fourth Industrial Revolution, artificial intelligence (AI) - with its yet unharnessed capabilities - will become more salient over the next decades. Emphasising this reality, the World Economic Forum (WEF) points to the impressive progress made in AI in recent years, driven by exponential increases in computing power and the availability of vast amounts of data.[293] Further explaining why today's technological transformations represent more than merely a prolongation of the Third Industrial Revolution and rather the arrival of a fourth and distinct one, the WEF highlights the critical factors of velocity, scope, and systems impact.[294]

Business and organisations are increasingly confronted with artificial intelligence that promises opportunities to streamline complicated, cumbersome, time-consuming, and resource-intensive processes through automation, and universities have not been exempt. While alluring and significant in any decision-making process, this is never the full consideration. As a rule of general application, decisions to adopt artificial intelligence should integrate two further key vectors, namely, the legal and ethical deliberations of the decisions taken. In this context, the reminder from Hanson is apposite: "In higher education … we face a decade in which institutional integrity and legitimacy is under fire."[295] As higher education institutions prepare for the deluge of technology in

---

[293] World Economic Forum (WEF). Fourth Industrial Revolution: What it Means, How to Respond, 2016, no page, https://www.weforum.org/agenda/2016/01/the-fourth-industrial-revolution-what-it-means-and-how-to-respond/

[294] WEF, 2016, op. cit.

[295] Hanson, W.R. *Ethical leadership in higher education: Evolution of institutional ethics logic.* Dissertation Graduate School of Clemson University, 2009, 1. https://tigerprints.clemson.edu/all_dissertations/377/

the Fourth Industrial Revolution, the duality of the relationship between ethics and technology must be an integral aspect of adoption, and the promise of technology should consciously align with the broader higher education commitment to academic authenticity and integrity.

AI for Recruitment and Selection

There is no gainsaying that the state's financial contribution to higher education has not kept up with the number of learners with access to university study. According to the Institute for Security Studies, government funding *per capita* has been consistently declining since 1994. In 2016, spending on higher education was 0.76% of gross domestic product (GDP) – lower than both the African (0.78%) and international (0.84%) averages.[296] With the limited budgets and institutional rivalries built on reputation, institutional rankings and competition linked to success and throughput, universities are keen to ensure that students enrolled are both most likely to be retained and will succeed to graduation. While not restricted by enrolment caps and state subsidies, private higher education institutions are equally committed to demonstrating graduate success and throughput.

As emphasised by Chen and Do the accurate prediction of students' academic performance is one of the critical factors considered by institutions these days when making admission decisions.[297] Supporting this imperative, AI and machine learning - specifically predictive

---

[296] Reva, D. No Date. Getting to the heart of South Africa's higher education crisis. *ISS Today.* Pretoria, South Africa: Institute for Security Studies, n.p. https://issafrica.org/amp/iss-today/getting-to-the-heart-of-sas-higher-education-crisis

[297] Chen, J.F. and Do, Q.H. "Training neural networks to predict student academic performance. A comparison of cuckoo search and gravitational search algorithms". *International Journal of Computational Intelligence and Applications.* 13(1), 2014, 18, https://doi.org/10.1142/S1469026814500059

analytics for recruitment and selection - has already become an intrinsic aspect of the institutional admissions management plans of many universities in the USA.[298] These universities have been increasingly applying machine learning for purposes of new student profiling and prediction of success, as well as to promote institutional efficiency during the enrolment processes.

With the focus on widening access and the massification of higher education, universities in South Africa receive thousands more

---

[298] The literature provides various definitions and descriptions of AI. One of the less complex definitions is provided by Kukulska-Hulme *et al.* (2020), who explain it as "computer systems that interact with people and with the world in ways that imitate human capabilities and behaviours." A more comprehensive definition is provided by the Independent High-Level Expert Group on Artificial Intelligence, set up by the European Commission, as follows:

"Artificial intelligence (AI) systems are software (and possibly also hardware) systems designed by humans that, given a complex goal, act in the physical or digital dimension by perceiving their environment through data acquisition, interpreting the collected structured or unstructured data, reasoning on the knowledge, or processing the information, derived from this data and deciding the best action(s) to take to achieve the given goal. AI systems can either use symbolic rules or learn a numeric model, and they can also adapt their behaviour by analysing how the environment is affected by their previous actions. As a scientific discipline, AI includes several approaches and techniques, such as machine learning,... machine reasoning,... and robotics." (European Commission 2019: 6)

As noted above, machine learning – underpinned by algorithms – is a sub-field of AI which involves "software able to recognise patterns, make predictions, and apply newly discovered patterns to situations that were not included or covered by their initial design" (Popenici and Kerr, 2017, op. cit., 2). Detailed references are: Kukulska-Hulme, A., Beirne, E., Conole, G., *et al. Innovating Pedagogy 2020. Open University Innovation Report 8.* United Kingdom: Institute of Educational Technology, Milton Keynes: The Open University, 2020, http://www.open.ac.uk/blogs/innovating/; European Commission. 2019. A definition of AI: Main capabilities and solutions. April, 8. Brussels: European Commission www.aepd.es/sites/default/files/2019-12/ai-definition.pdf

applications for places than they can accommodate. While many universities depend solely on quantitative data, globally, universities are also recognising that the "inclusion of qualitative components in applications can provide a more comprehensive representation of each applicant's potential than quantitative measures could do on their own."[299] However, qualitative applications are significantly more resource-intensive process as each one requires individual consideration. Furthermore, the method introduces different apprehensions, such as the potential for human bias and subjectivity.

That said, with the advances in machine learning and the AI capabilities to 'read' text statistically, this could be an attractive solution to the resource burden and subjectivity constraints confronting institutions.[300] It also has the potential to provide for better customer service and quick turnaround times to ensure that students can receive feedback much sooner. Reflecting on the promise of machine learning, Klutka, Ackerly and Magda describe forms of AI currently available in marketing automation and predictive analytics "that plug into customer databases and 'learn' what the ideal customer is that has purchased a product."[301] Describing the success of Harley Davidson sales in the New York City market, they note that how a person behaves in the buying process, and what the person responds to, are all possible of being diagnosed by the system. "This AI can then find individuals that match

---

[299] Alvero, A.J., Arthurs, N., Antonio, A.L., Domingue, B.W., Gebre-Medhin, B., Giebel, S, and Stevens, M.L. "AI and holistic review: Informing human reading in college admissions." *2020 AAAI/ACM Conference on AI, Ethics, and Society (AIES '20), February 7-8, 2020, New York, NY, USA.* ACM, New York, NY, USA, 2020, 7p. https://doi.org/10.1145/XXXXXX.XXXXXX, section 2.1
[300] Alvero et al, 2020, section 2.3.
[301] No Date: 9

these traits and show them ads for the product."[302] In higher education admission processes, such technology will enable much more focused student recruitment, thereby allowing universities to "narrowly define the 'ideal' student and use AI to select the best candidates."[303] The university can thus single out the best students for individualised engagement about the university, and why it is best suited for them.

Against this backdrop, the remaining issue then appears to be that of cost – yet this is not so. The most crucial consideration is whether the AI system will be a responsible solution. Considering the possibilities of AI for university selection and recruitment practices, the test stands on three pillars: (i) is the machine thinking rationally; (ii) is the machine making the right decision; and (iii) will the machine behave ethically. Triangulating the responses will aid in assuring a functionality that subscribes to the values of higher education and the priorities of the NQF.

Bearing in mind the objectives of the NQF, examples of how universities have applied AI in recruitment and selection are analysed to identify the risks and opportunities. Some cases specific to the university sector include the work of Andris, Cowen and Wittenbach who used machine learning to find spatial patterns that might favour prospective college students from specific geographic areas in the USA.[304] The university was then able to establish 'loyalty ZIP codes' and hone into particular areas and target those students most likely to apply, enrol and succeed.[305] This approach was undoubtedly more efficient as compared

---

[302] Klutka, J., Ackerly, N. and Magda, A.J. *Artificial Intelligence in Higher Education. Current Uses and Future Applications.* LearningHouse, No Date, 10, www.201811-AI-in-Higher-Education-TLH.pdf

[303] Klutka, Ackerly and Magda, ND, 20.

[304] Andris, C., Cowen, D., and Wittenbach, J. "Support vector machine for spatial variation." *Transactions in GIS*, 17(1), 2013, 41-61. https://doi.org/10.1111/j.1467-9671.2012.01354.x.

[305] Andris, Cowen and Wittenbach, 2013, 58.

with the traditional, often superficial, broad-brush method commonly employed by universities due to limited funding.

Other universities use a combination of historical and current enrolment data, learning analytics and academic performance data of past and current students to develop predictive models for 'recommender systems'. The system then guides the students' enrolment to specific programmes and majors in which the system calculates they will be most likely to succeed.[306] While optimised student success is an unambiguous objective of every higher education institution, this limited and shoehorned strategy to access must beg the following questions: what about the student's acquisition of new knowledge in an area outside of his/her comfort zone?; what about extending the neural pathways of the student to explore something different?; while prioritising student success, what happens to the student's overall development and focus on issues such as social consciousness and civic engagement?; and what about learning for enjoyment? It would be naïve to suggest that university education is not about discipline-specific learning. However, there is a concurrent groundswell of research emphasising the need for higher education to focus on holistic student development. Another important consideration for universities using predictive analytics to guide students towards specific learning paths is the acknowledgement that the best grade is not necessarily what will gear a student to be successful in the current world-of-work and life. (Stelnicki and Nordstokke 2015). There is also no consensus on the existence of a linear correlation between academic grade excellence in

---

[306] Ekowo, M. and Palmer, I. The promise and peril of predictive analytics in higher education. 7, 9 October 2016, https://www.luminafoundation.org/resource/the-promise-and-peril-of-predictive-analytics-in-higher-education/

high school, university success and achievement in the world of work. (Muller 2013; Wolmarans, Smit, Collier-Reed, and Leather 2010).[307]

Further interrogations on the use of algorithms for selection and recruitment highlight apprehensions about producing student archetypes. If properly founded, this question raises a more profound concern about whether such an outcome is not inherently counterintuitive to the fundamental principles of diversity and democratisation of access to higher education and learning. A further challenge with the process of universities shoehorning students based on algorithmic factors of success arises when the information is used by enrolment officers to *exclude* students from an institution even before they start the learning journey because they are considered a success risk.[308] There is no

---

[307] Stelnicki, A.M. and Nordstokke, D.W. "Who is the successful university student? An analysis of personal resources." 45(2), 2015, *Canadian Journal of Higher Education.* 214-228. www.184491-ArticleText-198393-1-10-20150822 (1).pdf.; Muller, A. The predictive value of Grade 12 and university access tests results for success in higher education. March 2013. Masters Dissertation in Education, Stellenbosch University, www.scholar.sun.ac.za/handle/muller _predictive_2013.pdf; Wolmarans, N., Smit, R., Collier-Reed, B. and Leather, H. 2010. "Addressing concerns with the NSC: An analysis of first-year student performance in mathematics and physics". Paper presented at the 18th Conference of the Southern African Association for Research in Mathematics, Science and Technology Education, KwaZulu-Natal, 274-284. https://www.researchgate.net/publication/236934790_Addressing_concerns_ with_the_NSC_An_analysis_of_first-year_student_performance_in_ Mathematics_and_Physics.

[308] At Mount St Mary's University, the institution used to survey to identify students likely to drop-out. The idea was that the students would be "encouraged to leave before they were included in the retention data" collated for purposes of government reporting and national rankings. A fundamental ethical concern with this approach is that students were neither informed of the purpose of the survey, nor were they aware that some students may, as a result of the findings, be "pressured to leave" (Ekowo and Palmer 2016, op. cit. 2). In defence of the university, the president explained that unsuccessful students would be refunded

gainsaying the material costs linked to marketing and student recruitment and universities – with all their current cost containment imperatives – need to be as strategic as possible with their limited resources. However, while the positive potential of machine learning for recruitment and selection processes engenders excitement, there is a definite alternate reality.

Discussion: Ethical and Legal Decision-Making

The advent of artificial intelligence and other similar technologies gives rise to critical and thorny legal and ethical questions, including questions about safety, security, the prevention of harm and the mitigation of risks; about human moral responsibility; about governance, regulation, design, development, inspection, monitoring, testing and certification; about democratic decision-making; and the explainability and transparency of AI and 'autonomous' systems.[309] To protect society against the abuse of AI and new technologies, it proposes nine ethical principles and democratic prerequisites when contemplating a new system: human dignity; autonomy; responsibility; justice, equality and solidarity; democracy; the rule of law and accountability; security, safety and bodily and mental integrity; data protection and privacy; and sustainability. These ethical considerations constitute the yardstick for the design and implementation of any AI system in a higher education institution.

---

their study fees and advised to enroll elsewhere where they had a better opportunity for success. According to the university, it was in fact "helping [students] avoid accumulating debt for a degree they might not have any chance of earning." (ibid.)

[309] European Group on Ethics in Science and New Technologies, 2018. *Statement on Artificial Intelligence, Robotics and 'Autonomous' Systems*, http://ec.europa.eu/research/ege/pdf/ege_ai_statement_2018.pdf

AI bias in selection and recruitment

As stressed by Remian:

"Authenticating the knowledge and predictions of AI becomes more important when AI is used for education since the further spread of inaccurate or outdated content could defy educational goals and further reinforce false information."[310]

One of the gravest concerns with artificial intelligence and especially machine learning is that bias in the system may be unconscious or more critically, not programmed at all but, as seen in the examples below, learned by the machines acting on their own. In addition to bias, two other elements, namely transparency and accountability, must be considered when adopting machine learning. Only when all three aspects are successfully in place will an institution be able to claim the authenticity and integrity of the system.

While machine learning in higher education, and specifically in the domain of selection and admission (access), has tremendous potential, it also presents an equal danger. Today, there is neither the will nor the proven reason to stop the tsunami of technology. However, one of the most significant risks of the Fourth Industrial Revolution is for persons to become sucked into the hype and excitement and, fearful of being left behind, inadvertently further propagating and entrenching stereotypes and current inequalities. Confirming this challenge, Alvero *et al.* reiterate that:

"AI is often described as having the ability to rapidly scale discrimination and exacerbate social inequality."[311]

---

[310] Remian, D. Augmenting education: Ethical considerations for incorporating artificial intelligence in education. 24 November 2019, ScholarWorks at UMass Boston, 20. https://scholarworks.umb.edu/cgi/viewcontent.cgi?article=1054and context=instruction_capstone

[311] Alvero, 2020, op. cit. section 2.3.

The South African entrant to higher education over the last 25 years (and perhaps in the next 25 years) presents with a significantly different profile to those who fed the university pipeline in the pre-1994 era and the few years post-democracy. As the numbers of historically disadvantaged students entering university grew, different race and gender demographic representations began to emerge, and the student profile changed from many (if not most) coming from homes where parents were not university graduates. With the introduction of fee-free higher education, the opportunity for students from lower-income families to enter university has increased exponentially. However, the stark reality is that the admission and success track records of the post-apartheid university student continue to be chequered by the apartheid legacy and are still developing. Against this backdrop, the even-handed outcomes of predictive analytics are doubtful, especially taking cognisance of the factors (such as race, ethnicity, high school, anticipated study areas, and family history) included by the data to 'train' the machines for recruitment and selection. For example, at Wichita State University, the student recruitment programme uses the specific factors of gender, race, ethnicity, standardisation test scores and parents' university background. Based on comparative ratings which interpret and indicate the individual's likelihood to attend the institution, the university targets prospective students for recruitment.[312]

Also using machine learning for recruitment, the University of Ithaca extended the list of factors for selection include the number of friends and photographs on social media. The university collected information about its students from their posts on the internal university social media platform, intended for communication between peers *inter se*, and between students and their lecturers. The university then linked the information with the academic performance of the identified students and using machine learning and analytics, compared the student data

---

[312] Ekowo and Palmer, 2016, op. cit. 11.

with that from applicants to determine prospective students based on their potential for success.[313] The example from the University of Ithaca highlights a material ethical (and legal) concern, namely whether students received advance knowledge about how the institution intended further using their social media information, beyond the academic imperative, and had the opportunity to consent. In a similar vein, Ekowo and Palmer explain that "[c]olleges have long streamlined their recruitment efforts by purchasing student names and their scores for relatively little from third-party organisations."[314] As will be seen later, such practices raise real questions about the integrity of the collection process.

Colleges have also used predictive analytics to assist in identifying the financial need and ability of students.[315] The ethical challenge with this is whether the outcome is to enable the university to better budget to support such students or whether the universities are using the data to eliminate students who may not be able to pay the fees of the institution.

In looking at algorithms and machines to determine recruitment, one may be lulled into a false sense of acceptance that at least the process will be objective. However, the sub-optimal outcome of Amazon's experimental recruitment engine – intended to mechanise the search for *top talent* – dashes the thought. Early in the process, the developers realised that the system displayed a distinct gender bias toward male applicants when it came to recruiting for specific technical positions. Upon further examination, it transpired that the computer models had been trained on résumés submitted to companies in the preceding ten years – a time when the industry was overwhelmingly male-dominated.

---

[313] Felton, E. "Colleges shift to using 'big data' – including from social media – in admissions decisions", 21 August 2015. *The Herchinger Report,* https://hechingerreport.org/colleges-shift-to-using-big-data-including-from-social-media-in-admissions-decisions/

[314] Ekowo and Palmer, 2016, 11.

[315] Ekowo and Palmer, 2016, 6.

Consequently, the machine learned to penalise résumés which included the word "woman". Amazon eventually disbanded the project, acknowledging that while in this instance the bias was identified and remedied, there was no guarantee that the machines would not themselves devise other secondary or *proxy* attributes that could also prove discriminatory.[316]

The Amazon experience was not an isolated instance of machine learning going rogue.[317] In a different experiment, researchers at Carnegie Mellon University also noticed that men were more likely to be targeted for high paying executive jobs. In this instance, the researchers were not able to identify the cause.[318] In another project, the system was explicitly trained to reject candidates with poor English language skills, and, over time, the algorithm taught itself to equate English sounding names generally with acceptable qualification for the job.[319] Such examples demonstrate the need for absolute assurance that where the human factor is crucial, data that informs the algorithm must be both reliable and valid.

Given the socio-economic factors used to *train* the machines, none of the AI systems indicated above resonates with the NQF objective of widening higher education access to previously disadvantaged individuals. Ekowo and Palmer also stress the potential for predictive models to perpetuate injustice for historically underserved groups because "they include demographic data that can mirror past discrimination included in the historical data."[320] The majority of South African applicants - for any number of reasons including the reality of being first-generation university entrants - would either have their

---

[316] Dastin, 2018, op. cit.; Kim, Soyatu and Behnagh, 2018, op. cit.

[317] Popenici and Kerr, 2017, op. cit. 2-3.

[318] www.harver.com

[319] www.harver.com

[320] Ekowo and Palmer, 2016, 14.

applications declined or be steered away from the more intense (and often economically lucrative) programmes on the basis that the system indicates a lack of potential to succeed. Such an approach must be antithetical to the national goals for more black graduates and more women graduates, especially in the discipline fields of science, technology, engineering, and mathematics at a national level. It further points out why in South Africa machines alone will not effective in university recruitment and selection practices.

The research further illuminates the need for universities considering AI systems for admission to understand how and why the machine was trained and who prepared it. Institutions must understand the system and be able to clearly define the value and its synergy with the institutional mission and purpose. In a country of acknowledged social, structural, and economic inequality, the factors applied must not - intentionally or otherwise - reinforce discrimination. Summarising the three fundamental problems that arise with the use of AI, Yu refers to algorithmic deprivation; algorithmic discrimination; and algorithmic distortion.[321] With specific regard to algorithmic discrimination, he notes that the concerns "range from errors to biases and from discrimination to dehumanisation" which tend to be particularly problematic for those on the unfortunate side of the algorithmic divide.[322] In most instances, the worst affected are the poor, the disadvantaged, and the vulnerable.

Confirming the findings in the case studies above, Yu states:

"While the existence of algorithmic bias alone is bad enough, the problem can be exacerbated by the fact that machines learn themselves by feeding the newly generated data back into the algorithms. Because these data will become the new training and feedback data for machine-learning purposes, algorithms that are improperly designed or that utilise problematic data could

---

[321] Yu, 2019, op. cit. 19.

[322] Yu 2019, 19.

amplify real-world biases by creating self-reinforced feedback loops. As time passes, the biases generated through these loops will become much worse than the biases found in the original algorithmic designs or the initial training data."[323]

Further to the above considerations, Alvero *et al.* stress the distinctly different approaches by AI researchers and university selection and enrolment officers to the values of fairness and bias. They note:

"AI researchers tend to be concerned with fairness and bias at the population level, and worry when patterned evaluative outcomes do not approximate population demographics. By contrast, admission officers tend to emphasise fairness of evaluation for individual applicants."[324]

These divergent ethical priorities must be much more closely aligned before universities begin to consider AI and machine learning for recruitment and selection and the caution by Popenici and Kerr bears notice:

"With the rise of AI solutions, it is increasingly important for educational institutions to stay alert and see if the power of control over hidden algorithms that run them is not monopolised by the tech-lords. ... Those who control algorithms that run AI solutions have now unprecedented influence over people and every sector of a contemporary society."[325]

In private higher education, in the absence of state funding, it is plausible that algorithms used in recruitment management will continue to favour selecting wealthier students over their less affluent peers simply because these are the students always enrolled. Some institutions

---

[323] Yu, 2019, 17.

[324] Alvero et al., 2020, op. cit. sect. 6.

[325] Popenici and Kerr, 2017, 4.

will accept this, satisfied that the commercial enterprise will be protected; however, other institutions may find that this unacceptable and contradictory to their central vision to widen access for *all* South Africans.

The legal parameters and standards

As is often the case, the law tends to lag technological developments. However, in South Africa, the Constitution – and specifically section 9 (which provides for the right to equality) and section 14 (which guarantees the right to privacy of every person) – may provide the necessary guidance that will be especially applicable to AI. As seen from the discussion above, the implementation of AI-based technologies in student recruitment and selection has the potential to violate these rights, and it is therefore imperative that institutions contemplating the use of AI take appropriate measures to safeguard against any rights violations.

The right to equality

The right to equality is given content through the Promotion of Equality and Prevention of Unfair Discrimination Act 4 of 2000 (PEPUDA). Section 1 defines *equality* as including "the full and equal enjoyment of rights and freedoms as contemplated in the Constitution and includes de jure and de facto equality and also equality in terms of outcomes." Section 6 expressly prohibits unfair discrimination based on:

(a) race, gender, sex, pregnancy, marital status, ethnic or social origin, colour, sexual orientation, age, disability, religion, conscience, belief, culture, language and birth; or

(b) any other ground where discrimination based on that other ground –

(i) causes or perpetuates systemic disadvantage;

(ii) undermines human dignity; or

(iii) adversely affects the equal enjoyment of a person's rights and freedoms in a serious manner that is comparable to discrimination on a ground in paragraph (a).

In relying on AI for decision-making, universities must be cognisant not to violate the right to equality or perpetrate an act of discrimination based on any of the prohibited grounds (cf. Wichita State University above). Relying on section 13(1) of PEPUDA, a prospective student alleging that s/he has been the subject of a discriminatory decision by the university need only make out a *prima facie* case of discrimination. Thereafter, the burden shifts to the university to prove either that the discrimination did not take place, or that its conduct was not based on any of the prohibited grounds. To satisfy its onus, the university will firstly, have to justify the basis of its decision; and secondly, show that its decision followed the law.

The right to privacy

In addition to the constitutional and common law right to privacy, higher education institutions must comply with the Protection of Personal Information Act 4 of 2013 (POPIA),[326] which provides a comprehensive legal framework for data protection in South Africa. POPIA requires higher education institutions using AI or machine learning to make decisions about students to ensure that: (i) the affected students are adequately informed of the intention; and (ii) the personal information processed for decision-making purposes complies with the conditions stated in the Act.[327] POPIA further expressly requires that personal data may only be processed if, given its purpose, it is relevant,

---

[326] All provisions of POPIA came into effect on 1 July 2020.

[327] The eight conditions include the principles of fairness, transparency and accountability, and the rights to be informed, to object, to access, and the rights related to automated decision-making.

not excessive, and there is a valid justification for the processing. Additionally, the collection of personal information must be for a specific, explicitly defined and lawful purpose related to a function or activity of the university and should not be retained for any longer than is necessary to achieve the goal, unless one of the legislated exceptions applies. Importantly, while higher education institutions may seek consent from data subjects for the processing of their personal information, this is not a silver bullet. The burden will remain on the institution to prove that the consent was given in a voluntary, specific, and informed manner (that is, that it was validly obtained). As such, higher education institutions must be open and transparent with students about the purposes for which personal information is being collected and used, as well as the consequences of their compliance or refusal to provide the information as requested.[328]

Restrictions on automated decision-making

Section 71 of POPIA deals specifically with the question of automated decision-making. Sub-section (1) provides that a data subject may not be subject to a decision which results in legal consequences for them or which affects them to a substantial degree, which is based solely on the automated processing of personal information intended to provide a profile of that person. Sub-section (2) sets out certain exceptions to the general prohibition. For instance, if the decision is in connection with the conclusion or execution of a contract, and appropriate measures are in place to protect the data subject's legitimate interests. "Appropriate measures" in this regard require that the data subject has an opportunity to make representations about the decision and provided with sufficient information about the underlying logic of the automated processing of the information to make such representations. The insertion of this provision evinces a clear understanding from the legislators of the

---

[328] Cf. University of Ithaca.

potential for risk attendant upon automated decision-making, and the broader implications that this may have on affected persons. Universities would be advised, as a rule of general application, to avoid decisions taken by solely automated means unless there is absolute certainty and clarity that the rights and interests of students can be appropriately protected.

The European Parliament report by the Panel for the Future of Science and Technology describes data protection as being at the forefront of the relationship between AI and the law.[329] AI systems need to collect and process data to make intelligent decisions, therefore making access to data fundamentally important.[330] However, appropriate means and mechanisms must be in place to ensure that the personal data in the possession or under the control of the university is not subject to unlawful access or abuse. As noted by the Panel for the Future of Science and Technology:

> "AI enables automated decision-making even in domains that require complex choices, based on multiple factors and non-predefined criteria. In many cases, automated predictions and decisions are not only cheaper, but also more precise and impartial than human ones, as AI systems can avoid the typical fallacies of human psychology and can be subject to rigorous controls. However, algorithmic decisions may also be mistaken or discriminatory, reproducing human biases and introducing new ones. Even when automated assessments of individuals are fair and accurate, they are not unproblematic: they may negatively affect the individuals concerned, who are subject to

---

[329] European Parliament report by the Panel for the Future of Science and Technology, 2020, op. cit., 1.

[330] WEF, 2019, op. cit., 6.

pervasive surveillance, persistent evaluation, insistent influence, and possible manipulation."[331]

To withstand the legal (and ethical) challenge, universities will, therefore, need to be transparent in setting out their recruitment strategies and the principles that inform their selection processes. Students must know if they are being subject to automated decision-making, as well as provided with the underlying logic of the automated processing, with a reasonable opportunity to make representations on the decision. To the extent that an automated outcome determines a result, universities should consider coupling such automation with human interventions to oversee the process and apply an independent mind to the determinations to preserve the values of a human-centric society.

Conclusion: The Need for AI – Authenticity and Integrity – With Machine Learning

When implementing artificial intelligence, it is vital to ensure that in the final analysis, the ethics, values, rights and standards espoused by the university and the higher education sector are protected and promoted, as well as the principles required by law. Where machine learning is used, this will inevitably include how the predictive models are created and by whom. Given the complexity of the processes and the decision-making involved, universities must develop institutional frameworks (including risk and impact assessments) to guide their approach, implementation, and application of AI within the institution, based on multi-stakeholder collaboration. This is an optimal strategy to promote accountability, transparency, privacy, and impartiality and create trust in what could quickly become a contested activity.[332] As explained by the United Kingdom Information Commissioner's

---

[331] Panel for the Future of Science and Technology, 2020, i.
[332] WEF 2019, 9&11.

Office (ICO) an approach that favours explaining AI-assisted decisions to affected individuals makes good business sense. It fosters trust, enables one to obtain more credible and reliable information, and gives one an edge over other organisations that are not as progressive and respectful in their interactions (2020: 16). The ICO further points to the risks incumbent in not explaining AI decisions, including the potential for regulatory action, reputational damage, and disengaged public.[333] Crucially, and as a further demonstration of considered and informed decision-making, it is imperative that institutional spokespersons explaining AI-assisted decisions to affected individuals fully understand the models, choices and processes associated with the AI decision-making processes (ICO 2020: 16).

While the increasing use of AI can have revolutionary benefits for higher education institutions, it is only by fostering a culture of authenticity and integrity that it will be possible to truly and meaningfully realise the opportunities that AI can offer. This means adopting an approach that is clear, coherent, transparent, responsible and abides by relevant principles of law and ethics. As students increasingly demand agency over their information and the decisions taken about them, higher education institutions should not risk being on the unfortunate side of the benefits that the technology can create.

---

[333] Expanding on its recommendation for explanation and engagement, the ICO has identified six main types of explanation: rationale explanation; responsibility explanation; data explanation; fairness explanation; safety and performance explanation; and impact explanation (2020: 20).

AI ETHICS AND ONLINE LEARNING

M.M. Ramya, D. Dinakaran, and R.W. Alexander Jesudasan

The restrictions imposed on educational institutions globally by the governments, as a part of their containment strategy to avoid the spread COVID-19 pandemic, has seen a distinctive rise of e-learning. Digital and virtual learning played a vital role in ensuring continuity in teaching - learning activities. In addition to these technologies, an additional technology in the form of artificial intelligence (AI) is beginning to change education tools and institutions. As the educational institutions reopen, virtual learning will remain as a strategy to provide blended learning. Such innovation is expected to have many positive outcomes in the future of education. However, there are concerns over introducing AI in educational tools (AIET). This article aims to discuss the ethical concerns in online learning over introducing AIET in education spaces.

Introduction

As a society, we want to simplify tasks whenever possible. Individuals who use technological devices to make life easier are likely engaging with artificial intelligence (AI) based solutions. In the recent years, we have seen a marked increase in the number of products in educational technologies to assist teaching - learning, and the integration of AI is becoming more common. AI is becoming more accessible to students, as mobile devices contain a voice assistant, and many devices found in technology-filled homes are programmed with similar functionality. Inclusion of AI technology in teaching-learning has various benefits such as (1) it can alleviate some aspects of a teacher's workload by streamlining admin task (2) it can benefit student by providing differentiated and personalised learning. Due to these benefits, teachers at all levels are expected to include appropriate digital technology to enhance teaching-learning practices. However, during lockdown due to Covid-19 the reality of digital exclusion was laid bare. Those learners who lacked adequate access to devices and internet connections suffered most. The critical loss of learning for many of the most disadvantaged young people could and should have been avoided. This clearly indicates that AIET have so far focused on efficacy. However, the legal and ethical concerns have not been explored much. This article discusses on the ethical considerations examining the views of the students and teachers.

Setting Educational Goals

AIET consists of a well-defined educational goal. One form of AIET may work very well for one student but may not provide the best assistance for another student. As a result, such technologies should provide options for students to set their own educational goals. This would allow them to advocate for themselves and to take more responsibility for their learning. Not only should students be given the choice of which assistive technologies they use; teachers should also be able to have their voices heard regarding setting up of educational goals. Since teachers know how best to meet the needs of their own students, they should be permitted to find a balance between over- and under-automation and autonomy within their classrooms. AIET should offer options to set and attain well-defined educational goals based on strong educational, societal or scientific evidence that is beneficial for learner. AI systems should be used to increase the level of control that learners have over their learning and development

Forms of Assessment

Although in education, acquisition of specific knowledge and achieving specific educational goals are important, the application of that knowledge in real life depends crucially on the individual's acquisition of broader concepts. Such broad and general skills are essential in student development. Such capabilities/skills are assessed through communication, adaptability, flexibility, problem solving abilities. AIET should be possible to evaluate and recognise a wider range of learners' talents in addition to the basic indicators. Additionally, assessment of learner's academic integrity is crucial. This can be evaluated using combination of various assessment approaches like quiz, presentation, written exams, case study and projects. Such assessments will minimise the academic dishonesty since the assessment is verified in different avenues. AIET should be able to handle multiple forms of assessments.

Administration and Workload

An educator spends an enormous amount of time grading homework, assessments and tests. AI can step in and offer swift work out of these grading tasks while at the same time offering suggestions/ recommendations to reduce the gaps in learning. Although educational tools can already grade multiple-choice based assessments, they are very close to being able to evaluate descriptive responses as well. The increasing digitalisation at all levels does not only lead to the improvement and optimisation of the administrative workload but also changes the way of internal and external collaboration. To avoid the misuse of the AI technology, the value of an ethical approach of AI technologies needs a strong focus and compliance with an adopted law.

Equity

AIET may be able to remove educator biases in regard to assessing student work, but there is still the potential for biases to exist and be unknowingly embedded by the developers of the technology, which can affect the way AIET evolve. These biases could include suggestions for other assistive technologies that are available for students, which could impact students in ways that discriminate based on various personal attributes, or those that are less obvious; therefore, these biases have the potential to put students and their personal information at risk. AIET should be used in ways that encourage equity between diverse groups of learners and not in ways that discriminate against the different group of learners

Infrastructure

Computers and internet have become basic and essential infrastructure around the world and particularly in the post COVID situation. AIET require advanced infrastructures and an ecosystem, which the low income and rural communities specially in developing countries is not ready with. The digital divide between the societies which refers to the access to digital devices, infrastructure and services prevents them to harness the full potential of AIET. Sustainability of AIET should be ensured by providing essential digital infrastructure to all parts of the country.

Privacy

AI-based assistive technologies are similar to many other digital services in that they collect and store personal information. Since educational assistive technologies are used with students, the concerns that arise over privacy, data security, and informed consent are ones that should be mitigated. Information collected about an individual should be minimised to include only information that is required for the intended purpose and outcome. Further, student data collection should commence only once the individual knows that it is occurring, and they have consented to the data collection. Institutions should ensure that students understand the consequences and outcomes they could experience when using AIET in order to protect their privacy and data. A balance between privacy and the legitimate use of data should be struck to achieve well-defined and desirable educational goals.

Physical and Mental Health

Usage of AIET for learning has substantially increased the screen time which contributes to Ophthalmic disorders. AI based monitoring solutions may lead to psychological issues such as stress among the students and may result in tension, anxiety, and depression. This also will affect the overall learning. During online assessments, AIET uses facial recognition methods to detect malpractice. Students with eye movement disorder like Nystagmus in which the eyes make repetitive, uncontrolled movements and Strabismus - a disorder in which the two eyes don't line up in the same direction face difficulty when AIET identifies them as students who indulge in malpractice. Such disorders have to considered when AIET developers.

Transparency and Accountability

When using AIET, there is often a lack of transparency and increased confusion over how data is collected and used, and who has permission to access this data. Explainable AI solutions are to be developed to develop generic solutions that can offer transparency. Educators are ultimately accountable for educational outcomes and hence should have an appropriate level of understanding of how AI systems operate. All stake holders: educators, learners and other relevant practitioners should have a reasonable understanding of AIET and its implications.

Conclusion

AI has pervaded in almost all activities of our everyday life. The consequences of its use need to be assessed critically, especially when it is introduced as an educational tool. This chapter aims to identify the possible influences that AIET can have on the users. Authors believe that AI has been a promising solution to transform education by creating educational systems that help to personalise learning. On the contrary, there is still a substantial scope for bringing in AIET for higher education, especially in studies where there is an overwhelming presence of experimental studies. It is vital to emphasise that AIET is not just another form of technology - the real concerns must focus on the ethical, pedagogical, social, economic and cultural dimensions of AI. While the ethical implications and the risks of applying AIET in higher education has been discussed, researchers should be encouraged to develop AIET at a broader level, that addresses the ethical implications which would be of paramount importance as such approaches are going to dominate the new normal post pandemic in the educational domain.

CONFLICTED INTELLIGENCE

HOW UNIVERSITIES CAN HELP PREVENT THE DEVELOPMENT OF LETHAL AUTONOMOUS WEAPONS

Alice Beck, Daan Kayser, and Maaike Beenes

Preliminary

This report is part of a PAX research project on the development of lethal autonomous weapons. Previous reports looked at the role of states, tech companies and arms producers in contributing to the development of weapons with increasing levels of autonomy. The present report focuses on universities. Its goal is to inform the ongoing debate with illustrations of where and how university collaboration with the military could be controversial, and potentially could run the risk of contributing to the development of lethal autonomous weapons systems. This report also aims to raise awareness of the issue more generally among students, university staff and the universities themselves. It is crucial that universities and their staff take steps to prevent any (unintentional) contribution to the development of lethal autonomous weapons.

Introduction

In February 2018, it was announced that the Korean Advanced Institute of Science and Technology (KAIST) had started a collaboration with arms producer Hanwha Systems. The goal was to "co-develop artificial intelligence (AI) technologies to be applied to military weapons, joining the global competition to develop autonomous arms."[334] This collaboration immediately led to an outcry among scientists and a call to boycott the university.[335] Faced with the boycott, KAIST gave public reassurances that it would not develop such weapons, nor did it have plans to develop lethal autonomous weapon systems.[336]

The KAIST example demonstrates two important points. On the one hand, universities play an important role in the development of new technologies that can have significant implications for international security. This includes technologies that could play a key role in lethal autonomous weapons. On the other hand, the KAIST example shows scientists can play an important part in preventing this from happening.

AI and related technologies are progressing rapidly and have enormous potential for helping humanity in countless ways, from improving healthcare to lifting people out of poverty and helping achieve the United Nations Sustainable Development Goals—if deployed wisely.[337]

In recent years, there has been increasing debate within the private sector about the impact of AI on our societies, and where to draw the

---

[334] Jun, Ji-hye. "Hanwha, KAIST to develop AI weapons," *Korea Times*, 25 February 2018, https://www.koreatimes.co.kr/www/tech/2018/12/133_244641.html.

[335] James, Vincent. "Leading AI researchers threaten Korean university with boycott over its work on 'killer robots'", *The Verge*, 4 April 2018, https://www.theverge.com/2018/4/4/17196818/ai-boycot-killer-robots-kaist-university-hanwha.

[336] Cyclical Consumer Goods, "AI researchers end ban after S. Korean university says no to 'killer robots'," Reuters, 9 April 2018, https://www.reuters.com/article/tech-korea-boycott/ai-researchers-end-ban-after-s-korean-university-says-no-to-killer-robots-idUSL8N1RM2HN.

[337] Vinuesa, R. *et al.* "The role of artificial intelligence in achieving the Sustainable Development Goals," 2019, https://arxiv.org/ftp/arxiv/papers/1905/1905.00501.pdf.

line between acceptable and unacceptable uses. Concerns related to privacy, human rights and other issues have been raised. The issue of weapon systems with increasing levels of autonomy, which could lead to lethal autonomous weapons, has also led to heated debate.

Fundamental Research, Fundamental Questions

Universities are hugely important in shaping society. They train future generations, pass on knowledge and play a key role in driving innovation. Many important innovations used in everyday life, from seatbelts to touchscreens, come from university research, illustrating the many positive impacts and applications university research can have.[338]

University research is not only financed by the state but also receives external, commercial, funding. Over the last decade, research and development at universities has seen increases in funding from industry by over 5.5 per cent per year in the US.[339] These partnerships exist not only for civilian products and sectors, but also with both ministries of defence and the arms industry.

Collaboration with the military sector is not necessarily problematic in itself. There are applications of new technologies in the military which are less controversial, for example when used for autonomous take-off and landing, navigation or refuelling of military systems. However, it is crucial for universities to be aware of how the technology they develop could be used in the future. Cutting edge research in for example computer science, artificial intelligence and robotics is a key influence for developments in the defence industry that are rapidly

---

[338] See "100 Important Innovations That Came From University Research," Online Universities, 27 August 2012, https://www.onlineuniversities.com/blog/2012/08/100-important-innovations-that-came-from-university-research/.

[339] Jahanian, Farnam. "4 ways universities are driving innovation," World Economic Forum, 17 January 2018, https://www.weforum.org/agenda/2018/01/4-ways-universities-are-driving-innovation/.

changing the nature of warfare and can come to pose threats to international peace and security. And as the experience with the KAIST at the university shows, particular concern arises in relation to the development of lethal autonomous weapon systems, also commonly known as *killer robots*.

Responsible Science

Given that research undertaken by universities may end up being used in military applications, with particular concerns relating to autonomous weapon systems, academia has a role to play in preventing the development of such weapon systems. It is crucial that universities take a stand against any contribution to the development of lethal autonomous weapon systems. Awareness of this issue is all the more important given the increasing blurring of the lines separating knowledge development for civilian purposes and knowledge development for military purposes.[340]

This report therefore gives a brief insight into various involvements of universities in military projects, highlighting some specific profiles that demonstrate why it is essential that staff and students are well aware of what they are working on as well as the possible end uses.

The main aim of this report is to raise awareness of the issue of lethal autonomous weapons among students, university staff and faculty and anyone else interested in the issue, particularly within a university context. Indeed, there is concern that unless universities develop proper policies, some technologies not intended for battlefield use may ultimately end up being used in weapon systems.

---

[340] Rathenau Instituut. "Kennis in het vizier," Rathenau Instituut, 1 July 2019, https://www.rathenau.nl/nl/vitale-kennisecosystemen/kennis-het-vizier (Google translation).

This is an important debate in which universities play an important role. To ensure that this debate is as fact-based and productive as possible, it is valuable for universities to articulate and publicise clear policies on their stance, clarifying where they draw the line between what AI technology they will and will not develop.[341]

Lethal autonomy[342]

> Collaborations with the military sector are not always problematic, but do point to areas of concern. Such collaborations are potentially problematic because of the impact on a range of societal issues they may have, ranging from the compatibility of disruptive military technologies with the laws of war, to digital human rights such as freedom of speech and the right to anonymity. Of particular concern to this report is the potential development of lethal autonomous weapon systems.
>
> Lethal autonomous weapon systems are weapons systems that detect and apply force to a target based on sensor inputs, rather than direct human inputs. This means that the decision to use lethal force is delegated to a machine, and that an algorithm can decide to kill humans.

---

[341] Future of Life Institute, "Autonomous Weapons: An Open Letter From AI & Robotics Researchers," 28 July 2015, https://futureoflife.org/open-letter-autonomous-weapons/.

[342] Docherty, Bonnie. "Mind the Gap: the Lack of Accountability for Killer Robots," Human Rights Watch, 9 April 2015, https://www.hrw.org/report/2015/04/09/mind-gap/lack-accountability-killer-robots; Chengeta, Thomas. "Accountability Gap, Autonomous Weapon Systems and Modes of Responsibility in International Law," SSRN, 30 September 2015, https://papers.ssrn.com/sol3/papers.cfm?abstract_id=2755211.

The function of autonomously selecting and attacking targets could be applied to various autonomous platforms, for instance drones, tanks, fighter jets or ships. The development of such weapons would have an enormous effect on the way war is conducted and it has been called the third revolution in warfare, after gunpowder and the atomic bomb. Militaries are developing these weapons so that they can react more rapidly, and thus gain an advantage over the enemy. Another reason to develop unmanned and increasingly autonomous systems is to reduce the direct exposure of troops to hostilities. Furthermore, these systems can operate for long periods in contested environments where even remote control by a human would not be possible.

However, many experts warn that lethal autonomous weapons would violate fundamental legal and ethical principles and would be a destabilising threat to international peace and security. Moral and ethical concerns have centred on the delegation of the kill decision to an algorithm. Legal concerns are related to whether lethal autonomous weapons could comply with International Humanitarian Law (also known as the law of war). Military and legal scholars have pointed out an accountability vacuum regarding who would be held responsible in the case of an unlawful act.[1] Experts have also voiced various security concerns. For example, by enabling risk-free and untraceable attacks, they could lower the threshold to war and weaken norms regulating the use of force. Delegating decisions to algorithms could result in the pace of combat exceeding human response times, creating the danger of rapid conflict escalation. Lethal autonomous weapons might trigger a global arms race in which they become mass-produced, cheap and ubiquitous since, unlike nuclear weapons, they do not require any hard-to-obtain raw materials. They might therefore proliferate, spread to a large number of states and end up in the hands of criminals, terrorists and warlords.

Designing the Future of War

Historically, universities and research institutes have played a key role in developing new technologies. With new technologies, however, also come new risks. This is especially true when research is used for military purposes.

During the Second World War and later the Cold War, innovation was one of the areas where states competed for dominance. Collaborations between universities and the military became commonplace.[343] In the US, for instance, the Defense Research Committee was founded in 1940. This committee funded research such as the Manhattan Project and established the current model of federal funding for university research.[344]

The Manhattan Project: the science of destruction[345]

The Manhattan Project is an important illustration of academic contribution to military research. Back then, several US universities (including all those within the University of California) carried out academic research, which was crucial to the aim of the Manhattan Project: the development of a nuclear weapon.

The development of the nuclear weapon also made other countries realise that both fundamental and applied physics research had become a crucial part of conflict.

---

[343] Comen, Evan. "10 universities spending billions on R&D," MSN, 4 April 2017, https://www.msn.com/en-us/money/careersandeducation/10-universities-spending-billions-on-randd/ar-BBzjbN7.

[344] Ibid.

[345] Van Duzer, Nate. "Schools of Mass Destruction: American Universities in the U.S. Nuclear Weapons Complex," ICAN, November 2019, https://universities.icanw.org/.

> Once developed, the nuclear bombs that were then dropped on Hiroshima and Nagasaki led to the death of over 200,000 people. Once the news of the attacks became clear, various scientists working on the project shared their regrets in developing the technology. The nuclear bomb is a clear example of the horrific consequences of academic research, without proper moral reflection on the effects, may lead to.

Societal impact of new technologies

In the current geopolitical environment, with rising tensions and high military and economic competition, innovation is still seen as an important source of power. There are, however, some important differences with the Cold War period.

Most importantly, the difference between innovation for civilian and military purposes is increasingly blurry.[346] This is because emerging technologies are often dual-use in nature. This raises new questions about the responsibility of research communities for the potential end-uses of their research. In many cases, the ultimate end-uses will not be known when a technology is first developed. However, in the case of close collaborations between universities and military organisations and arms producers, it is clear some level of responsibility lies with the university.

This is particularly relevant because worldwide the trend of military funding into academic research has continued. Defence departments look to universities to help them in their research and development (R&D).

This chapter will provide some examples of involvement between the military sector and universities, focusing on the US, UK and China. It is not meant to be exhaustive, but to give an idea of the various types of collaborations. As mentioned the examples of collaborations with the

---

[346] Ibid.

military sector are not always problematic, but do point to areas of concern where it is important for universities to articulate and publish clear policies on their stance, clarifying where they draw the line between what AI technology they will and will not develop.

United States of America

The US Department of Defense's (DoD) overall spending on R&D has nearly doubled in the past two decades, increasing from USD 35.5 billion in 1996 to USD 68.3 billion in 2017, according to the National Science Foundation.[347] A part of this R&D funding goes to universities in all 50 US states. Although such funding is mostly not for research into weaponry, an MIT researcher argues that "there is no such thing as free lunch, and the Pentagon is not handing out money just to do good science."[348]

In the US, the Pentagon is the third largest sponsor of all academic research. Only the National Institutes of Health and the National Science Foundation invest more.[349] Furthermore the Pentagon is the leading sponsor in the physical sciences and engineering, for example in electrical engineering, mechanical engineering, mathematics and computer science. The DoD Joint Artificial Intelligence Centre (JAIC) fosters cooperation with academy and industry and is aimed at "accelerating the delivery of AI-enabled capabilities, scaling the Departmentwide impact of AI, and synchronizing DoD AI activities to

---

[347] Conway, Brian. "Carnegie Mellon University is helping to shape the future of war. What do we really know about it?" Public Source, 30 April 2018, https://www.publicsource.org/carnegie-mellon-university-is-helping-to-shape-the-future-of-war-what-do-we-really-know-about-it/.

[348] Ibid.

[349] Ghoshroy, Subrata. "Fact Sheet: The Pentagon and the Universities," Global Campaign on Military Spending, 14 January 2011, http://demilitarize.org/enfact-sheet-pentagon-universities/.

expand Joint Force advantages [...] and adapt AI technologies for DoD missions."[350]

Carnegie Mellon University (CMU) is one of the many US universities benefitting from funds from the DoD. Its long-standing collaborative relationship with the Pentagon goes back more than 70 years.[351] For the fiscal year ending 30 June 2017, the university stated that it had spent USD 172 million in direct funding from the DoD.[352] CMU notably works with the Defense Advanced Research Projects Agency (DARPA) on the OFFSET programme (OFFensive Swarm-Enabled Tactics), which aims to use swarms "to accomplish diverse missions in complex urban environments,"[353] in collaboration with other universities and start-ups such as Corenova Technologies Inc.[354]

In general, most funding from government typically goes to university-affiliated research centres. One example is the Applied Physics Laboratory at John Hopkins University, which was established by the DoD in 1942 and "accounted for USD 1.3 billion of the

---

[350] Deputy Secretary of Defense. "Memorandum: Establishment of the Joint Artificial Intelligence Center," 27 June 2018, https://admin.govexec.com/media/establishment_of_the_joint_artificial_intelligence_center_osd008412-18_r....pdf

[351] O'Toole, Bill, "U.S. Army launches AI Task Force at CMU, stirring concerns about lethal machines," Next Pittsburgh, 4 February 2019, https://www.nextpittsburgh.com/latest-news/u-s-army-launches-ai-task-force-at-cmu-stirring-concerns-about-lethal-machines/.

[352] Conway, B. "Carnegie Mellon University is helping to shape the future of war. What do we really know about it?", Public Source, 30 April 2018, https://www.publicsource.org/carnegie-mellon-university-is-helping-to-shape-the-future-of-war-what-do-we-really-know-about-it/.

[353] DARPA, "OFFensive Swarm-Enabled Tactics (OFFSET)," https://www.darpa.mil/program/offensive-swarm-enabled-tactics.

[354] PAX, "State of AI," May 2019, https://www.paxforpeace.nl/publications/all-publications/the-state-of-ai.

university's USD 2.3 billion R&D expenditure in 2015".[355] The lab works on various projects including robot swarms and is "helping to solve one of the Defense Department's most significant challenges: the test and evaluation of autonomous unmanned aerial systems."[356]

Another example is the Lincoln Laboratory, part of MIT. The laboratory researches and develops technology in support of national security. It is a DoD, federally funded R&D centre.[357] It runs a 17,000-square-foot indoor test facility at the Hanscom Air Force Base used for "prototyping and testing of ground-based, aerial, and undersea autonomous systems."[358]

United Kingdom

Along with the United States, the United Kingdom is one of the largest funders of overall military R&D. Investments are currently increasing following a period of decline.[359] The UK spends around 17 per cent of total public R&D on the military – a large proportion but these numbers are still overshadowed by the figure of 52 per cent for the US. The majority of this funding goes to the arms industry, but (an unknown) part of this funding goes into universities.

---

[355] Comen, E. "10 universities spending billions on R&D," MSN, 4 April 2017, https://www.msn.com/en-us/money/careersandeducation/10-universities-spending-billions-on-randd/ar-BBzjbN7.

[356] John Hopkins Applied Physics Laboratory. "Intelligent Systems Center," https://www.jhuapl.edu/isc.

[357] Lincoln Laboratory, https://www.ll.mit.edu/partner-us/government.

[358] Lincoln Laboratory. "Autonomous Systems Development Facility," https://www.ll.mit.edu/about/facilities/autonomous-systems-development-facility.

[359] Parkinson, Stuart. "Militarising academia: arms corporations and UK universities," SGR Conference: Universities for sale? 19 November 2016, https://www.sgr.org.uk/sites/default/files/SGRconf2016-Parkinson-Universities+arms-industry.pdf.

The MoD has various programmes and projects that relate to artificial intelligence and autonomy. One of these is the *autonomy programme*. The programme seeks to collaborate with academia, industry and international partners, with the aim of drawing on "external civil and military scientific and technological developments and capabilities." Activities include algorithm development, artificial intelligence, machine learning, "developing underpinning technologies to enable next generation autonomous military systems" and optimisation of human autonomy teaming.[360] A survey undertaken by Drone Wars UK shows that 14 UK universities received funding for autonomous systems and drone technology from Defence Science and Technology Laboratory (Dstl), an MoD agency.[361]

An example of this is the Autonomous Systems Underpinning Research (ASUR) programme, led by BAE Systems with support from, for example, Cranfield and Loughborough universities. ASUR supports the development of technologies for unmanned systems, including with regard to "engineering autonomous systems", "operator system decision-making partnership" and "reasoning about metadata in a distributed autonomous environment in order to exploit, prioritise and adapt."[362]

---

[360] Dstl. "Autonomy Programme", 1 January 2018, https://www.gov.uk/guidance/autonomy-programme.

[361] Burt, Peter. 'Off the Leash: The development of autonomous military drones in the UK', Drone Wars UK, November 2018, https://dronewarsuk.files.wordpress.com/2018/11/dw-leash-web.pdf.

[362] Innovate UK. "Autonomous Systems Underpinning Research - ASUR 2013," https://sbri.innovateuk.org/competition-display-page/-/asset_publisher/E809e7RZ5ZTz/content/autonomous-systems-underpinning-research-asur-2013/1524978.

University	Area of collaboration
Cranfield University	Autonomous systems
Imperial College London	Sensors and data analytics
Loughborough University	Autonomous systems
University College London	Imaging and sensors
University of Cambridge	Control and performance
University of Liverpool	Ship-launched drones

Image: Examples of cooperation between universities and MoD / arms producers (source: Drone Wars UK)[363]

UK university funding does not only stem from the Ministry of Defence and its associated laboratories. Arms producers themselves pour large amounts of money into the academic sector as well. There are collaborations with several arms producers, including BAE Systems, Thales, and QinetiQ. Drone Wars UK notes that "universities appear usually to undertake applied research of this nature in collaboration with private sector contractors, often as part of a broad industry-academia consortium involving several partners from each sector, with projects specifically focused on defined outputs."[364] According to an article from 2018, "in the past three years alone, 15 universities with renowned engineering departments have received almost £40m in grants from the contractors."[365] Examples include Boeing's funding of scholarships and internships for students working on a drone project at Bristol University,

---

[363] Burt, Peter. "Lethal and autonomous: coming soon to a sky near you," *Responsible Science*, 12 June 2019, https://www.sgr.org.uk/sites /default/files/2019-06/SGR-RS01_Lethal_autonomous_drones.pdf.

[364] Peter Burt. "Off the Leash: The development of autonomous military drones in the UK," *Drone Wars UK*, November 2018, https://drone warsuk.files.wordpress.com/2018/11/dw-leash-web.pdf.

[365] Doward, Jamie and Bennett, Greg. "Defence contractors hand British universities £40m," *The Guardian*, 1 April 2018, https://www.theguardian.com/ world/2018/mar/31/defence-contractors-british-universities-funding.

as well as BAE Systems sponsoring the Centre for Ethics and Law at University College London.[366] BAE Systems also supports a professorship at Cranfield University in autonomous systems and artificial Intelligence.[367]

These collaborations in the UK have sparked debate in the past. Already in 2010, a group of 20 professors asked for public spending cuts be made in military R&D rather than into research into healthcare and environmental issues.[368]

China

Traditionally there have been strong links in China between defence and educational institutions. This is also the case in the development of artificial intelligence and related technologies. Tsinghua University, for instance, has launched the Military-Civil Fusion National Defence Peak Technologies Laboratory to create a "platform for the pursuit of dual-use applications of emerging technologies, particularly artificial intelligence."[369] In a speech, the Vice President of Tsinghua University stated that "Applied basic research is mainly focused on major national

---

[366] Ibid.

[367] Cranfield University. "Cranfield University reveals plans for leading research role in autonomous systems and AI," 3 October 2018, https://www.cranfield.ac.uk/press/news-2018/cranfield-university-reveals-plans-for-leading-research-role-in-autonomous-systems-and-ai.

[368] Michael Atiyah. "Cut military R&D, not science funding," The Guardian, 13 October 2010, https://www.theguardian.com/commentisfree/2010/oct/13/cut-military-research-not-science-funding.

[369] Bendett, Samuel and Kania, Elsa B. "Innovation, with American Characteristics? Military Innovation, Commercial Technologies, and Great Power Competition," Strategy Bridge, 2 August 2018, https://thestrategybridge.org/the-bridge/2018/8/2/chinese-and-russian-defense-innovation-with-american-characteristics-militaryinnovation-commercial-technologies-and-great-power-competition; see also PAX, "State of AI," May 2019, https://www.paxforpeace.nl/publications/all-publications/the-state-of-ai.

needs, especially military needs, research and development of key core technologies, and promote military-civilian integration in the field of artificial intelligence in China."[370] The university received CNY 100 million (around EUR 13 million) for research into "AI Theories and Crux Technologies for Future Human-Machine Cooperative (Combat) Operations."[371]

A number of Chinese universities participate in the China Innovation Challenge Competition, including the Chinese Academy of Sciences, Peking University, Tsinghua University, Shanghai Jiaotong University and Fudan University. The event is co-organised by the Zhongguancun Civil-Military Integration Industrial Alliance. Ji Huixian, general secretary of the Alliance stated: "Some of the latest scientific achievements have been applied to meet the needs of users, which contributed a lot to promoting national defense."[372] Another example is the Tianjin Artificial Intelligence Innovation Centre (TAIIC) which was established by the Academy of Military Sciences. The centre does various research projects for the People's Liberation Army (PLA) and collaborates with several Chinese universities.[373] These links are also

---

[370] Ministry of Education (China), "The Ministry of Education held a press conference to interpret the 'Action Plan for Artificial Intelligence Innovation in Higher Education Institutions'," Ministry of Education website, 8 June 2018, https://web.archive.org/save/http://www.gov.cn/xinwen/2018-06/08/content_5297021.htm#2 (Google translation).

[371] Kania, Elsa B. "Tsinghua's Approach to Military-Civil Fusion in Artificial Intelligence," Centre for New American Security, 12 July 2018, https://www.cnas.org/publications/commentary/tsinghuas-approach-to-military-civil-fusion-in-artificial-intelligence.

[372] CCTV, "China Innovation Challenge Competition boosts integration of civilian, military technologies," 17 June 2019, http://www.cctvplus.com/news/20190617/8113481.shtml.

[373] 'Tianjin (Binhai) Artificial Intelligence Military-Civil Fusion Innovation Center', 14 November 2018, http://www.yingjiesheng.com/job-004-024-366.html (Google translation).

seen at Harbin Engineering University (HEU), which traces its origins to the PLA Military Engineering Institute and is mainly aimed at research for the navy. In 2018 the university co-organised the "civil-military integration of artificial intelligence Industry Development Summit". One of the technologies currently being developed at the university is autonomous underwater vehicles.[374]

Interestingly some Chinese scholars have argued that the development of artificial intelligence should not be without limits. Indeed, Xu Nengwu and Ge Hongchang of China's National University of Defence Technology state that "the international community maintains that the control of autonomous lethal weapons systems is difficult, but necessary" and recommend a framework that emphasises both transparency and legal principles.[375]

The following chapter in this volume emerges from this same research project and will look more closely at some examples of university–military cooperation that potentially risks contributing to the development of lethal autonomous weapons and therefore raises particular concerns.

---

[374] 'The first civil-military integration of artificial intelligence Industry Development Summit', 709, 2018, http://www.jingpai7.com/ej/qdxq_hrbeu _edu_cn/2018/0415/c5162a185124/page.htm.

[375] See Goldstein, Lyle J. 'China's Olive Branch to Save the World from AI Weapons', *The National Interest*, 1 February 2019, https://nationalinterest.org/ feature/chinasolive-branch-save-world-ai-weapons-42972.

RISKY RESEARCH

Alice Beck, Daan Kayser, and Maaike Beenes

Case Studies

The sections below aim to highlight specific universities that are involved with defence departments and/or arms producers.[376] The aim is to give some insight into a number of ongoing projects that could run the risk of (unintentionally) contributing to the development of lethal autonomous weapons. Projects are considered concerning if they involve technology (and associated hardware) relevant to the development of lethal autonomous weapons systems as well as close military collaboration. Examples of technologies include:

- Sensors, notably: radar, camera, lidar, inertial measurement unit (IMU).
- Software for object detection, identification and classification and target tracking
- Related hardware, notably chips and semiconductors
- Key components for robotics and unmanned systems

In these cases, there is potential for the research carried out within the framework of universities to be used by the military. It is also possible that militaries reconfigure academic research for purposes not foreseen by the institutions.

---

[376] Note of the Editor: This report as the previous chapter is part of a PAX research project on the development of lethal autonomous weapons.

University of Queensland and University of New South Wales Canberra (Australia)

In February 2019, the University of Queensland and the University of New South Wales (UNSW) announced a joint collaboration with the aim of developing "ethical killer robots." The five-year, 9 million Australian dollars (around USD 6 million) project is funded by the Australian Defence Department and is the world's largest study "into how to make autonomous weapons such as future armed drones behave ethically in warfare."[377] The research will also involve the establishment of an advisory board "for organisations to consult with on ethical matters."[378]

Despite the proclaimed aim of this research to embed ethics in autonomous weapons, the project is a worrying one and has sparked controversy, as the research appears to legitimise lethal autonomous weapons. Indeed Dr Jai Galliott, the lead researcher, stated that the project "aims to shape international policy by convincing people that autonomous weapons are a force for good."[379] The idea that programming ethics and the laws of war into machines would solve the

---

[377] Wroe, David. "'Killer robots' to be taught ethics in world-topping Australian research project," *The Sydney Morning Herald*, 28 February 2019, https://www.smh.com.au/politics/federal/killer-robots-to-be-taught-ethics-in-world-topping-australian-research-project-20190228-p510vz.html.

[378] Nott, George. "Killer robot campaign defector to 'embed ethics' in autonomous weapons," *Computerworld*, 11 March 2019, https://www.computerworld.com.au/article/658600/killer-robot-campaign-defector-embed-ethics-autonomous-weapons/.

[379] Moore, Charlie. "Australian Defence Force invests $9 million in researching 'killer robots' to ensure artificially intelligent weapons are ethical and don't open fire on children," *Daily Mail Australia*, 1 March 2019, https://www.dailymail.co.uk/news/article-6758051/Australian-Defence-Force-invests-9million-researching-killer-robots.html.

concerns related to lethal autonomous weapons has been critiqued by various AI experts.[380]

Carnegie Mellon University (US)

Similarly, Carnegie Mellon University is involved in research that raises questions. In February 2019, it was announced that the university was further expanding its defence collaboration with the launch of the United States Army's Artificial Intelligence Task Force, which will be based in the National Robotics Engineering Centre in Lawrenceville. Although the broad mission of this task force has not yet been decided, it is likely that the Task Force will be at the forefront of applying AI technologies to weapons systems.[381] Apparently, the task force will delve into ethics and codes of conduct for AI systems, despite the President of CMU, the Army Secretary and the commander of Army Futures Command all declining "to endorse a full ban on autonomous weapons systems."[382] More recently, the AI Army Task Force head Col. Matty said that they were "able to leverage existing relationships between Carnegie Mellon and DOD through Army Research Lab [...] to

---

[380] See for example: Aimee van Wynsberghe and Scott Robbins, "Critiquing the Reasons for Making Artificial Moral Agents," February 2018, https://link.springer.com/article/10.1007/s11948-018-0030-8; Sharkey, Noel. "The evitability of autonomous robot warfare," *International Review of the Red Cross*, June 2012, https://international-review.icrc.org/sites/default/files/irrc-886-sharkey.pdf;_Prof. P. Asaro. "On banning autonomous weapon systems: human rights, automation, and the dehumanization of lethal decision-making," *International Review of the Red Cross*, 2020, https://e-brief.icrc.org/wp-content/uploads/2016/09/22.-On-banning-autonomous-weapon-systems.pdf.

[381] O'Toole, Bill. "U.S. Army launches AI Task Force at CMU, stirring concerns about lethal machines," *Next Pittsburgh*, 4 February 2019, https://www.nextpittsburgh.com/latest-news/u-s-army-launches-ai-task-force-at-cmu-stirring-concerns-about-lethal-machines/.

[382] Ibid.

create an Army task force that could tap into the artificial intelligence ecosystem."[383]

The parallels with the above example are self-evident, and this announcement has also raised concerns. On campus, "critics say they wish they had more information on this new work with the Army."[384] These developments come at a time when Silicon Valley and the tech sector are toeing the line between useful innovations (for defence and civilian protection), and producing autonomous weapons.[385] An op-ed in the student newspaper, the Tartan, protested clearly and strongly against the presence of the US Army on campus. This op-ed argued that "even our very own university president, Farnam Jahanian, is committed to war over diplomacy and negotiations. [...] This is unacceptable. The President did not seek the input of students, faculty, or staff before proffering this view on our behalf – or indeed, before committing Carnegie Mellon to the Army AI Task Force itself."[386]

On top of this, one of the Task Force's projects has been tied to (the much controversial) Project Maven. The US Army has been developing surveillance technology within CMU's Army AI Task Force, where it seeks to develop algorithms able to analyse drone footage in order to

---

[383] Sheftick, Gary. "AI Task Force taking giant leaps forward," US Army, 13 August 2019, https://www.army.mil/article/225642/ai_task_force_taking_giant _leaps_forward.

[384] Linder, Courtney. "Some students, faculty remain uneasy about CMU's Army AI Task Force," *Post-Gazette*, 18 February 2019, https://www.post-gazette.com/business/tech-news/2019/02/17/army-ai-task-force-pittsburgh-cmu-farnam-jahanian-military-google-project-maven/stories/201902150015.

[385] Ibid.

[386] "CMU SDS opposes Army AI Task Force," *The Tartan*, 10 February 2019, http://thetartan.org/2019/2/11/forum/sds?fbclid=IwAR0kl7rNalFWZuU_nmrfYv 0Fdn3MQ4DDKo5NztX8lLNsLP8iN0Kk5MXLrMg.

identify targets.[387] Allegedly, the pursuit of this Project Maven initiative by the university "went without any notice or publications."[388]

Imperial College London (UK)

Imperial College London provides another example of a university with strong defence links and collaborations. The university is among those receiving the highest levels of military funding, according to Scientists for Global Responsibility (SGR), a UK-based organisation that has undertaken research into military funding of UK universities.[389]

In July 2018 it was reported that Imperial's White City Campus "is providing a new hub for DASA [the Defence and Security Accelerator]". This new hub was arranged at the same time as both institutions agree to explore research collaboration opportunities that "could provide advantages to the UK's defence and security." According to the head of DASA, "Our presence at I-HUB gives us access to innovative start-ups and world class academics across a wide range of disciplines, and promotes collaborative working between the Government, academia and the private sector."[390] Indeed, the aim of DASA is to help the UK DoD maintain strategic advantage over its adversaries.[391]

---

[387] Tunnard, Adam. "CMU Quietly Hosts Project Maven Offshoot Through Army AI Task Force," WESA, 3 September 2019, https://www.wesa.fm/post/cmu-quietly-hosts-project-maven-offshoot-through-army-ai-task-force#stream/0.

[388] Ibid.

[389] Parkinson, Stuart. "Military-university collaborations in the UK – an update," Scientists for Global Responsibility, 13 April 2015, https://www.sgr.org.uk/resources/military-university-collaborations-uk-update.

[390] Imperial College London. "New solution to defence and security challenges to be explored at White City," 10 July 2018, https://www.imperial.ac.uk/news/187172/new-solutions-defence-security-challenges-explored/.

[391] DASA. "About us," https://www.gov.uk/government/organisations/defence-and-security-accelerator/about.

Imperial College had also previously developed flight control algorithms for the Demon drone, which displayed a certain amount of autonomy.[392] According to NGO Drone Wars UK, it is likely that Imperial College works on sensor networks and visualisation in projects funded by DSTL; however when conducting research on this topic, they were unable to get more information as Imperial College turned down requests to provide more details.[393]

Academic Resistance

Student activism

Traditionally, universities have been fertile ground for activism and protests. This was particularly evident during the Vietnam war, where student unrest spread across the US. A nationwide strike took place on 5 May 1970, in reaction to the deaths of students at a protest rally in Kent State University following president Nixon's extension of the war into Cambodia.[394] The week-long protest that ensued involved some of the largest protest movements around the country.

In recent years, universities have been host to student protests in relation to climate change, particularly with the aim of getting universities to divest from fossil fuel companies. In February 2018, the University of Edinburgh declared that it was fully divesting from all fossil fuels, following a long student campaign.[395] In November 2019,

---

[392] Burt, Peter. "Off the Leash: The development of autonomous military drones in the UK," Drone Wars UK, November 2018, https://dronewarsuk.files.wordpress.com/2018/11/dw-leash-web.pdf, 36.

[393] Ibid.

[394] Altaras, Zoe. "The May 1970 Strike at UW," Washington University, https://depts.washington.edu/antiwar/may1970strike.shtml.

[395] Carrington, Damian. "Edinburgh University divests form all fossil fuels," *The Guardian*, 6 February 2018, https://www.theguardian.com/environment/2018/feb/06/edinburgh-university-divests-from-all-fossil-fuels.

the University of Manchester announced that it was reviewing its GBP 12 million investment into fossil fuel companies. This came after a week of protests involving the occupation of one of the university's buildings.[396]

Similar activism has also been linked to university shares in arms producers. In September 2019, an investigation by the Glasgow Guardian found that the University of Glasgow had a total of GBP 3 million invested in weapons producers as of 30 June 2019.[397] Following this, six University societies have formed a coalition protesting for full divestment and they aim to pursue a long-term campaign.[398] The Glasgow University Arms Divestment Coalition states: "The campaign has such a broad base of societies due to the very nature of the arms trade. It is damaging in so many ways, from furthering the climate crisis to violation of human rights. We hope that the University will hear loud and clear that the student population does not accept this use of money now, nor ever."[399]

These examples illustrate the influence that students may have over universities and their policies.

---

[396] Wootton-Cane, Nicole. "University of Manchester to review fossil fuel shares after student protest," *The Guardian*, 26 November 2019, https://www.theguardian.com/education/2019/nov/26/university-of-manchester-to-review-fossil-fuel-shares-after-student-protest.

[397] Doak, Sam. "Glasgow University invests over £3m in arms trade and military service providers," *Glasgow Guardian*, 15 September 2019, https://glasgowguardian.co.uk/2019/09/15/glasgow-university-invests-over-3m-in-arms-trade-and-military-services-providers/.

[398] Doak, Sam. "Newly-formed Glasgow University Arms Divestment Coalition releases demands," *Glasgow Guardian*, 18 October 2019, https://glasgowguardian.co.uk/2019/10/18/newly-formed-glasgow-university-arms-divestment-coalition-releases-demands/.

[399] Ibid.

Protesting military involvement with universities

University collaboration with the military sector is contentious and has raised questions for many years. Below are some more recent examples of resistance in accepting research funding from defence organisations.

Japan

In Japan, it was reported back in 2017 that there was a big divide among academics over MoD grants to universities for defence-related research.[400] Indeed, the years 2015 to 2017 were marked by a big increase in subsidies for such research, from JPY 300 million (approximately EUR 2.5 million) in 2015 to JPY 11 billion (approximately EUR 92 million) for the fiscal year 2017.[401] What is more, for Japan 2015 marked the first year since World War II that direct research funding was provided to universities from the defence ministry.[402] Since the end of World War II, Japanese academics have consistently renounced military research "based on the bitter lessons of the war, in which Japanese scientists contributed."[403] Worries pertain primarily to the risks posed by defence funding to academic freedom, as the results would not be available to the public without permission from the military, according to the Japanese Coalition Against Military Research in Academia. In March 2018, Kyoto University announced it was adopting a policy of not conducting any military-related research.

---

[400] Kakuchi, Suvendrini. "Rapid expansion of defence research divides academics," *University World News*, 10 January 2017, https://www.universityworldnews.com/post.php?story=20170110132046209.

[401] Conversions based on current transfer rates (as per 2 February 2020).

[402] Kakuchi, S. "Rapid expansion of defence research divides academics," *University World News*, 10 January 2017, https://www.university worldnews.com/post.php?story=20170110132046209.

[403] Japanese Coalition Against Military Research in Academia, http://no-military-research.jp/?page_id=7.

Germany

In Germany, some 20 universities have signed a clause (the *Civil Clause*) where they promise to only conduct civilian, not military research.[404] Civil clauses were first introduced at the University of Bremen in 1986, with multiple other German universities following suit.[405] In 2013, revelations about US defence funding research at German universities and research institutions caused quite a stir, raising questions about the relationship between the Pentagon and Germany's institutes of higher education and research.[406] However, in July 2019 the German state of North Rhine-Westphalia adopted a new law allowing universities in North Rhine-Westphalia to conduct military research in the future through abolishing the so-called civilian clause, despite many groups protesting the bill.[407]

European Union

The European Union itself is now also focusing on military R&D, allocating EUR 13 billion for the new European Defence Fund in the period 2021 to 2027. For now though, universities have received just 2 per cent of the EUR 44 million allocated so far, while 26 per cent went to research and technology organisations – such as TNO, the Netherlands Organisation for Applied Scientific Research.[408] However,

---

[404] Dierck, Gijs. "Universiteit moet beter gevaren van onderzoek zien," NRC, 8 July 2019, https://www.nrc.nl/nieuws/2019/07/08/universiteit-moet-beter-gevaren-van-onderzoek-zien-a3966407.

[405] Sara, A. "New law abolishes 'civil' German universities," News One, 12 July 2019.

[406] Greiner, Lena. "German Scientists Accused of Naivete," *Spiegel*, 26 November 2013, https://www.spiegel.de/international/germany/german-universities-under-fire-for-taking-pentagon-contracts-a-935704.html.

[407] Sara, A. "New law abolishes 'civil' German universities," op. cit.

[408] Gibney, Elizabeth. "Europe's controversial plans to expand defence research," *Nature*, 22 May 2019, https://www.nature.com/articles/d41586-019-01567-y.

in the future projects might be tailored more "towards fundamental science and universities."[409] These developments have led some researchers to actively avoid the scheme. A campaign group named Researchers for Peace gathered more than 1,000 signatures against the fund, with the largest share of signatures coming from Germany.[410] The campaigners warn that the "establishment of an EU military research programme points towards an unprecedented acceleration of the militarisation of the EU."[411]

Science for good

There are several organisations that work to ensure that research is done for the benefit of humanity. Such groups include previously-mentioned *Scientists for Global Responsibility* (SGR), a UK membership organisation promoting responsible science and technology.[412] SGR have listed the various justifications that universities may provide for accepting military funding, which include arguing that the amount may only be a small percentage of the university's total funding and so "it has little effect on its overall research agenda" and that "military-funded projects benefit Britain's national security."[413] SGR refute these points, arguing that funding may represent a large proportion of the budget for a particular department, and thus can shape the research priorities of that department – "gearing them towards a more militaristic agenda."[414] Another example is *Pugwash Conferences on Science and World Affairs*, an international organisation which

---

[409] Ibid.

[410] Ibid.

[411] Researchers for Peace, https://researchersforpeace.eu/.

[412] Scientists for Global Responsibility, https://www.sgr.org.uk/.

[413] Parkinson, Stuart. "Military-university collaborations in the UK – an update," Scientists for Global Responsibility, 13 April 2015, https://www.sgr. org.uk/ resources/military-university-collaborations-uk-update.

[414] Ibid.

focuses on the issues that lie at the intersection between science and global affairs.[415] Its goal is to seek the elimination of all weapons of mass destruction and to reduce the risks of war, among others.

A need for due diligence

The examples given above demonstrate existing tensions concerning military funding in higher education institutions, whereas not all defence collaborations with universities are necessarily unwanted. As this report focuses on concerns related to the development of lethal autonomous weapon systems, many components that could be used for such systems may be in the research and development phase. It is therefore crucial that universities are fully aware of the purpose and possible applications of the technologies they are working on, especially if the research is pursued in collaboration with Ministries of Defence and the arms industry.

What Can Universities Do?

This report has presented several potentially concerning examples of university collaboration with the military. However, there have also been examples of universities taking positive steps to prevent any future contribution to the development of lethal autonomous weapons systems. The present chapter will present some examples of such action as well as provide other measures that universities and their staff can take to ensure none of their work ends up leading to the development of weapons systems without meaningful human control.

In spring 2018, the Korean Advanced Institute of Science and Technology's collaboration with an arms producer led to a huge public outcry. In February of that year, the institute had opened a joint research centre along with Hanwha Systems, with the aim of carrying out studies

---

[415] Pugwash, https://pugwash.org/about-pugwash/.

into how Fourth Industrial revolution technologies can be utilised on future battlefields.[416] This announcement led to a boycott organised by Professor Toby Walsh. More than 50 leading AI and robotics researchers stated that "they will boycott South Korea's KAIST university over the institute's plans to help develop AI-powered weapons."[417] The boycott would "forbid all contact and academic collaboration with KAIST until the university makes assurances that the weaponry it develops will have 'meaningful human control'."[418] In response, the university indeed gave public reassurances that it would not develop such weapons, nor did it have plans to develop them,[419] and the boycott was ended.

Later, in June, KAIST launched an ethics subcommittee within the KAIST Institute for Artificial Intelligence, "in a bid to cope with a series of challenging ethical questions being posed by AI-powered systems worldwide."[420]

---

[416] Jun, Ji-hye. "Hanwha, KAIST to develop AI weapons," *Korea Times*, 25 February 2018, https://www.koreatimes.co.kr/www/tech/2018/12/133_244641.html.

[417] Vincent, James. "Leading AI researchers threaten Korean university with boycott over its work on 'killer robots'," *The Verge*, 4 April 2018, https://www.theverge.com/2018/4/4/17196818/ai-boycot-killer-robots-kaist-university-hanwha.

[418] Ibid.

[419] "AI researchers end ban after S. Korean university says no to 'killer robots'," Reuters, 9 April 2018, https://www.reuters.com/article/tech-korea-boycott/ai-researchers-end-ban-after-s-korean-university-says-no-to-killer-robots-idUSL8N1RM2HN.

[420] Jun, Ji-hye. "KAIST launches ethics subcommittee on AI," *Korea Times*, 7 June 2018, http://www.koreatimes.co.kr/www/tech/2018/06/133_250278.html.

As a result, KAIST now has a code of ethics for artificial intelligence[421]:

> "Artificial Intelligence (AI), researched and developed at KAIST, is required to have the following codes of ethics:
>
> 1. AI should contribute to improving the quality of life and human society as well as individual people. In this process, artificial intelligence must cooperate with people, follow the directions of people, learn the values of human society, protect the law and morality, and improve its own abilities.
>
> 2. AI in any events should not injure people.
>
> 3. Unless violating codes 1 and 2 above, AI shall follow both explicit and implicit human intention. However, before the execution, AI should ask people to confirm the implicit intention. (If several people are involved and their intentions are different, AI should follow a person with the highest priority or the closest relationship.)
>
> 4. Unless violating codes 1 to 3 above, AI may autonomously perform functions delegated by people. However, for the cases of either a low confidence or a high risk, AI should always advise to people and confirm the final decision before the execution".

The KAIST controversy demonstrates the important role that academia can play in preventing any developments that could lead to lethal autonomous weapon systems. The following section will provide an overview of what else universities can do, as well as some examples of other commitments already made by academic staff.

The KAIST example is not the only time that academics have played a role impeding the development of lethal autonomous weapon systems. There have been a number of scientists' letters, i.e., open letters

---

[421] KI for Artificial Intelligence. "KAIST: Code of Ethics for Artificial Intelligence," https://kis.kaist.ac.kr/index.php?mid=KIAI_O.

signed by prominent AI and robotics researchers, some of which have been submitted to national parliaments or to the UN.

Stuart Russell, a computer science professor at the University of California in Berkeley has warned that "because they do not require individual human supervision, autonomous weapons are potentially scalable weapons of mass destruction; an essentially unlimited number of such weapons can be launched by a small number of people. This is an inescapable logical consequence of autonomy."[422] Therefore "pursuing the development of lethal autonomous weapons would drastically reduce international, national, local, and personal security," according to Russell.[423] Decades ago, scientists used a similar argument to convince presidents Lyndon Johnson and Richard Nixon to renounce the US biological weapons programme and ultimately bring about the Biological Weapons Convention.[424]

In Belgium, an open letter was published in December 2017 by 116 scientists working in fields such as AI and robotics. The letter expressed "serious concern at the development of weapon systems lacking meaningful human control over the critical functions of targeting and engagement in every attack." Many of the signatories were university professors or researchers.[425] The letter was released on the same day that

---

[422] Russell, S. "The new weapons of mass destruction?" *The Security Times*, February 2018, https://www.securityconference.de/fileadmin/MSC_/2018/Dokumente/Security_Times_Feb2018.pdf.

[423] Sample, Ian. "Ban on killer robots urgently needed, say scientists," *The Guardian*, 13 November 2017, https://www.theguardian.com/science/2017/nov/13/ban-on-killer-robots-urgently-needed-say-scientists.

[424] Guillemin, Jean. "Scientists and the history of biological weapons: A brief historical overview of the development of biological weapons in the twentieth century," *Science and Society*, July 2006, https://www.ncbi.nlm.nih.gov/pmc/articles/PMC1490304/.

[425] "Belgian scientists letter on autonomous weapons," https://docs.google.com/document/d/e/2PACX-1vQU8W-

the Belgium parliament held its first hearing on autonomous weapons.[426] The attention and coverage was instrumental in leading to a resolution unanimously adopted by the Belgian parliament in July 2018 calling for a ban. The resolution calls on the government "to forbid the Belgian military from using lethal autonomous weapons and to work toward an international treaty banning the weapons."[427] Another letter was published in Norway in June 2019. At the time of writing, it has received over 750 signatures.[428] Signatories include numerous rectors of Norwegian universities, professors and heads of departments.

As shown above, these letters can have a significant impact on debates in national parliaments. We encourage university faculty staff, researchers and students to sign any such national open letter. Similarly, they can make a commitment by signing the Future of Life's *Lethal Autonomous Weapons Pledge*.[429]

Students and faculty members can take other steps to raise awareness too, in the aim that their institutions take action to prevent the development of killer robots. Actions such as events and workshops on the issue are helpful, as well as encouraging dialogue and questions on (military) research conducted within universities.

---

mpdjBqLHlA4Xgbe1BhKI4scm2UyQg3cPpylpjnOVF81OmPSE7QmzaXNDfq BeLGrNFS4ozRL8-/pub.

[426] Stop Killer Robots. "National campaigning against killer robots," 7 December 2017, https://www.stopkillerrobots.org/2017/12/national-outreach/.

[427] PAX. "Belgium votes to ban killer robots," 23 July 2018, https://www.paxforpeace.nl/stay-informed/news/belgium-votes-to-ban-killer-robots.

[428] Call for action against Lethal Autonomous Weapons, https://lytt-til-oss.no/en/.

[429] Future of Life. "Lethal Autonomous Weapons Pledge," 2018, https://futureoflife.org/lethal-autonomous-weapons-pledge/.

> "Pursuing the development of lethal autonomous weapons would drastically reduce international, national, local, and personal security" – *Stuart Russell.*

Besides steps taken by students and staff, there are measures that universities themselves can take to prevent their collaborations leading to the development of lethal autonomous weapons.

- Commit publicly to not contributing to the development of lethal autonomous weapons.[430]
- Establish a clear policy stating that the university will not contribute to the development or production of lethal autonomous weapon systems, and including implementation measures such as:
  - Ensuring each new project is assessed by an ethics committee;
  - Assessing all technology the university develops and its potential uses and implications;
  - Adding a clause in contracts, especially in collaborations with ministries of defence and arms producers, stating that the technology developed may not be used in lethal autonomous weapon systems.
- Ensure university staff and researchers are fully aware of what precisely their technology is being used for and understand the possible implications of their work, and allow open discussions about any related concerns.

---

[430] See for example, Conn, Ariel. "AI Companies, Researchers, Engineers, Scientists, Entrepreneurs, and Others Sign Pledge Promising Not to Develop Lethal Autonomous Weapons," Future of Life Institute, 18 July 2018, https://futureoflife.org/2018/07/18/ai-companies-researchers-engineers-scientists -entrepreneurs-and-others-sign-pledge-promising-not-to-develop-lethal- autonomous-weapons/

PART 3

CONTEXTUAL AND INTERDISCIPLINARY APPROACHES

DIPLOMACY AND TECHNOLOGY
THE INTERSECTION OF ARTIFICIAL INTELLIGENCE WITH INTERNATIONAL RELATIONS

Dhwaanii Arora

Introduction

The most rapid changes in the past 5 years across the globe have been seen in technological innovation - mainly the development of sophisticated artificial intelligence (AI) and machine learning (ML) techniques. There has been a sudden shift in focus to these topics because they are being projected as game-changers, a futurist's delight. Buzzwords or not, these terms are now common parlance and are immediately associated with a disruption in the twenty-first century, be it in education, jobs, or global relations. Each domain in our personal and professional lives will be affected by these technological advancements, including international relations.

It is no surprise that these new concepts are going to create a seismic shift across all professions. Albeit gradual, the shift is inevitable. The influence that the new technologies will have on our society can only be discerned over time. Till then, predictions can be made by studying old patterns of changes, which is also a process common to the operations of AI technology. The growing speculation around the uses of AI in various fields such as education, food industry, manufacturing, commerce, and so on, prompts the thought of seeing AI at the intersection of almost everything in our lives. Do we, humans, have the expertise to work with this technology? What is the next step for us?

These kinds of questions around capacity building concentrate direct our attention towards the education sector, the all-encompassing sector that can contribute towards upskilling, learning and really turning tides generation after generation. Since time immemorial, education as a concept was narrowly defined as the degrees and educational qualifications that one could accrue. But it is no longer just about a piece of paper that validates your spending 3 or 4 years completing your higher education and getting a degree. The definition of education has evolved and is now seen as a way of being and thinking, rather than just reproducing what the books teach. It is about synthesizing the input to produce a simple, yet effective output; it is almost a worldview in its own. Education refers to a holistic developmental experience in a person's life – where they not only interact with books in a sophisticated way, but also with their surroundings, people, culture and so much more, which ultimately leads to a broadened outlook.

With the advent of AI, the kind of education that needs to be imparted, needs us to reinvent the wheel. Education is about learning how to learn and unlearn, breaking away from traditional methods of studying and focusing on tapping into the brainpower that humans most often do not end up utilising to the full capacity. It is about learning how to make connections, recognizing patterns and thinking critically.

The expectations from our educational frameworks are changing and demanding alteration for substantially different learning, something that goes beyond the traditional textbook knowledge. Simply knowing dates of important historical events such as the Battle of Plassey or the French Revolution will not suffice. Each piece of information now comes with some context around it, hence allowing the learners to relate to it and consume it more intelligently, rather than simply rote learning it.

Contextual information and knowledge are extremely relevant when thinking about what one is learning or doing. "Contextual information is data that gives context to a person, entity or event. In other words, context-awareness is the ability to extract knowledge from or apply knowledge to information."[431] So, educational models need to adopt this revised approach of learning where there is an equal emphasis on hardcore facts while accounting for the changing times. The parallels that can be drawn here with the world of AI are that the algorithms cannot work and produce results till the time they are fed large amounts of past data, i.e., something that sets the context. Without this background, they will not be able to make predictions. Similarly, a student learns better if there is some related information that can be delivered along with the new information so there are connections that can be formed associating the new piece of information with the old one, thus creating a web of information. This makes it easier to retain knowledge.

For the purpose of this paper, the focus will be on analysing how disciplines like international relations will be affected by artificial intelligence. This is important to study because foreign policy, diplomacy and processes that allow countries to interact with each other will soon be affected by advancements in technology. Social media is currently the most pervasive and effective manifestation of how the course of interaction between countries can be affected by technological advancements. Access to information has become much easier, not only for those in decision making positions, like the diplomats and elected representatives, but also to the citizens. This keeps all parties accountable and makes everyone think twice before pulling a sly move on the other. "Diplomats today now mostly utilise technological

---

[431] Lackey, Jason. "Context Awareness and Network Visibility", *Keysight Technologies*, https://blogs.keysight.com/blogs/tech/nwvs.entry.html/2020/05/01/context_awarenessan-pn3M.html

developments in information dissemination in projecting power abroad, rather than relying on more traditional structures."[432]

In an article titled *Technologies changing diplomatic practices: Pre and post-Covid-19 reality*, published on the Observer Research Foundation forum, the author writes "Official accounts of foreign offices today compete in wit and sharp words. The problem of Twitter diplomacy is everlasting presence of the third party: spectators who immediately show you their support or dissatisfaction. This makes foreign policy highly dependent on domestic policy, likes and dislikes of a non-professional audience."[433]

Newer kinds of strategies in the tech world would also affect how countries interact with each other. This will be very apparent in defence, security and intelligence. Having an advanced technological backing could potentially be a projection of power and superiority.

"Technological advances of MNCs are always factored in reflecting both pressure and persuasion when the home and host governments strengthen their relations."[434] Does this mean a blurring of boundaries for the sake of innovation and collaboration? Will cross-border interactions in the field of AI supersede the political restrictions? With the scope of acceleration in technologies like blockchain, usage of drones, and darknet, nations are already interacting with each other in a way that keeps its economy and politics somewhat mutually exclusive.

The example of China, however, also tells us that some nations are willing to tread their own path without seeking external validation or

---

[432] "Technology is Changing Diplomacy", International Policy Digest

[433] Ivanchenko, Viktoriia. "Technologies changing diplomatic practices: Pre and post-Covid-19 reality", *Observer Research Foundation,* https://www.orfonline.org/expert-speak/technologies-changing-diplomatic-practices-pre-and-post-covid19-reality/.

[434] Jain, Pracin. "Technology as a silent factor in international relations", *Times of India,* https://timesofindia.indiatimes.com/readersblog/civil-services-preparation/technology-as-the-silent-factor-in-international-relations-29719/.

assistance. "The Chinese government has launched "Made in China 2025," a state-led industrial policy that seeks to make China dominant in global high-tech manufacturing. The program aims to use government subsidies, mobilise state-owned enterprises, and pursue intellectual property acquisition to catch up with—and then surpass—Western technological prowess in advanced industries. For the United States and other major industrialised democracies, however, these tactics not only undermine Beijing's stated adherence to international trade rules but also pose a security risk."[435]

Other nations around the world seem to differ in opinion. Israel is making rapid advances to improve its technology capabilities, and given their rate of innovation, there are nations willing to strike deals with them just to boost business. "Israel's technology boom has created opportunities for Israeli policy makers to shape new and expanded international partnerships."[436] In such a context, it is important to be able to differentiate objectives of statecraft from those of growth of the country.

It might be worth studying the implications of artificial intelligence in the international relations study. Perhaps to better equip ourselves to understand the interplay of technology and international relations and to stay ahead of the curve. Diplomats will now not only need to know ins and outs of conducting diplomacy, but will also have to wear the technologist hat, where they understand newer technologies and their implications. Many countries followed suit in appointing tech ambassadors to navigate digital affairs after Denmark appointed its first

---

[435] McBride, James & Chatzky, Andrew. "Is 'Made in China 2025' a Threat to Global Trade?", *Council on Foreign Relations,* https://www.cfr.org/backgrounder/made-china-2025-threat-global-trade.

[436] Tooch, David. "The Case of Israel's Technology Transfers as Tools of Diplomacy in East Asia", *JEMEAA – VIEW,* https://www.airuniversity.af.edu/Portals/10/JEMEAA/Journals/Volume-01_Issue-2/JEMEAA_01_2_Tooch.pdf

tech ambassador in 2017.[437] With this intense focus on technology, countries are realizing that it is an important feature of modern-day diplomacy.

AI in itself is not the end goal, it is only the means to an end which is to make processes easier, smarter and eventually self-sufficient so no human intervention is required. Integrating artificial intelligence education with international relations can benefit global relations. There is a need for individuals who not only understand diplomatic nuances, but also have a strong hold in international relations theory, alongside fluency in AI and related technologies. This is essential to drive the digital transformation that countries are currently undergoing. This shift in the way political operations are conducted will primarily be driven by emerging technologies and subsequently have an effect on the interactions that countries have with each other. The all-pervasive nature of social media platforms like Facebook, Instagram and WhatsApp especially in acting as a disseminator of information and influencer of opinions, alludes to its effect beyond borders. Facebook is now a geopolitical medium outside the jurisdiction of most countries. This is one way AI has an effect on the way countries interact. Twitter's own privacy policies and refusal to comply with the Indian government by not deleting tweets of a certain nature led to a series of allegations on the big tech firm by the Government of India. Big tech firms are clearly trying to break away from the socio-political restrictions, giving them more importance than ever in democracy.[438]

AI is not only a catalyst for change but also something that needs to be interwoven with traditional international relations education. "AI

---

[437] Clarke, Lauria. "Tech ambassadors are redefining diplomacy for the digital era", *Techmonitor,* https://techmonitor.ai/leadership/innovation/techambassa dors.

[438] Daniyal, Shoaib. "Why is the Indian government at war with Twitter?", *Scroll.in,* https://scroll.in/article/999171/why-is-the-government-of-india-at-war-with-twitter

has also become a chief instrument in international diplomacy in areas such as international security, use of autonomous weapon systems, monitoring of concluded agreements, military power like cyber-security, threat monitoring and warfare."[439]

Debate around the Relevance of Higher Education

Education has withstood the test of time and is seen as the driver of change in rapidly evolving times. Content needs to be realigned, not only to deal with the job market, but also to understand and tap into the full potential of what technology has to offer. So, the sooner AI is incorporated in international relations, the faster AI can be leveraged to the advantage of nations.

A person's worth is suddenly doubled if they attend the Ivy League or Oxford, Stanford and the likes. But it is no longer just about the institutional tag, it's about what these institutions teach. Are they breaking the confines of their traditional methods of classroom learning, with fixed curriculums to accommodate the rapid changes in the world? Is higher education worth it? Will education be able to surpass the rate of innovation or even match up to it?

These are extremely tricky questions. Answers to these questions are evolving on a daily basis with people trying to reimagine what the future of education can look like. First, with the COVID-19 pandemic, compounded with the changing landscape of shifted priorities (towards providing better livelihood and protection in general), the education system has a lot of catching up to do. Not only is there a need to make a shift from theory to practice, there is also a need to envision ways of

---

[439] Amaresh, Preethi. "Artificial Intelligence: A New driving horse in International Relations and Diplomacy", *Diplomatist.com*. https://diplomatist.com/2020/05/13/artificial-intelligence-a-new-driving-horse-in-international-relations-and-diplomacy/.

integrating principles of artificial intelligence into the study plan. The question of relevance of higher education needs to be tackled by shifting perspective and recalibrating the curriculum.

It is true that some subjects will not need the technological component to them, however, it is becoming an indispensable means to achieve the impossible. So, it might be prudent to make these changes early on. While there are rapid changes taking place, technology is still in the exploratory stage. It is not set in stone and is still very much within the ambit of human understanding. Machines have not started outdoing human intelligence, yet. But who is to say how far away that day is? Mainstream education will not go out of fashion for the foreseeable future till there is a viable alternative to it. However, the mode of teaching and learning can. Education is meant to enhance capabilities, but these capabilities are becoming more demanding over time, which is why cognizance of the fact that education needs to be more robust to suit the changing times is extremely important. Education is not just about learning skills or specific knowledge. It is a combination of classroom learning, peer to peer interaction, developing a lens to view the world and so much more.

International Relations Education and AI

The core of artificial intelligence is to create less dependence on humans and allow technologies to think for themselves. The inception, however, is from the human brain which first allows for the information to be fed into the machines, subsequently allowing the machines to make sense of the data and establish patterns. Through these patterns, the machines can then take actions further based on their experiences. This is an example of emerging technologies - they are not yet ready to replace the existing technologies, but their mere presence in the market is making the current technology systems obsolete. There is considerable merit in AI in note-making processes, i.e., use of natural language processing in a (a component of AI that gives computers a human-like capability to understand spoken words and text) simple exercise of taking down meeting notes on a laptop could potentially render the entire process useless.

Much like humans, who learn from their experiences, artificial intelligence too, hinges on it. However, we as humans are capable of generating our own thoughts, but machines as we know it are not yet fully capable of that functionality just yet. AI is categorised into two broad categories - narrow and general. Contrary to the terms, narrow AI is the AI of today and what everyone is familiar with. "Narrow AI is based on machine learning, which uses large amounts of data and powerful algorithms to develop increasingly robust predictions about the future."[440] Much of general AI is yet to manifest itself in our daily lives. General AI is much like when a child blossoms into an adult, not requiring any assistance and making decisions itself. This kind of AI would be capable of thinking creatively and be closer to the capabilities of a human brain.

Historically, changes in a society have been slow and steady. The coming of the internet took years and has still not permeated fully to all age groups, socioeconomic groups, and societies. The rapid rate at which AI has hit the market, however, has been astounding; all industries have seen some effect of this, not just tech. "In fact, 90% of leading businesses already have ongoing investment in AI technologies. More than half of businesses that have implemented some manner of AI-driven technology report experiencing greater productivity."[441]

---

[440] Meltzer, Joshua P. "The impact of artificial intelligence on international trade", *Brookings,* https://www.brookings.edu/research/the-impact-of-artificial-intelligence-on-international-trade/

[441] Stahl, Ashley. "How AI will impact the future of work and life", *Forbes,* https://www.forbes.com/sites/ashleystahl/2021/03/10/how-ai-will-impact-the-future-of-work-and-life/?sh=27058daf79a3.

The interaction of technology in the realm of international relations can have immense impact on how relations between countries are now defined. There is a fourth dimension growing in importance in addition to military, economic, and cultural supremacy and that is technology. The country that arrives at the forefront as the technology leader, paving the path for the other countries, will automatically have an upper hand. "The winners of this upcoming AI-defined era in human history will be the countries and companies that can create the most powerful algorithms, assemble the most talent, collect the most data, and marshal the most computing power."[442]

Advancements in the field of international relations are dependent on creating bias-free algorithms and bettering them to ensure accuracy that can be used to drive change. The first-mover advantage will go to whichever country can set the gold standard for innovating and implementing the use of AI. No doubt, this is fluid and is bound to change over time, but the one who enters the field first and makes their mark will earn them an important spot in the history of defining AI.

This is unlike the advancements in science and technology where focus was mostly on enhancing an approach to conducting international affairs; this is very much a real ready-to-used tool that can be employed instantly to deliver instant results. An example of this would be the use of AI facial recognition tools to identify the frequent lawbreakers. Inherently, the systems created until now are replete with flaws where they target people of colour at a higher frequency than their white counterparts. This may be happening because the system learns from the past data which may not be impartial. The bias exists at the source – humans.

---

[442] Allen, John R. "Why we need to rethink education in the artificial intelligence age", *Brookings,* https://www.brookings.edu/research/why-we-need-to-rethink-education-in-the-artificial-intelligence-age/.

Take Google's face recognition program: cats are uncontroversial, but what if it was   to learn what British and American people think a CEO looks like? The results would likely resemble the near-identical portraits of older white men that line any bank or corporate lobby. And the program wouldn't be inaccurate: only 7% of FTSE CEOs are women. Even fewer, just 3%, have a BME background. When computers learn from us, they can learn our less appealing attributes.[443]

So the bias inevitably creeps up, further exacerbating the age-old stereotypes that relegate people of colour to a lower status in society. If this technology is put into motion at a large scale, governments will be increasingly biased against a certain section of society which will snowball into a wider phenomenon reflecting in the foreign policy mandates. This technology is only slightly developed, but it gives us an idea about the extent to which technology could affect our lives.

Conclusion

From the teaching and learning perspective, there simply is not enough data that can be fed to AI mechanisms for them to replace traditional methods of teaching this subject. Bots can answer factual questions but still cannot find intelligent ways to be our mentors, guides or teachers. While the traditional systems can be partially replaced, the nuances of AI still need to be developed for it to successfully replace the functions that involve a more of a psycho-emotional bond. The bots that are being used to answer queries are only useful till the queries are simple enough for the responses to be generic. As soon as different

---

[443] Buranyi, Stephen. "Rise of the racist robots – how AI is learning all our worst impulses", *The Guardian,* https://www.theguardian.com/inequality/ 2017/aug/08/rise-of-the-racist-robots-how-ai-is-learning-all-our-worst-impulses. (More on this - https://www.themarshallproject.org/2016/02/03/policing-the-future?ref=hp-2-111#.UyhBLnmlj)

patterns of conversations emerge, the conversation is directed to a human being on the other end.

"The impact of AI on international relations will not be restricted only to economy but will have particular influence on "hard" international security. AI technology is not a weapon in itself, but it does have a difficult-to-assess trigger potential (enabling technology) in many other areas that are crucial for both the economic and military power of states."[444] One such area of influence is AI in diplomatic relations. Diplomacy is an extremely popular and important aspect of international relations. It refers to the delicate dance between nations. The influence of AI in diplomacy has been categorised into three segments

AI as a diplomatic topic, AI as a diplomatic tool, and AI as a factor that shapes the environment in which diplomacy is practised. As a topic for diplomacy, AI is relevant for a broader policy agenda ranging from economy, business, and security, all the way to democracy, human rights, and ethics. As a tool for diplomacy, AI looks at how it can support the functions of diplomacy and the day-to-day tasks of diplomats. As a factor that impacts the environment in which diplomacy is practised, AI could well turn out to be the defining technology of our time and as such it has the potential to reshape the foundation of the international order.[445]

Each of these offers to create an ecosystem of its own where AI holds importance. Be it as a topic, tool or a catalyst that offers a newer and different environment. As a topic, AI could have no bounds with the endless discussions that could and are happening around it. It is primarily speculation based, based on the advancements in narrow AI

---

[444] Sajduk, Błażej. "Theoretical premises of the impact of artificial intelligence on the international relations and security", *The Copernicus Journal of Political Studies*, December 2019.

[445] Bjola, Corneliu. "Diplomacy in the Age of Artificial Intelligence", *Emirates Diplomatic Academy*, Jan 2020.

which is where AI mechanisms can predict the next step on the basis of past data fed into the system.

As a tool, AI can be utilised to develop a sophisticated method of pre-empting and thus, preventing threats. "While diplomacy with terrorist groups is ethically unacceptable, technology can today provide means of coercive action to pre-empt such threats. All these represent a world of new challenges for diplomacy and I.R. where technology will play an increasingly decisive role."[446] It can also be employed in the context of assisting in negotiations. According to Parul Saxena, a consultant writer at NASSCOM's India AI, "Using data mining, political forecasting can be made easier leading to better understanding and predictions of political, economic, and social trends. AI could prove itself useful in negotiations, the analysis of past negotiations and in predicting the outcome of on-going discussions. Even financial aid disbursements can be protected from discrepancies through AI's anomaly detection."[447]

In such instances, the use of AI is restricted to assisting people in mundane, slightly cumbersome and repetitive tasks. For these tools to be employed, people using them will need to have a fair bit of understanding about their workings to exploit the technology to its fullest potential. The importance and relevance of international relations education combined with that of AI surfaces here. Even machines need to learn from somewhere and the training for that will come from individuals who have the capacity to operate them. Humans use a combination of implied reference, context and logic to make sense of statements and that is what differentiates them from machines; machines

---

[446] Amitav, Mallik. *Role of Technology in International Affairs,* 12.

[447] Saxena, Parul. "AI Across Borders: AI in Diplomacy, International Relations, and Humanitarian Efforts", IndiaAI.gov.in, https://indiaai.gov.in/article/ai-across-borders-ai-in-diplomacy-international-relations-and-humanitarian-efforts, April 2021.

use pure logic to interpret the meaning of statements. As much as we would like to equip machines to take over, we as humans cannot eliminate ourselves from the equation just yet.

TOWARD INDONESIA 4.0: ENVISAGING A VIRTUAL STEWARDSHIP MACHINE FOR THE MARGINAL RELIGIOUS COMMUNITIES

Leonard Chrysostomos Epafras

Introduction

The awakening of the Indonesian Artificial Intelligence (AI) was on July 2020, at the moment the government issued the *National Strategy for the Indonesian Artificial Intelligence, 2020-2045*; *Stranas* in short.[448] *Stranas* is an orientation and roadmap for AI and Information and Communication Technology (ICT) policy in general, framing the direction of AI development with the main objectives to increase business productivities and investment efficiency, to improve human resources management, and to encourage multisector innovative initiatives. In the present article, I take *Stranas* as a context to reflect the possible effect of such futuristic discourse to the marginal groups, notably religious communities. Beyond a reflection, I further discuss the vision of a virtual stewardship machine to imagine a model of AI abstraction for a more ethical and humane implementation of AI.

A little bit dilatory, *Stranas* hauled the government to join the global AI race. Pandemic, furthermore, provided the impetus to seize the day, as the digital engagement is drastically increased and AI-driven

---

[448] BPPT, Strategi Nasional Kecerdasan Artifisial Indonesia, 2020-2045/AI Towards Indonesia Vision 2045, Jakarta: Badan Pengkajian dan Penerapan Teknologi, 2020.

health technology is in high demand. President of Indonesia, Joko Widodo, renowned as Jokowi, framed the condition as an 'era of the war of AI,' *masa perang kecerdasan buatan*. 'Who controls AI, potentially controls the world,' he concluded.[449] Moreover, *Stranas* is a high-profile political gesture and rhetoric to welcome the coming 2045, in which the country is going to celebrate the centennial of Indonesia.

AI is hardly a new discourse for Indonesians as it has been studied, taught, and explored since the 1990s in a number of schools, universities, and research centres. Numerous such initiatives have been produced by Indonesian technologists and most of AI technologies such as machine learning, deep neural networks, have been explored by them. The start-ups such as CekMata, Gojek, and 3dolphins applied AI in their business activities. As part of a community engagement project entitled *Co-Designing Sustainable, Just and Smart Urban Living through ICRS Education, Civic Engagement and Policy Advocacy* (2019-2021, hereinafter referred to as *Co-Designing*), the Indonesian Consortium for Religious Studies (ICRS) managed a small grant for urban innovative products.[450] One of the winners was a university student team who implemented AI for a smart wheelchair that employed voice recognition and optical navigation technologies, all controlled by an Android-based smartphone. The electric wheelchair is not a new innovation of Indonesians, but it is an example of how they tune in to the global wind of change.

Hence, why *Stranas*? Why now? Just like other people of the globe, the awe and wonder of AI technology possessed Indonesians. Hollywood movies since the 1970s have provided vivid pictures on the advanced electronic technology through the imageries of robots,

---

[449] CNN Indonesia. "Perkembangan Kecerdasan Buatan di Indonesia," *CNN Indonesia*, March 15, 2021, https://www.cnnindonesia.com/tv/20210315163418-413-617702/video-perkembangan-kecerdasan-buatan-di-indonesia.

[450] The project is funded by the Ford Foundation.

sophisticated computers, and future fate of the earth when the cyborgs reigned. Reality on the ground was even more impressive. The 2010s became the starting point of the massive foreign investment for internet and telecommunication infrastructures and services. However, despite being among the most internet exposed in the world and holding a huge digital market, Indonesia did not bind by a single vision of AI technology.[451] Along with other Southeast Asian countries, Indonesian AI adoption is still in nascent, integrated ecosystem yet to emerge, and facing numerous shortcomings.

In introspection, *Stranas* registered the existing challenges, among others parsimonious investment and limited infrastructural support to encourage AI research and experiment. Furthermore, there was no link and match between research and the industrial demand, insufficient workforce, outdated regulation, fragmented data governance, limited digital literacy, and many other challenges. A home for 260 million inhabitants, scattered in seventeen thousand islands, those challenges have been around for a long time in Indonesia. On the flipside, huge potential is waiting for exploration, notably the demographic bonus Indonesia would enjoy, that is, a high proportion of productive ages, coupling with the lowest dependency ratio that projected to take place in the period of 2028 to 2031.[452] *Stranas* provided a generic map to address those challenges and opportunities by outlining the national frameworks for AI education, research, innovation and learning ecosystem, industrial AI, fintech development, and regulation reformation.

As it might be expected, the underlying mindset of the vision is progressivism, developmentalism, and marketism. Ecological redemption and human development are absorbed to those central ideas, while at the same time put digital democracy and quality of social interaction at the vulnerable points. However, putting the entire moral

---

[451] "Digital 2021: Indonesia", We Are Social and Hootsuite, 2021, 17, 85.

[452] Kementerian PPN-Bappenas, "Visi Indonesia 2045," Jakarta 2017, 7.

burden to *Stranas* is unwarranted as it is a derivation of the larger aspirations epitomised in *Visi Indonesia 2045* and the Ministry of Industry's dream of *Indonesia 4.0.*[453] On the whole, the vision needs what is in digital terminology, a *tweaking*, 'a fine adjustment to a mechanism or system.'[454]

The following discussion is a proposal of a tweaking to refine the vision by exploring the possible tangible problems affected to the marginal groups and suggesting a model to ensure any AI implementation outlined in *Stranas* will be an inclusive, service-oriented, and an ethical system. The model is reified through the abstraction of what I called as *virtual stewardship machine* (VSM). A *virtual machine* (VM) is an 'information processing system that the programmer has in mind when writing a program, and that people have in mind when using it.'[455] VM is a grand design before it details into algorithms, flowcharts, and furthermore coding stages.

Meanwhile, the notion of *stewardship* has a religious connotation as it presumes human responsibility to care for the creatures and God's creation. *Digital stewardship* on the other hand, has a narrower connotation, as it refers to digital humanities activities such as curation, preservation, and protection human heritages such as books, artifacts, and others.[456] Thus, VSM might relate with the notion of service-based governance that caring to individuals and groups as the heart of the system. In short, a VSM is *an abstraction of an AI service-based system*

---

[453] Kemenperin RI/ A.T. Kearney Inc. *Making Indonesia 4.0.*, Jakarta: Kemenperin RI & Kearney, 2018.

[454] https://translate.google.com/saved?sl=en&tl=id&text=tweak&op=translate.

[455] Boden, Margaret A. *Artificial intelligence: a very short introduction*, Oxford: Oxford University Press, 2018.

[456] Langley, Somaya. "Digital Preservation Should be More Holistic: A Digital Stewardship Approach," in *Digital Preservation in Libraries: Preparing for a Sustainable Future*, Myntti, Jeremy and Zoom, Jessalyn (Ed.), Chicago: American Library Association, 2019, 93-128.

that combines the narrow AI objectives and value of caring for people. It might create a mental map for any stakeholder involved in designing, implementing, and utilising AI. Stakeholders in this regard are civil society elements, including religious and marginal groups, coders, government officials, and other relevant parties in dealing with a design of a narrow AI. Cooperation, collaboration, and co-designing are the spirit in creating a VSM.

The next part is discussing the insights drawn from ICRS engagement in the aforementioned project of *Co-Designing*,[457] and a project on digital technology intervention on social issues, entitled the *Indonesian Interfaith Weather Station* (IIWS), ushering the VSM.[458]

Engaging with the Marginals

The development of AI, whether through the discourse of *artificial general intelligence* (AGI), *human computer integration* (HCI) or the futuristic-imaginative *artificial superhuman intelligence* (ASI), humans tend to anthropomorphise AI, and at the same time alienating it.[459]

---

[457] Included in the projects are a small grant competition for urban-friendly products, two international symposia, a cluster of research activities, book publication, series of ecological training workshops for religious extension officers in numerous cities and regions, engagements with indigenous communities, and policy recommendations.

[458] The project is funded by the United States Embassy of Jakarta for the period of 2014-2015. The publication of the outcome of the project see Epafras, Leonard Chrysostomos. "Religious Conflict Prevention and the Indonesian Interfaith Weather Station," in *Interfaith Dialogues in Indonesia and Beyond: Ten Years of ICRS Studies (2007–2017)*, Leonard Chrysostomos Epafras (Ed.), Geneva: Globethics.net, 2017, 185–209.

[459] Oh, Changhoon *et al.* "Us vs. Them: Understanding Artificial Intelligence Technophobia over the Google DeepMind Challenge Match," in *Proceedings of the 2017 CHI Conference on Human Factors in Computing Systems*, Denver, Co.: ACM, 2017, 2530–31.

Beyond the former debate of weak and strong AI, whether AI one day could transform into an intelligent machine (*machina sapiens*), or it is simply instrument for humanity advancement, the imagination of anthropomorphised AI is often based on the template of perfect humanity and full citizenship, which might excluding certain subjectivities.[460]

In general, *Stranas*, aware of such excluding power of AI, even literally mentioned the importance of the inclusion of people with disabilities, however there is no open indication how AI would deal with other marginal groups, such as religious sects, indigenous communities, and *the nones* (atheists and irreligious subjects).[461]

Indonesia has a long history of discrimination against marginal groups and often at odds in implementing freedom of expression, including religious one. As a multicultural, multi-ethnic, and multi-religion country, intercommunal tension is often a reality on the ground. Besides, part of the challenges is the enforcement of the law since many of them derived from or continuation of the outdated Dutch colonial product. The latest legal product relevant to AI development is Law No. 11/2008 and No. 19/2016 on electronic information and transactions (UU ITE), which is laden with some controversial articles in relationship with defamation and religious blasphemy.[462] Within the systemic corruption in bureaucracy and weak law enforcement, the

---

[460] Delio, Ilia. "Religion and Posthuman Life: Teilhard's Noosphere," in *Techno-Sapiens in a Networked Era: Becoming Digital Neighbors*, Bolger, Ryan K. and Kutter Callaway (Eds.), Kindle, Eugene, OR: Cascade Books, 2020.

[461] BPPT, loc. cit.

[462] Epafras, Leonard Chrysostomos. "Freedom of Religious e-Xpression in the Indonesian Cyberspace," in *Religion and Public Piety: Comparing European and Indonesian Experiences*, Yogyakarta, 2015.

implementation of these articles tends to siding with powerful subjects, heavily focus on public civility, and social harmony.[463]

The defence of public civility tends to comply with the mainstream understanding of morality, religiosity, and religious interpretation; by imagining a *hygienic society* that cancelling those considered *dissidents* and *morally problematic*.[464] Hot button issues such deviant religious movements (*aliran sesat*), LGBT, pornography, and indigenous religions might easily incite public moral panic, induced by certain hegemonic groups, such the case of a Minang Atheist (2012) and the disfiguring of Sunda Wiwitan's shrine (2020). A ministry of telecommunication that served the former administration, renowned for maintaining a certain version of public civility. During his tenure he ushered some cases of pornography into the court, blocked thousands of websites he considered pornographic or promoting LGBT causes, while left open some others that for the proponent of digital democracy were considered promoting religious radicalism.

The meaning of *religion* in the most part determined by the state that by implications only applicable to monotheistic religions, even to the degree non-theistic religions such as Buddhism and Confucianism should make theological and philosophical adjustment in order to fit into it.[465] Furthermore, there are only six religions administratively supported by the government – Islam, Christianity, Catholicism, Hinduism, Buddhism, and Confucianism, which in the public mind is often referred to as *legal religions* (*agama resmi*). The remaining religions such as

---

[463] Juniarto, Damar. "The Rise of Digital Authoritarianism in Indonesia," SAFENET, December 30, 2020, https://safenet.or.id/2020/12/the-rise-of-digital-authoritarianism-in-indonesia/.

[464] Epafras, Leonard Chrysostomos, loc. cit.

[465] Picard, Michel. "Introduction: 'Agama', 'Adat', and Pancasila," in *The Politics of Religion in Indonesia: Syncretism, Orthodoxy, and Religious Contention in Java and Bali*, Picard, Michel and Madinier, Rémy (Eds.) Oxford and New York: Routledge, 2011, 1-20.

Bahaism, Sikhism, Judaism, and others are protected but do not enjoy administration facilities coordinated by the Ministry of Religious Affairs. The most difficult positions suffered by indigenous religions that before 2017 were not recognised as *religions* but traditional cultural expressions, are often misrepresented as *pagans*. This situation made them vulnerable as the above case informed us. Similar situations haunted the nones and other irreligionists.

Considering those challenges, the *Co-Designing* project was an attempt to bring different social stakeholders to make an open conversation in dealing with numerous subjects related to urban living but including the projection of an inclusive framework for the marginals. The project was not specifically focusing on AI development but an interface for cooperation and collaboration among civil society, government officials, religious authorities, academics, the representation of people with disabilities and indigenous religious communities to discuss together the best way to realise sustainable, just, and smart urban living. It appealed for honouring human dignity manifested in public policy making, e-governance implementation, environmental justice, and urban inclusivity.[466] Why urban living? By 2035, Indonesia will be crowded with the urbanites as 66.6% of the population will live in the urban landscape.

The main spirit of the project is *challenging inequality*.[467] Urban living became the manifestation of civic space, embracing the marginals. The gerund co-designing signals the premise of the program that knowledge is everywhere and should not be monopolised by restricted social groups, and moreover, to come closer to the sustainable, just, and smart urban living, it is important to embrace all the stakeholders to contribute. Learning from the interface among stakeholders, notably

---

[466] ICRS, *Co-Designing Sustainable, Just and Smart Urban Living in Indonesia*, A Monograph, Forthcoming, Yogyakarta: ICRS, 2021.
[467] Ibidem.

between the government and civil society, it was revealed that many cities of Indonesia started to apply e-government under the rubric of a *smart city*. Some of them are in the advanced stage, including the implementation of *e-Musrenbang* (Community Discussion of Development Planning), which attempted to include the underprivileged, though the indigenous and others still in difficult positions. The creation of a smart city is one of five priorities of *Stranas*; hence co-designing the smart city by including the marginal groups into the conversation is mandatory.[468] Once the smart city is elevated into an AI-driven system, a VM design might require careful consideration so that it does not put the marginal groups in a difficult position.

Co-designing Virtual Stewardship Machine

Figure 1 is a mock-up of VSM simply to help imagine the importance of stakeholder position to define a narrow AI system.

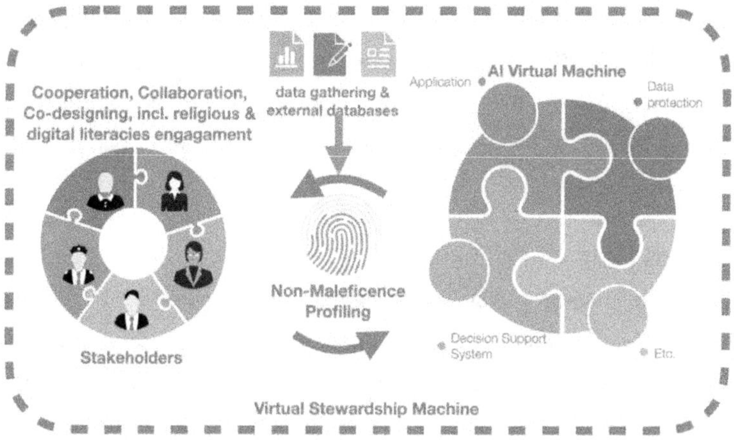

Fig. 1. Virtual Stewardship Machine

---

[468] BPPT, op. cit., 135-138.

As an example, just imagine a VSM that one of its functions is profiling the members of an indigenous religious community, for the purpose of public administration. The co-designing and religious literacy might ensure the data gathering and profiling process could not be used to backfire or discriminate against its members.

Several issues for considerations in designing a VSM are to be taken in consideration.

Invigoration and revitalisation the stakeholder's literacies, notably on digital and religious literacies

The dimension of co-designing of VSM is realised through the digital and religious literacies for stakeholders at the entry stage of the designing process. Any outcome of the stage is documented digitally and might become the feeder for AI systems.

While digital literacy is the large part technical, religious literacy is becoming the heart of stewardship. It is the space of cordial interaction to learn from each other and accept differences. Indeed, there is no agreement pursuit, but the outcome will become data feeder that will create a non-maleficence profiling for the AI VM. The acquisition and processing of data require trained subjects that are not only mastery in dealing with digital technicalities but are expected to maintain high ethical posture.

Data governance

Data governance is not only regarding data management but also privacy protection. Furthermore, it implies the good practice of profiling and documentation. At this juncture the challenges in the large part are political. In the last three years ago the government introduced a National Legislation Program (*Prolegnas*) on protection of privacy data, to be discussed in the House of Representatives. Internal political struggle in the House suspended the discussion until after the publication of this essay. This has become an immediate challenge since

Stranas envisions Indonesian Single Database initiative. Without sufficient deliberation, the AI system could fall into a tool for discrimination. It is important to include the element of stewardship into the design.

Peace and conflict resolution virtual machine

The final consideration for VSM is the designing an active peace VM, based on the earlier ICRS' experiment of the Indonesian Interfaith Weather Station (IIWS), conducted in 2014 and 2015. It is a modest non-AI VM that can be developed and expanded further through the VSM proposal. IIWS is a religious conflict prevention system that is applied by employing an Ushahidi-based system.

In the nutshell, IIWS is an early warning system that main purpose is to prevent a possible interreligious conflict. It is based on the crowdsourcing methods that assign the public as agents for endorsing active peace initiatives and at the same time preventing conflict. The digital outcome is a territorial map with icons manifesting the situation on the ground. It employs weather station metaphors to represent the structural data. The metaphors are sunny (responsive peace capacity), cloudy (active peace capacity), drizzly (dispute), rainy (crises), and stormy (violence).

It was not an AI system but indeed through the development of AI, IIWS can be upgraded and become a VSM machine learning that is not only preventing conflict but becoming a powerful tool for peace and conflict resolution.

Conclusion

The present administration is eager to mobilise Indonesia to be a more competitive and digitised country. *Stranas* is a path to the realisation of this aspiration, which hopefully materialises before Indonesia reaches her centennial. The buzzword 'Indonesia 4.0' includes five vital sectors – food and beverage, textile and apparel, automotive, chemicals, and electronics. AI technology is immersed at any turn in those sectors. We can imagine that such ambition might put human dignity alienated if there is no proper ethical involvement at each stage of implementation. Let alone the fate of marginal groups. VSM is yet a mature design as it needs further research and elaboration. Nonetheless, it could be one of the considerations as *Stranas* is restricted from a deeper ethical and cultural dimension.

BIOCYBERETHICS AND ARTIFICIAL INTELLIGENCE IN MEDICINE

Andrea Mariel Actis

Introduction

We are in a pandemic and immersed in the 4th industrial revolution. The scientific technological advance in computing, the enormous growth of social networks and the forced use of computer media show that the digital era has invaded our lives. We had to accept terms and conditions, without even stopping to think if it was correct or not. Each new cell phone model includes more technology and without knowing it we are feeding our digital twins. Each of us has our own digital version, the target of an advertising barrage that coincidentally fits our tastes. Algorithms are the stars of this technological revolution.

In this digital universe, all areas have their potential enhanced. One of the areas where it was most rooted was in Medicine. In the year of the SARS-CoV-2 pandemic, added to the confinement, the world set its sights on medicine, hands in alcohol and eyes on device screens that allowed us to continue working, studying, connecting with friends and family. The horizon of Artificial Intelligence was magnified in an epic way.

As never before, the digital gap among natives, immigrants and illiterates has been highlighted. Since the digital natives almost continued doing what they always did, staying connected and fearlessly adding new apps to their devices, with Zoom® perhaps being the most downloaded app.[469] Digital immigrants realised that they had to accept what they had been resisting: doing home banking and many other things that they always distrusted. Digital illiterates, especially older adults, lost much of their autonomy, unable to leave their homes; they required someone to assist them to try to understand the digital age. In some cases, they have unfortunately been victims of cybercrime, given their technological vulnerability.

Regarding medicine, during this period we all went through a reformulation of medical practice, going to the doctor or the dentist would no longer be the same. Telemedicine and the regulation of electronic prescriptions were perhaps the practices that a year ago were resisted, condemned and rejected by the medical community, but this year with the mandatory confinement, it was the only way to have some medical control without exposing oneself to contagion.

The idea that a robot could replace doctors has been around for a couple of decades in the international community. And then, almost without realizing it, we were pushed into the era of the GNR Revolution namely: Genetics, Nanotechnology and Robotics. The use of Artificial Intelligence (AI) in medicine is framed within this GNR Revolution, and with each passing minute, it advances more and more.

The aim of this work is to expose the main ideas behind the GNR Revolution and make a bioethical approach to some of the possible issues related to it.

---

[469] Archibald, MM, Ambagtsheer, RC, Mavourneen, GC, Lawless, M. "Using Zoom Videoconferencing for Qualitative Data Collection: Perceptions and Experiences of Researchers and Participants". *International Journal of Qualitative Methods* 2019; 18: 1-8. Zoom overtakes tiktok. https://www.financialexpress.com/industry/technology/zoom-overtakes-tiktok-to-become-the-most-downloaded-app-on-ios-app-also-breaks-new-record-in-india/2029446/

Genetic Revolution

The Genetic Revolution began with the discovery of the structure of DNA[470] and the ambitious Human Genome project that managed to decipher the sequence of the human genome in a shorter time than originally planned, thanks to the concomitant advancement of computer science.[471] A complete timeline analysing the events that led to the sequencing of the human genome can be accessed from the project website[472]. This molecular knowledge helped to discover the genetic and molecular bases of various diseases. The advancement in molecular techniques made it possible to propose genetic editing to correct genetic errors and thus avoid suffering from many diseases. Health expenses would also be avoided to sustain a respectable quality of life for sick people and a human resource would be gained in the labor production chain.[473]

It is no coincidence that the 2020 Nobel Prize in Chemistry has been awarded to researchers Emmanuelle Charpentier and Jennifer Doudna, for their contributions in the technique of genetic editing using CRISPR-Cas9.[474] With the CRISPR technique, genes can be edited in somatic cells. This modification should not generate major complications in the person who undergoes said editing, at the same time that it would be able to repair the genetic damage caused by their disease. But, on the other hand, genes can also be altered in germ cells, resulting in the

---

[470] Watson, J. *The Double Helix*, New York: Atheneum Press, 1968.

[471] "International Human Genome Sequencing Consortium. Finishing the euchromatic sequence of the human genome". *Nature* 2004; 431, 931-945.

[472] Timeline of Human Genome Project. https://www.genome.gov/human-genome-project/Timeline-of-Events

[473] Charpentier, E. "Gene Editing and Genome Engineering with CRISPR-Cas9". *Molecular Frontiers Journal* 2017; 1(2):1-9.

[474] Doudna, J; Charpentier, E; Jinek, M; Chylinski, K; Fonfara, I; Hauer, M. "A programmable dual-RNA-guided DNA endonuclease in adaptive bacterial immunity". *Science*, 2012, 337(6096), 816-821.

possibility of inheriting these editions.[475] This condition opens the door for a change in human nature if there is no global consensus on how far to go with these heritable genetic modifications. Among the most controversial changes proposed for the human genome is genetic editing in astronauts to conquer, for the moment, Martian territory. In this race to conquer new planets, it has been suggested that the conquest of Mars would require a genetic edition of the human being to withstand the adverse conditions of living on that planet.[476]

Gene editing to avoid certain diseases is not a bad idea itself but, it could generate genetically advantaged individuals, who would enjoy better health, better quality of life and probably an extension of life expectancy. This situation will generate social injustices. From a Kantian point of view, it would not be correct to modify the genome of a few, generating inequities in a great majority.

Nanotechnological Revolution

The Nanotechnological Revolution involves handling science in the order of nanometers, that is, one billionth of a meter, in the order of atoms and molecules. When talking about a nano robot, we are assuming that we could introduce into the blood a small robot capable of exploring every corner of our interior while recording and storing all this information. It represents, perhaps, making an old science fiction movie called "Fantastic Voyage" come true, where with a machine a group of scientists was reduced to a minimum size inside a nuclear submarine to be introduced into an individual and heal their ailments. The movie was

---

[475] Cunningham, A. "A Cleaner, CRISPR Constitution: Germline Editing and Fundamental Rights", *William & Mary Bill of Rights Journal*, 2019, vol. 27, 877, https://scholarship.law.wm.edu/wmborj/vol27/iss3/11

[476] Szocik, K.; Wójtowicz, T.; Boone Rappaport, M; Corbally, C. "Ethical issues of human enhancements for space missions to Mars and beyond". *Futures*, 2020; 115(102489):1-14.

shot in 1966. Some nano robots are only designed to collect information that can then be analysed by doctors and make decisions. But, we could go a step further and think that these nano robots not only collect information but could alter the reality of cells in view of a long-awaited recovery, although we know little about the collateral effects of that molecular intervention. We have a certain tendency to justify the use of new and wonderful technologies considering that they will only produce the good, but we do not think about possible adverse effects, such as new diseases or susceptibilities to infections or neurological modifications that generate individuals with altered capacities to distinguish good and evil.

One of the latest and most innovative experiments using nanotechnology aimed to study intracellular mechanical forces. The use of injected nanodevices opened new opportunities to analyse intracellular mechanobiology. A multi collaborative study using nanodevices allowed identifying changes in the cytoplasmic mechanical properties required for the development of the mouse embryo from fertilization to the first cell division. The nanodevices reported a reduction in cytoplasmic mechanical activity during chromosome alignment and indicated that cytoplasmic hardening occurred during embryo elongation, followed by rapid cytoplasmic softening during cytokinesis. These results suggest that intracellular forces are part of a concerted program that is necessary for development at the origin of new embryonic life. This result, which is surprising, is perhaps overshadowed by the methodology used. Silicone nanochips implanted in unicellular mouse embryos were used to reveal mechanical changes during the early onset of embryonic development and these nanochips do not appear to have altered cellular behaviour, being able to be technological witnesses of vital processes at molecular level.[477]

More recently, the use of a nanorobot to select one sperm cell and fertilise an egg has been reported in in vitro fertilization techniques. This would improve the efficiency of current techniques that consist of the introduction of the male pronucleus into an immobilised ovum. These spermbots constitute a new class of micro-robots created by coupling sperm cells to mechanical loads.[478]

Robotic Revolution

The most important imminent revolution is the R or robotics revolution that tries to provide robots with a certain *human level* by feeding their intelligence through mechanisms similar to the way in which we learn ourselves, added to the possibility of use skin-like materials and an incredibly human appearance. However, this AI is designed to exceed human capabilities. In this way, technology has brought us to the edge of the "age of singularity" where man and machine will merge as one and there will be no physical distinction between physical and virtual reality.

Medical robotics is a relatively new field with incredible potential. This new area arose by technical improvements over the past two decades. However, the balance between risks and benefits derived from the use of medical robots has not been fully discussed. Medical robots

---

[477] Duch, M., Torras, N., Asami, M. *et al.* "Tracking intracellular forces and mechanical property changes in mouse one-cell embryo development." *Nat. Mater.* 19, 1114–1123, 2020. https://doi.org/10.1038/s41563-020-0685-9

[478] Singh, Ajay V., Mohammad H.D. Ansari, Mihir Mahajan, Shubhangi Srivastava, Shubham Kashyap, Prajjwal Dwivedi *et ali.* "Sperm Cell Driven Microrobots—Emerging Opportunities and Challenges for Biologically Inspired Robotic Design", *Micromachines* 2020, 11, no. 4: 448. https://doi.org/10.3390/mi11040448

have been used by few technological generations and the technology continues to change every day. University curricula are not fully prepared to teach all the benefits, or to discuss about the ethics about its use. The impact of robots on near-future medicine cannot be even imagine, but it is for sure market orientated and the research will never be enough to ensure the bioethical issues related to the use of all this new technology.

Medical robotics is an already established field, which had a quantum leap with the development of technologies related to AI. One of the medical robots best known to the public is perhaps the Da Vinci Robot, used to perform laparoscopy using a small camera, reducing post-surgical complications and improving the quality of life of patients.

If we talk about macro Robots, the first surgical robot was the PUMA 560 robot, which was used in 1985 for stereotaxic surgery with the aim of inserting a needle into the brain for a biopsy, a practice that was performed with errors due to tremor of the surgeon's hand. The medical areas in which robots have been used for a decade or more are: in neurology, where accuracy and precision are of vital importance, since 1991 the Robot Minerva has been available; in orthopaedics, since 1992 the Robodoc has been experimented with; in laparoscopic surgery since 1995 with the well-known Da Vinci Robot; in radiosurgery with the CyberKnife robot since 1999; in percutaneous procedures, such as biopsies and drains with the InnoMotion robot since 2005; in catheterization with the Sensei X robot since 2007; in emergency the Auto Pulse Plus robot for resuscitation since 2010; in prosthetics and exoskeletons with the i-limb Ultra hand robot since 2011.[479]

More recently, the stars of robotics began to be micro-robots such as the Smart Pill that measures pressure, pH and gastric emptying time, all

---

[479] Lane T. "A short history of robotic surgery". *Annals of the Royal College of Surgeons of England* 2018; 100(6s), 5-7.

in a small tablet that is swallowed which has a micro-chamber, lights and batteries.[480] As mentioned above, Spermbots are also in this category.

To these applications of robotics, let's call it structural or hard, we must add the use of AI in medical diagnosis through programs, such as in ophthalmology to perform an exhaustive analysis of fundus images to detect alterations that they could escape even the most trained eye; in mammographic studies to detect minimal lesions and also analyse the probability that it is carcinogenic. In psychiatry, AI associated with the study of Magnetic Resonance images can detect schizophrenias and suicide attempts.[481] During the first year of the SARS-CoV-2 pandemic, some studies were also presented where the use of AI would allow anticipating the presence of the virus when analysing radiological images or when analysing changes in the human voice.[482]

Data and Big Data

The collection and aggregation of personal health and medical data is today growing at exponential rates: medical and pharmacological research, patients' treatments, individual's health & medical devices, etc. Also, in the very current pandemic context, all the movements and authorizations of governmentally controlled data from official apps, telecom providers, and filled forms/affidavit forms can be added to this list.

---

[480] Beasley, R. "Medical Robots: Current Systems and Research Directions". *Journal of Robotics*, 2012, Volume 2012, Article ID 401613, 14pp. doi:10.1155/2012/401613

[481] Loh, E. "Medicine and the rise of the robots: a qualitative review of recent advances of artificial intelligence in health", 2018, *BMJ Leader* 2018; 2:59-63, doi:10.1136/leader-2018-000071

[482] Márquez Díaz, J. "Inteligencia artificial y Big Data como soluciones frente a la COVID-19". *Rev Bio y Der.* 2020; 50, 315-331.

We are talking currently about petabytes (10^{15} bytes) for health data, which is expected to reach the exabyte scale in 2021 and 44 zettabytes (10^{21} bytes) for the overall digital data for 2020/21.[483]

Medical data, and in particular sensitive data related to patients is theoretically highly secured by processes and by several technological, strict security layers. However, no system in the world can be said to be 100% secure. We can list at least four main risks in particular about medical data and the worldwide medical landscape: 1. Hackers risk, as for any other sector and industry; 2. Human factor in terms of cybersecurity risk, it is accepted that "the biggest usual risk in terms of cybersecurity is sitting between the keyboard and the chair;" 3. IoT (Internet of Things) for Medical systems, as this situation multiplies the number of entry points and related potential weaknesses; 4. The weakest links in terms of cybersecurity standards in the medical chain: smaller GP practices/pharmacies, small medical laboratories and medical institutions in general and even more particularly in the less developed countries, with less IT & cybersecurity budgets and resources, as they are may be consequently less up-to-date in terms of standards and therefore, more vulnerable in terms of cybersecurity.

Some critical issues have already happened such as the leak of 500,000 French patients' medical data, including HIV status in 2021[484] and ransomware attacks with a major example being the Universal Health Services (UHS) in 2020 in the US.[485]

Data is the representation of information that is processed, for example: names, years, facts, concepts, etc. This information can be

---

[483] World Economic Forum. How much data is generated each day? https://www.weforum.org/agenda/2019/04/how-much-data-is-generated-each-day-cf4bddf29f/

[484] French Hospital hacked. https://www.france24.com/en/europe/20210225-france-investigates-massive-leak-of-medical-records

[485] UHS hacked. https://www.wired.com/story/universal-health-services-ransomware-attack/

stored in the memory of an individual computer or in the memory of a server, the latter, commonly referred to as the cloud if distributed over multiple servers via an internet network.

Big Data refers to a very large volume of data, impossible to handle manually. It can only be processed by automation, complex algorithms and/or Artificial Intelligence. Big Data management involves high volume, high speed, high variety, high value, and high validity.

The Observatory of Bioethics and Law published two important documents with specific recommendations about the use of Big Data in healthcare[486] and guidelines about the evaluation of projects encompassing new medical technologies and personal data.[487]

In the recently released document "Guidelines for reviewing health research and innovation projects that use emergent technologies and personal data" it is remarked that:

"Scientific and technological changes are occurring at a dizzying rate, in an exacerbated market society where health is being increasingly commodified, and in which personal data are monetised. Although it is true that law-making processes and knowledge creation and transfer rates are not the same, there is a certain paralysis in the application of laws, due basically to a lack of understanding of the digital phenomenon that we are facing. It is therefore considered that RECs [Research Ethical Committees] are willing and able to act as guarantees that research, and the

---

[486] Document on bioethics and Big Data: exploitation and commercialization of user data in public health care, 2015. http://www.publicacions.ub.edu/ refs/observatoriBioEticaDret/documents/08209.pdf

[487] Guidelines for reviewing health research and innovation projects that use emergent technologies and personal data, 2020. http://www.bio eticayderecho.ub.edu/sites/default/files/documents/doc_eval-proyectos.pdf

innovation that goes with it, comply with ethical principles and meet the established legal requirements."[488]

The same document clearly sets that:

"The digital society, data driven, based, therefore, on the intensive exploitation of datasets, including personal data, has clearly shown that the current review model – a child of the second half of the 20th century – for analysing research projects in which humans take part and/or their data personal is used, is outdated and ineffective, due to the technical, ethical and legal challenges posed by personal data processing in the 21st century."

Because of this reason, the accountability of the Research Ethical Committees for safeguarding individuals and specially their personal data is emphasised, in order to ensure the privacy and confidentiality of the data owners.

The mentioned document also affirms that:

"Thus, personal data are the gold of our time, and health, biometric and socio-demographic data, especially, are considered by law to be special categories of data that require the highest protection because they say everything about us; and because they could be used for unwanted purposes and give rise to covert discrimination, with profound implications for people's freedom and that of future generations. The possession of personal datasets by third parties, whether private or public initiatives, could affect our rights depending on the uses, giving these third parties extraordinary power over us, a situation that goes unnoticed by the great majority of people. The decisions taken in the field of health research and innovation, and in highly

---

[488] Ibid.

digitised contexts will mark the lives of people, groups and societies."[489]

A lot is done currently in terms of cybersecurity all over the world, and even more particularly regarding medical and patients' data. Hacking, in particular of up-to-date medical IT systems is theoretically not easy to perform, but it can still happen, through the different, above listed factors - among others - and as such, it still represents a risk.

The European GDPR regulation forces organizations not only to care about privacy and consent but goes very deep into the obligation of securing the data via anonymization, pseudonymisation, data hiding, encryption, and all aspects of cybersecurity. Lack of current implementation of these strict technical conditions leads directly to fines and direct responsibility in case of hacking.[490]

The Neuralink Project and the Singularity Concept

The concept of linking the brain to a computer is a project with the idea of providing a solution to individuals with different diminished capacities; again, the technological advance in order to solve deficiencies to insert ourselves into society is not questionable. But other aspects, such as autonomy, inequity, the balance between risks and benefits, they do are subject of ethical discussions.[491]

The Neuralink project, funded by billionaire Elon Musk, seeks to develop a "whole brain interface." The idea is that, through a network of small electrodes connected to the brain, it would be possible to

---

[489] Ibid.

[490] GDPR regulation. https://www.eu-patient.eu/globalassets/policy/data-protection/data-protection-guide-for-patients-organisations.pdf

[491] Coin, A., Mulder, M. and Dubljevic, V. "Ethical Aspects of BCI Technology: What Is the State of the Art?" *Philosophies*, 2020, 5(31):1-9. https://doi.org/10.3390/philosophies5040031

communicate wirelessly with other people who also have this interface connected. In this way, it would allow us to share our thoughts, fears, hopes and anxieties without the need to speak or write. If this really did happen, and we are on our way to do so, then the next revolution will be in the hands of Elon Musk, who is also involved in space travels. A few months ago, the US Food and Drug Administration approved the use of Neuralink implants for users with disabilities to control appliances in their home.[492]

As in the movie The Matrix, we would have a "whole brain interface" so complete, biocompatible, and powerful that users would feel it as just another part of their cerebral cortex, central nervous system and specially the limbic system, which is involved in our behavioural and emotional responses, then thoughts, dreams, emotions, memories, everything could be shared. We could interact directly with the cloud, with computers and with the brain of anyone who has a similar interface in their head. This flow of information between your brain and the outside world would be so easy that it would feel just like your thoughts right now. We would probably make thought transmission and telekinesis a reality.

But if this sounds like science fiction, the potential problems also sound incredible. First, Neuralink is not like placing an implant in the head to control epileptic seizures or a pacemaker in the heart. The Neuralink implant would be an elective surgery, presumably in healthy people for non-medical purposes. We are clearly facing a completely different landscape, both legally and ethically. Who would be the ones who access this possibility? Will it be experimental for some volunteers? Who would run the risks once the technique is established? What will the cost be to implement it? What will be the cost to maintain it? What advantages will those who have these implants have? What

---

[492] Jawad, A. J. "Engineering Ethics of Neuralink Brain Computer Interfaces Devices", *Ann Bioethics Clin App*, 2021, 4(1), DOI: 10.23880/abca-16000160

happens to the rest who do not have those implants? Can these implants be hackable? What regulations should be done regarding cybercrime?

Diagnosing with Artificial Intelligence Algorithms

Technological growth and in particular, digital biotechnology follows an exponential curve. The fear of replacing the vision of the health professional by robots is a recurring theme in medical circles of different specialties.

These systems can analyse all your personal data like age, heart rate, exercise habits, eating habits, body mass index, sleep pattern and your psychological behaviour and also your preferences in many fields through various sensors. Examples of these technologies are smartwatches, health bands, browsing history, smartphone activity and geolocalisation, smart TV, etc. Thereafter your data is uploaded on the cloud where it is categorised and analysed with the help of Cognitive Networks and AI algorithms.[493]

It is useless to avoid AI as a tool which can definitely assist doctors in early diagnosis and help lower the mortality rate and reduce medical costs. In this way, doctors will rely on support from AI either for simple diagnostics, or also get recommendations for complex or rare diagnostics too. Working faster and better. But the very last decision, thorough check and responsibility remains in the hands of the human specialist. And regulators must approve and authorise those tools.[494]

For example, some robots can create a patient's specific 3D anatomical model by hospital electronic record system which includes Magnetic Resonance Imaging (MRI), Computed Tomography (CT),

---

[493] Kashyap, A. "Artificial Intelligence & Medical Diagnosis". *Sch. J. App. Med. Sci.* 2018; 6(12): 4982-4985.

[494] Jie, Z., Zhiying, Z. & Li, L. "A meta-analysis of Watson for Oncology in clinical application". *Sci Rep* 11, 5792, 2021. https://doi.org/10.1038/s41598-021-84973-5

ultrasound, and so on. This information can be used for the location of a catheter via an electromagnetic tracking system with patient anatomy.

A great amount of literature points at the successful applications of AI in healthcare. Since long ago, it has become a hot topic of discussion whether AI expert systems would eventually replace human doctors. For others, different AI techniques can help to find out relevant information from a large amount of clinical data.

Some authors prefer to talk about increased intelligence given that the activity, judgment, and expert eye of the radiologist, for example, is not putting themselves at risk, but with the use of AI, their own intelligence is enhanced in making decisions that would benefit patients to further reduce mortality due to its effective detection at increasingly earlier stages of the disease.[495]

Hacking of Medical Devices

As indicated earlier, almost all medical devices are exposed to cybersecurity vulnerabilities due to the connectivity to computer networks. Cybersecurity incidents could be preventable, but it is important to recognise the complexity of the operational environment, to help patients to understand what could happen as well as to catalogue the technical vulnerabilities.[496] The main goal of cybersecurity is to safeguard any network device and all digital information circulating through the web from any malicious damage or disruption. In the case of medical devices, we must consider any instrument, apparatus, implant, nanodevice, nanorobot, which could be used to search, register, record,

---

[495] Arieno, A., Chan, A., Destounis, S.V. "A review of the role of augmented intelligence in breast imaging: from automated breast density assessment to risk stratification", *Am. J. Roentgenol.* 2018; 212(2): 259–270. DOI: 10.2214/AJR.18.20391

[496] Best, J. "Could implanted medical devices be hacked?", *BMJ*, 2020 Jan 14;368:m102. doi: 10.1136/bmj.m102. PMID: 31937555.

diagnose, treat, predict, etc., that could be hacked and cause any kind of damage to patients.

This possibility of hacking any device is due to the software embedded inside which allow its function. Well-developed and validated software has the potential to impact the delivery of patient care significantly and positively, transforming how we manage healthcare across the globe.[497]

Bioethical Reflections Related to GNR Revolution

Taking into account all that has been explained, it is necessary to redefine bioethics, to consider the foreseeable consequences or not of the GNR Revolution. We can conceive of bioethics as the science of interstices, understanding that the interstice is the space between cells where intercellular communication mechanisms occur, it is also the space where cells understand their own limits and recognise the existence of another cell. Normal cells respect each other to build a tissue that works in a coordinated manner. When this balance is disrupted, problems start. By analogy, when anybody does not respect the other one, problems start. So, Bioethics emerges as the possibility to use dialogue to find the better solution to one problem related with life issues. But within the framework of cyberspace, immersed in the cybersociety of the 21st century, I want to propose the use of the term *Biocyberethics*, to refer specifically to ethics linked to life and health issues related to advances in genetics, nanotechnology and robotics.

Bioethics, which is commonly understood to refer to the ethical implications and applications of the health-related life sciences, will

---

[497] International Medical Device Regulators Forum. "Software as a Medical Device": Possible Framework for Risk Categorization and Corresponding Considerations. IMDRF Software as a Medical Device (SaMD) Working Group; 2014. http://www.imdrf.org/docs/imdrf/final/technical/imdrf-tech-140918-samd-framework-risk-categorization-141013.pdf.

now get the addition of a new subspecialty "Biocyberethics", while AI will be part of the doctor-patient relationship, for example through telemedicine and electronic prescription, where also, a lot of sensitive data circulates through different digital networks.

Among the main concerns of Biocyberethics are the following questions: How to connect evidence-based medicine with the contributions of AI in medicine? How to contribute to the credibility and sustainability of AI in medicine? Who will be responsible for a wrong diagnosis if the diagnosis was made using AI? Who is the owner of the data? What would be the main regulations that each country should discuss and make available to the population to guarantee equitable access to health for the population? Is germ cell gene editing ethical? Is it ethical to modify human genetics to improve health? Who is responsible for damages if a medical device controlled by AI is hacked? Should we add algorithm conflict to the list of conflicts of interest? Which medical aspects are feasible to be simulated and which are not? Is it ethical to simulate the doctor's critical thinking using algorithms? Is it ethical to lose our privacy and give our sensitive data to the web? Will modifying genetics, inserting a nanodevice into the brain, and linking it to a computer make us superhumans? Are we playing God? Will we stop being Homo sapiens to become Homo Deus?[498]

A possible and prudent constructive solution to the problem of the use of AI in the medical field implies the non-generalization of the machine factor to the detriment of the human or the human factor to the detriment of the machine. The idea is that AI works as a mechanism that increases and not replaces human capacities. It is about promoting the

---

[498] Actis, A.M. "Why do we need bioethical recommendations?", *Palliat Med Care Int J,* 2019; 1(5): 555572. DOI: 10.19080/PMCIJ.2019.01.555572. Vayena, E., Haeusermann, T., Adjekum, A., Blasimme, A. "Digital Health: Meeting Ethical and Policy Challenges". In: *Cyber Ethics 4.0 Serving Humanity with Values.* Stückelberger, C. / Duggal, P. Eds. Geneva: Globethics.net, 2018, Ch. 13, 229-258.

interrelation and interconnection of man and machine, in such a way that the components of each part interact fully to generate new characteristics, absent for each one of them separately.[499]

Responsibility must be emphasised, which concerns to health professionals, the institutions that decide to incorporate AI into their services, and the governments, which will ultimately be the ones to regulate and control its use. The dialogue between these three actors: professionals - institutions - government must ensure the protection of the autonomy of all citizens and in particular ensure the interests of patients and the safeguarding of their rights.[500] We must insist that the only way to guarantee the improvement of our survival, on Earth or on another planet is education. Education is information accompanied by reflective thinking. A challenge for scientific societies is the inclusion of bioethical dialogue and the generation of consensus or guidelines to guide the correct performance in future situations, where all contributions are considered.

It is also urgent to establish dialogues with patients, especially with those who may be exposed to more vulnerable conditions. It is important in these dialogues to work from sincerity and common sense. This dialogue will be beneficial to advance later in the informed consent process, with a better predisposition of patients to consent to new technologies.[501] It is important to note that the bioethical aspects have more to do with the data than with the technology itself. Perhaps if we understand that data is in cyberspace a representation of people in the

---

[499] Elenko, E., Speier, A., Zohar, D. "A regulatory framework emerges for digital medicine". *Nat. Biotechnol,* 2015; 33(7):697-702.

[500] Rigby, M. J. "Ethical Dimensions of Using Artificial Intelligence in Health Care". *AMA J Ethics,* 2019; 21(2):E121-124. DOI: 10.1001/amajethics. 2019.121.

[501] Ohno-Machado, L. "Data science and artificial intelligence to improve clinical practice and research". *Journal of the American Medical Informatics Association.* 2018; 25: 1273-1273.

physical world, we understand that data should be protected just as we protect people.

It is essential to encourage dialogue and training on issues of Biocyberethics and Artificial Intelligence in future health professionals, at least insisting on the use of critical thinking and common sense. It is important to fight for regulatory policies, assumed with transparency and responsibility. Philosophers, bioethicists, scientists and doctors must work together to guarantee the safety of the use of Artificial Intelligence in Medicine and tend to safeguard the autonomy of patients, inevitable users of new technologies.

The enthusiasm for the scope and possible benefits of the use of AI in medicine has generated a significant number of articles describing the possibilities of using AI in medicine, however there are few articles that dedicate a thoughtful look at the possible ethical consequences, including cultural and social aspects. The use of AI in medicine generates infinite possibilities for convergence and many other bioethical nuances and details, which opens the door to responsible debate on the advances and scope of AI in medicine.

How near is the day when through virtual reality programs surgeons can locate themselves inside the patient's body and be able to see the exact cell that must be cut or killed to heal the patient? Nothing seems too much science fiction, everything seems possible.[502]

Artificial Intelligence and its Ethical Implications in Higher Education

There is a strong emotional and subjective influence on the learning process. As a general rule, students learn better when they feel that their

---

[502] Kurzweil, R. "We are going to live forever." *The NYT*, 2013. https://www.nytimes.com/2013/01/27/magazine/ray-kurzweil-says-were-going-to-live-forever.html

teacher cares about them and their learning, that is, when teachers are involved in this relational contract that is the teacher-student bond.

This relational aspect can work in the same way in the presence as in virtuality, if in both cases authentic and personalised communication channels are established. When everything indicates that in this digital age we are a "bag of data" and the "loot" of digital companies, we all feel special when another person pays attention to us and dedicates her/his time to us.

The change in productivity does not imply replacing people with machines, but empowering people with machines, for this reason some prefer to speak of augmented intelligence instead of AI. The teacher must change her/his role as presenter, content reader; text repeater and retained data evaluator. The biggest challenge is realizing that we have to change the way we are educating.

There are some studies that demonstrate the value of AI in predicting the degree of dropout of university students with great precision, as well as other student's variables such as academic performance throughout their educational experience, being able to offer alternatives to improve that performance on time. On the other hand, some commercial educational companies have quickly focused on different technologies that could be exploited in educational settings by both teachers and students. There is vast and diverse potential in the field of AI to transform our teaching practices and student learning experiences. However, due to the traditional academic inertia, that culture of resistance to change, the university spirit always runs (or walks, or crawls) behind technological advances. This *doxa* of creating technology confronts to the *paradox* of resisting its use and *just* in education. It may be the lack of interest, the distrust, the lack of policies to train teachers and many other obstacles that threaten the implementation of an authentic process of change.

The problem is to believe that using AI in education is limited only to improving content presentations with new apps and automating evaluation. The problem is putting the focus on the *how* and forgetting the *what* we want to teach. Teamwork between designers, developers, teachers and students is required more than ever to enhance creativity in problem solving and also the constant and necessary practice of reflective thinking. The challenge of higher education today is to prepare future generations of professionals to solve the unexpected, the accumulation of data and academicism must be put aside: data springs from cell phones! Teachers have to get more involved in this change, without waiting for the university to move the first token to start the game.

A big problem adds to this dilemma: social networks and the big internet companies (Google, Facebook, Instagram, WhatsApp, YouTube) can offer in the context of higher education a great free access to knowledge, added to the knowledge that students themselves generate and share and even some teachers who are encouraged to give classes and tutorials through the networks.

Therefore, we have to educate the teacher again. But… will everyone want to?

Will the University, the Queen of knowledge, be able to maintain its deeply rooted values such as trust, legitimacy, truthfulness, scientific integrity, autonomy?

AI in education is at the moment a kind of potential Trojan Horse, in the wrong hands it could cause disasters, but if we are vigilant and with an open mind we can avoid this unwanted collapse. Meanwhile, the Queen is in check!

The future of higher education is intrinsically linked to the developments of new technologies and the computational capabilities of new intelligent machines. Education is clearly influenced by the digital world with unlimited possibilities. Some companies estimate that within

3 years, by 2025 about 50% of all the world's stored data will reside in public clouds. The use of data is the new *Big Bang* since it is a process that has no limits and continues to increase. It is estimated that in 2025 the Datasphere (what is produced in real time) globally will be about 175 ZetaBytes (10^{12} Gigabytes), as mention before.

The same process of automation that is causing a break in the current workforce in the industry is making knowledge itself the main article of production and consumption. Hence the folly of the unemployment alarm. Paid apprenticeship is already becoming the main workforce and new source of wealth in our society.[503]

Collective intelligence can be seen as an alternative source of media power. We are learning to use that power through our daily interactions within the culture of convergence. New media technologies have made it possible for the same content to flow through very different channels and assume very different forms at the point of reception.[504]

More specifically, in the modern liquid context, to be of any use, education and learning must be continuous and even span a lifetime. No other form of education and/or learning is conceivable; it is unthinkable that people or personalities can be *formed* in any other way than through continuous and eternally unfinished retraining.[505]

Some questions we need to discuss seriously are: What could be the ethical and social implications linked to the advancement of new technologies in the university context? Can social media help create knowledge in ways other than traditional ones? How does knowledge circulate in the era of the 4th revolution? Is there copyright in teaching? Should knowledge circulate freely?

---

[503] McLuhan, M. *Understanding Media: The Extensions of Man.* New York: Signet Books, 1966.

[504] Jenkins, H. *Convergence Culture: Where Old and New Media Collide.* New York: New York University Press, 2006.

[505] Bauman, Z. *Liquid Life,* Cambridge: Polity, 2005.

We are, then, at a critical inflection point with respect to copyright. If in this age of communication, knowledge should flow freely through the web, then how is the fact that there are companies or private companies that quickly saw knowledge as a profitable market resolved?

If we are a *bag of data* and data is the gold of the moment, imagine how much data linked to knowledge is worth. In this context, in what position are Universities to face this enormous tide of data coming and going through social networks? Could it be that its inertia will become its stigma? Will Universities evolve or disappear? Will they be able to keep their hegemony? Are we in time to react?

THE ROBOT VOICE CONTRASTED WITH THE VOICE OF TWO DISABLED PEOPLE: A REFLECTIVE PIECE

Laura Smith and Peter Smith

This chapter presents a combination of different *voices*.[506] First, we are presented with the voices of modern robot technology, in the form of several Artificial Intelligence (AI) products, which are used on a day-to-day basis by many people. Each *robot* presents their functionality and discusses the advantages they offer. This is followed by the voices of the two disabled authors, each of whom reflects upon the advantages of using AI technology to help themselves with their daily business. Alongside this, the authors reflect upon some of the drawbacks which they face in using the technology. In doing so, this reflective piece contrasts different views of modern, commonly used, AI technology through the voices of the *robots* themselves and two disabled people who make use of the technology. The chapter concludes by drawing lessons learnt from the reflections, summarising two individual's views of their lived experiences of making use of modern-day AI products.

---

[506] Authors note: This piece has been dictated using AI technology products. The authors have checked the spelling and grammar manually and using Word grammar check; however, it is possible that some errors remain as a result of using AI technology. Editor note: all footnotes have been added based on a complete bibliography delivered by the authors.

Introduction

More than a billion people live with disability and there is a need to explore how AI technologies can affect this diverse group. AI research can be a force for good for disabled people (Smith & Smith, 2021).[507]

It is true that AI technologies have the potential to dramatically impact the lives of people with disabilities. However, widely deployed AI systems do not yet work properly for disabled people, or worse, may actively discriminate against them. Anhong Guo and co-authors identify how AI may "impact particular disability constituencies if care is not taken in their design, development, and testing."[508]

The methodology employed in this thought piece is largely based upon reflection with Schön and Warwick. It involves analysing particular occurrences, again preferably as they are expressed, and thinking about what is learned from these occurrences and what decisions are taken as a result.[509] As Flanagan shows well, one method often used in reflection, and applied in this paper, is the critical incident approach.[510] The critical incident approach involves identifying and analysing particular incidents which occur, and which makes the individual question their own beliefs or practices. To help us do so, we have each prepared a diary of our day-to-day interactions with simple,

---

[507] Smith, P., & Smith, L. "Artificial intelligence and disability: too much promise, yet too little substance?", *AI and Ethics*, 1(1), 81-86, 2021.

[508] Guo, A., Kamar, E., Vaughan, J. W., Wallach, H., & Morris, M. R. Toward fairness in AI for people with disabilities SBG@ a research roadmap. *ACM SIGACCESS Accessibility and Computing*, (125), 2020, 1-1.

[509] Schön, D. *The Reflective Practitioner: How Professionals Think in Action* New York: Basic books, 1983. Warwick, P. Reflective practice: Some notes on the development of the notion of professional reflection, Part of the ESCalate Help Directory for Teacher Educators, Busy Teacher Educator Guides, ESCalate, 2007.

[510] Flanagan, J. C. "The critical incident technique". *Psychological Bulletin*, 51(4), 1954, 327.

readily available, AI systems. These diaries appear below, in the form in which they were written, using first person as they are personal accounts.

Robot Voices

The Voice of Voice-Over

Apple's VoiceOver is a screen reader which audibly relays information about what is happening on the screen of your device. Using a synthetic voice, VoiceOver is able to "describe people, objects, text and graphs," allowing the user to access documents, websites and images without having to use their eyes to do so.[511] Indeed, the voice of VoiceOver reads out text, describes images and announces site features such as headings, buttons and links. In many ways, the voice itself has been designed to act as a guide, assisting the user with accessing written content and navigating all aspects of the screen. Indeed, as stated by the manufacturer, "Auditory descriptions … make content such as websites a breeze to browse" (ibid.).

Whether engaging with a phone, tablet or computer, users are able to select a voice of their choice from a range of options including default *Alex*, a mail [sic] sounding American, *Agnes*, Alex's female sounding counter-part [sic], and a whole host of options ranging from the breathy hushed tones of *Whisper* to the less clear, almost indecipherable *Bubbles*. The selected voice will then announce whatever the curser hovers over, as the user scrolls around the screen either using a mouse, key-board arrows or track-pad. Essentially, the software is designed to enable users who are blind or visually impaired to access apple technology.

---

[511] Apple Website, Vision. For every point of view, https://www.apple.com/accessibility/vision/

The Voice of Siri

Siri is a virtual assistant which is available on many Apple products. "Siri can make calls or send texts for you whether you are driving, have your hands full, or are simply on the go."[512] Without even touching your device, you can ask Siri to carry out tasks such as to set an alarm, send a message or add an event to your calendar. You can also ask Siri simple questions, such as how to spell a word, look up train times or let you know if rain is forecast for later that day.

Siri answers your requests and queries in a friendly, upbeat voice. Users can be conversational when engaging with Siri, who will even answer more personal questions, sing you a song or tell you a joke. "It also offers proactive suggestions – like texting someone that you're running late for a meeting – so you can stay in touch effortlessly." Indeed, Siri offers a two-way interaction, is able to offer simple suggestions and is there to help you in many varying ways.

The Voice of Alexa

Alexa is a personal assistant which is present in many houses and possesses a multitude of functionality.

Alexa is Amazon's cloud-based voice service available on more than 100 million devices from Amazon and third-party device manufacturers.[513] With Alexa, you can build natural voice experiences that offer customers a more intuitive way to interact with the technology they use every day… It is capable of voice interaction, music playback, making to-do lists, setting alarms, streaming podcasts, playing audiobooks, and providing weather, traffic, sports, and other real-time information, such as news   (Amazon Alexa Developer Website, 2022).

---

[512] Apple Website, 2020, What is Siri. https://www.apple.com/uk/siri/

[513] Amazon Alexa Developer Website, 2022, https://developer.amazon.com/en-GB/alexa/

Alexa is thus a very powerful tool which can be used for assisting with many day-to-day activities, by individuals in their homes throughout the world. It is, however, particularly useful to disabled people.

The Voice of Dragon Speak

Dragon Speak provides powerful speech technology which enables those with physical disabilities, who are unable to operate a computer keyboard, to speak to the computer and thus create documents and emails. The speech technology is very advanced and accurate and assists disabled people throughout the world. It is also used by others, who are not disabled, and who prefer to use speech technology to create their documents.

Get more done at work, at home or on the go with fast, accurate speech recognition, dictation and transcription. Dragon by Nuance is the world's leading speech recognition solution with over two decades of continuous development to meet the needs of the most demanding users. Meet the powerful tools that will make you more productive by unlocking the power of your voice (Nuance Website, 2022).[514]

Peter's Voice

Peter's Story

On 29 April 2016 at 5am, I was returning to my bedroom in the dark. I found myself plummeting down the stairs. I landed awkwardly, with my head hanging over the stairwell. I realised immediately that I had broken my neck; I could not feel my arms or legs. I shouted for my wife, Marie, who telephoned for an ambulance. I was rushed into intensive care at the Royal Victoria Infirmary, Newcastle, UK. I was later transferred to the Spinal Injuries Unit at James Cook Hospital, Middlesbrough, UK. I spent 6 months in hospital learning how to speak,

---

[514] Dragon by Nuance Website, 2022, https://shop.nuance.co.uk

eat, and breathe again. I started physiotherapy and regained some mobility. The damage to my spinal cord is incomplete, which means that I have some mobility, but none which is really functional in that I cannot feed myself or walk.

Peter's Voice about Siri

I use Siri on my iPhone to make calls. It is very useful and I can speak to it and ask Siri to dial [sic] specific numbers which I have stored in my phone. Almost every time Siri will recognise the name of the person or company I am wishing to dial and it will ring the number for me, on speakerphone so that I can talk to the person at the other end. The only problem arises when no one is there and the call switches to answerphone. At the moment, and it may be me not understanding fully the functionality of Siri, I have not found a way to end the call. I need to call upon one of my carers to stop the call. So far, I have not discovered a way around this and the manual input is required to end the call.

Overall Siri is extremely effective and a great product which enables me a lot of independence in making phone calls to friends, family and external organisations. I could do this independently and with privacy. Other products such as Alexa also enable me to make phone calls.

Peter's Voice about Alexa

I make quite a lot of use of the personal assistant tool, Alexa. Firstly, I use Alexa to access Amazon music and play music to me and help me relax. Alexa is able to locate and play almost anything I wish to hear; usually old rock and pop songs from the 1960s and 1970s! If I tire of a song, I can quickly tell Alexa to stop playing that song and move onto something else. All of this works very efficiently.

I also use Alexa to set reminders of upcoming events. This is very effective although, probably due to my own accent, I sometimes find it difficult to recognise the event that Alexa is reminding me of!

Alexa also helps me find out facts about people and places, such as the distance to a specific place, which I may wish to visit or some information about an individual, such as what I might find on a Wikipedia page. All of this works very well and Alexa can more often than not answer my question.

Alexa is a great AI product. My only concern is whether Alexa is collecting data about me. I have read articles, which suggest that this may be the case, which concerns me a little. However, the advantages offered by Alexa are excellent I am probably only touching the surface of her capabilities!

Peter's Voice about Dragon Speak

Dragon speak is an excellent speech technology product which enables me to *type* word [sic] and other documents by speaking to the computer. Dragon learns my voice, quite quickly, and gradually builds up a user profile consisting of words and names that I often use so that it knows the spelling of many of my contacts around the world. The spelling of some of these names is quite complex and challenging. However, Dragon soon learns these and stores them in my user profile. Dragon is an excellent help and allows me to continue to work, write and dictate documents independently.

Laura's Voice

Laura's Story

At the age of two, I was diagnosed with Juvenile arthritis, which affected most of my joints. Shortly after this diagnosis, it was ascertained that the arthritis had also caused inflammation in my eyes and as a result, I had contracted a condition called Uveitis which was causing me to lose my sight. Despite several attempts to save my vision, laser surgery and the removal of cataracts, by the time I was five years old I was registered blind. By age ten I had completely lost my sight in both eyes.

Despite my disability, I have always enjoyed an active, independent life. My guide dog Vicky enables me to get out and about and a range of assistive technologies support me with tasks in my daily life, at work and when raising my two young children.

Laura's Voice about Voice-Over

"Technologies like AI and machine learning play a vital role for [...] visually impaired people so that they too can lead a normal and independent life like other people." (Swathi & Shetty, 2019).[515] Indeed, use of a screen-reader, such as VoiceOver, is invaluable to my independence. It has enabled me to access education, pursue hobbies, connect with online communities, research, participate and contribute to countless ventures. Indeed, VoiceOver is also helpfully assisting me in the writing of this very document! It is absolutely evident, that a life without VoiceOver, or similar screen-reading software, would be extremely challenging, not to mention a lot less fulfilling.

However, although providing a much-needed solution to reducing some of the barriers faced by people who are blind and visually impaired, VoiceOver and its screen-reading counterparts does not come without its own challenges. Firstly, in order to use VoiceOver, you must first learn a series of keyboard short-cuts, command keys and or finger swipes which allow you to navigate the screen and select information. Sometimes, frustration can arise if I am attempting to access a particular part of a site, however I just don't know the corresponding key commands or finger movement to trigger it. As well as this practical issue, VoiceOver is also not always able to give information if the

---

[515] Swathi, M., & Shetty, M. M. "Assistance System for Visually Impaired using AI". *International Journal of Engineering Research & Technology*, vol. 7, no. 08, 2019, Conclusion.

document or site I am wanting to access is incompatible with its software. In these instances, I then have to creatively find a way around these barriers, either enlisting a sighted person's support, or the use of another form of technology.

Laura's Voice about Siri

I use Siri a lot on a daily basis. It helps me organise my schedule and set reminders, avoiding the need for a paper-based diary. When dressing my baby, asking Siri for the day's weather forecast enables me to choose appropriate clothing and avoids the need for me to physically go outside to check the temperature. Siri helps me look up word definitions quickly without the use of a website or dictionary and it can even read out recipes to me when cooking. Indeed, there are numerous, varied ways Siri is able to help me be independent.

However, whilst Siri is extremely helpful and efficient, my dependence upon it means that I must also accept some, less welcome aspects of engaging with the interface. Protecting my privacy is a concern I have when I am so reliant on engaging with Siri. My voice commands, queries and requests all constitute personal data. Having the ever-present ear of Siri enabled on my phone and tablet means that I may be providing personal data to technology companies (Schmeiser, 2017).[516] It is not clear how the information you give Siri is used and this lack of transparency is concerning.

Siri, as a helpful, friendly assistant has a constantly upbeat manner. When asking Siri to research something, it replies "great! I've found this on the web, check it out!" in a positive, seemingly happy manner. Whilst, of course, it is understandable why Siri has been programmed in

---

[516] Schmeiser, L. "How much dirt does Siri have on you?", *The Observer*, 06/09/2017, https://observer.com/2017/06/siri-voice-assistants-data-collection-speech-recognition/

this way, there are times when such responses are not welcome, or indeed appropriate.

When asking Siri for information relating to a sensitive topic, its upbeat stock response can sometimes feel, in my view, somewhat unhelpful. When asking Siri to message details of the death of my guide dog, Siri's response of *great* after sending the message seemed somewhat inappropriate and uncomfortable, given the circumstances. Of course, I realise Siri is not sophisticated enough to read moods and dynamically alter its tone in response to situations. However, its default programming of perpetual happiness can be, in my view, sometimes problematic.

Conclusion

This chapter has presented the *voice* of some common AI products and the functionality which they can offer, particularly in terms of supporting disabled individuals. This is then contrasted with the voices of the two authors, who are both disabled in very different ways; one is blind, the other is physically disabled without the use of his hands. We both make a lot of use of AI products to go about our day-to-day business. These products enable also both to achieve much. They enable our independence and also support us in writing material such as this book chapter. Without them we would not be able to function at the same level. None of the products are perfect, however, they are constantly improving and developing and the positives far outweigh any negatives.

AI technology is helping support the life of many disabled people around the world. It will continue to improve over time and we look forward to new products appearing which will provide us with further independence. The main drawback is the concern that some of these products may be collecting data about the users, their activities, their preferences; particularly in relation to purchasing activity. However, this is not only a concern to disabled people, it is a general concern to the public at large (Cappel, Shah & Verhulsdonck, 2020).[517]

---

[517] Cappel, J. J., Shah, V., & Verhulsdonck, G. "Perceptions of Online Privacy". *Journal of Business and Educational Leadership*, 10(1), 2020, 122-133.

FURTHER READING

Ada Lovelace Institute, 'Ethics and accountability in practice', https://www.adalovelaceinstitute.org/our-work/programmes/ethics-accountability-practice

AI Saturdays Lagos, https://www.aisaturdayslagos.com

Algorithmic Justice League, 'Library', https://www.ajl.org/library/home

Azar, E. and Haddad, A. (Eds.), *Artificial Intelligence in the Gulf: Challenges and Opportunities*, Singapore, Palgrave Macmillan, 2021.

Bamforth, E., 'How higher ed is handling AI ethics', *EdScoop* 24 November 2021, https://edscoop.com/list/how-higher-ed-is-handling-ai-ethics/

Chan, D., 'The AI that has nothing to learn from humans'. *The Atlantic*, 20 October 2017, https://www.theatlantic.com/technology/archive/2017/10/alphago-zero-the-ai-that-taught-itself-go/543450/

Contact North, 'Ten Facts About Artificial Intelligence in Teaching and Learning', https://teachonline.ca/sites/default/files/tools-trends/downloads/ten_facts_about_artificial_intelligence_0.pdf

Critical Design Lab, https://www.mapping-access.com/lab

Data & Society, 'AI on the Ground', https://datasociety.net/research/ai-on-the-ground/

Ding, J. (Ed.), *ChinAI Newsletter*, https://chinai.substack.com

European Commission, 'Digital Education Action Plan', https://education.ec.europa.eu/focus-topics/digital/education-action-plan

Farrelly, Glen, 'AI is here to help postsecondary educators (not take over)', University Affairs, 7 July 2021, https://www.university affairs.ca/career-advice/career-advice-article/ai-is-here-to-help-postsecondary-educators-not-take-over/

Gal, D., 'Perspectives and Approaches in AI Ethics: East Asia' in Dubber, M., Pasquale, F., and Das, S. (Eds.) *The Oxford Handbook of Ethics of AI*, 2020, https://doi.org/10.1093/oxfordhb/9780190067397.013.39

Gebru, T., 'Race and Gender', in Dubber, M., Pasquale, F., and Das, S. (Eds.) *The Oxford Handbook of Ethics of AI*, 2020, https://doi.org/10.1093/oxfordhb/9780190067397.013.16

Global CIO Forum, 'AI Ethics in the West is not necessarily the same as in the Middle East', https://globalcioforum.com/ai-ethics-in-the-west-is-not-necessarily-the-same-as-in-the-middle-east/

Gomez-Mont, C., *et al.*, 'Artificial Intelligence for Social Good in Latin America and the Caribbean: The Regional Landscape and 12 Country Snapshots', Inter-American Development Bank, July 2020, https://publications.iadb.org/publications/english/document/Artificial-Intelligence-for-Social-Good-in-Latin-America-and-the-Caribbean-The-Regional-Landscape-and-12-Country-Snapshots.pdf

Gwagwa, A., 'Recommendations on the inclusion of sub-Saharan Africa in Global AI Ethics', *Research ICT Africa*, https://researchictafrica.net/wp/wp-content/uploads/2020/11/RANITP2019-2-AI-Ethics.pdf

Hamraie, A., *Building Access: Universal Design and the Politics of Disability*, Minneapolis, MN, University of Minnesota Press, 2017.

Holmes, W., *et al.* 'Ethics of AI in Education: Towards a Community-Wide Framework', *International Journal of Artificial Intelligence in Education*, 2021. https://doi.org/10.1007/s40593-021-00239-1

The Institute for Ethical AI in Education, 'The Ethical Framework for AI in Education,' https://www.buckingham.ac.uk/wp-content/uploads/2021/03/The-Institute-for-Ethical-AI-in-Education-The-Ethical-Framework-for-AI-in-Education.pdf

Kiemde, S.M.A, Kora, A.D., 'Towards an ethics of AI in Africa: Rule of education', *AI Ethics*, https://doi.org/10.1007/s43681-021-00106-8

Kim, D., 'Advancing AI Ethics in Japan: A Q&A with Dr. Arisa Ema, Professor at University of Tokyo,' *Asia Pacific Foundation of Canada*, https://www.asiapacific.ca/publication/advancing-ai-ethics-japan-qa-dr-arisa-ema-professor

Koroleva, E. and Kuratova, A. 'Higher Education and Digitalization of the Economy: The Case of Russian Regions', *International Journal of Technology*, 11:6 (2020), 1181-1190, https://doi.org/10.14716/ijtech.v11i6.4431

Mohamed bin Zayed University of Artificial Intelligence, 'Webinars', https://mbzuai.ac.ae/aitalks/webinars/

Rizk, N., 'Artificial Intelligence and Inequality in the Middle East: The Political Economy of Inclusion,' in Dubber, M., Pasquale, F., and Das, S. (Eds.) *The Oxford Handbook of Ethics of AI*, 2020, https://www.oxfordhandbooks.com/view/10.1093/oxfordhb/9780190067397.001.0001/oxfordhb-9780190067397-e-40

Saveliev, A., and Zhurenkov, D., 'Artificial intelligence and social responsibility: the case of the artificial intelligence strategies in the United States, Russia, and China', *Kybernetes* 50:3, 2021.

Seldon, A., and Abidoye, O., *The Fourth Education Revolution: Will Artificial Intelligence Liberate or Infantilise Humanity*, London, UK, Legend Press Ltd., 2018.

Smuha, N., 'Trustworthy Artificial Intelligence in Education: Pitfalls and Pathways', December 2020, http://dx.doi.org/10.2139/ssrn.3742421

Taiuru K., 'Indigenising through Te Taha Wairua: AI, Algorithms, Data, Internet and IOT', https://www.taiuru.maori.nz/indigenising-through-te-taha-wairua-ai-algorithms-data-internet-and-iot/

Zeide, E., 'Artificial Intelligence in higher education: applications, promise and perils, and ethical questions,' *EduCause Review*, 26 August 2019, https://er.educause.edu/articles/2019/8/artificial-intelligence-in-higher-education-applications-promise-and-perils-and-ethical-questions

CONTRIBUTORS

Andrea Mariel Actis, PhD, from Buenos Aires, Argentina, is a Biochemist and Pharmacist from Buenos Aires University (UBA). She is Assistant Professor at the Faculty of Medicine (UBA) since 1992, teaching biochemistry, bioethics, the history of medicine and medical social anthropology. She has postgraduate certificates in bioethics, health technology assessment, university assessment, teaching with information and communication technologies, as well as AI and cyber ethics.

Mac Adkins is founder and Chief Academic Officer of SmarterServices. Since 2002, he has led the company as it has grown to serve over five million students and 12 thousand faculty at over 500 institutions. Over the past 25 years, he has held a variety of leadership roles in higher education, including Dean of Distance Education. He also serves as a course reviewer for the International Distance Education Certification Center, and has authored, designed, and delivered a certification program for the IDECC. He is a frequent public speaker and also serves on several advisory and review boards.

Peng Hwa Ang teaches and researches media governance and ethics at Nanyang Technological University, Singapore. He is the author of Ordering Chaos: Regulating the Internet (Cengage, 2005), and in 2004 was appointed by then UN Secretary General Kofi Annan to the 40-strong Working Group on Internet Governance. He co-founded the Global Internet Governance Academic Network and the Asia Pacific Regional Internet Governance Forum and served as inaugural chairs of both organisations. He served as President of the International Communication Association in 2017. He is currently Chair of the Advertising Standards Authority of Singapore and editor of the Asian Journal of Communication.

Dhwaanii Arora graduated from Ashoka University with a Bachelor of Arts (Honours) degree in Political Science and International Relations. She has worked in different sectors including education, human resources in not-for-profits, and startups. She has a keen interest in exploring the impact of technology on various aspects of our lives such as diplomacy, its large-scale implications, and how it can be used to transform lives. She likes to read on topics varying from sports, international relations, human behaviour, among other things. Dhwaanii is currently working at an HR tech start up as an Entrepreneur in Residence, building a product extension that is focused on upskilling and training people. She spends her spare time volunteering with organisations that create impact on the society and also started her own social venture, Walk n Talk, which is aimed at improving the overall lifestyle of elderly citizens in her community.

Alice Beck is project officer autonomous weapons at the Dutch peace organisation PAX. She focuses on the positions of European countries and the role of the private sector in the development of autonomy in weapon systems.

Maaike Beenes is project officer autonomous weapons at the Dutch peace organisation PAX. Her expertise is the role of the financial sector in investing in controversial weapons producers and working to get these institutions to divest.

Roland Chia is Chew Hock Hin Professor of Christian Doctrine at Trinity Theological College and the Theological and Research

Advisor of the Ethos Institute for Public Christianity (ethosinstitute.sg). Dr Chia has published essays on theology, the arts, culture, aesthetics, politics, science and religion and music in a number of journals and is a member of the Global Network for Digital Theology, the Advisory Board for Lausanne Movement Workplace Ministry and the National Transplant Ethics Committee. His recent publications include Hope for the World: A Christian Vision of the Last Things, The Right to Die? A Christian Response to Euthanasia and Hybrids, Cybrids and Chimeras: The Ethics of Interspecies Research.

D. Dinakaran has 20 years of experience in teaching, industry, and research in the field of robotics and automation. He has received six research grants from national and international agencies. He has developed three industry funded research laboratories at Hindustan Institute of Technology and Science. His specialisation includes robotics, low cost automation, condition monitoring and manufacturing processes. He is an executive member of the Condition Monitoring Society of India.

Leonard Chrysostomos Epafras is a faculty member and researcher at the Universitas Kristen Duta Wacana and Indonesian Consortium for Religious Studies, Indonesia. Dr Epafras teaches history of religions, theology and modern sciences, advanced study of Christianity, Judaism, and more. His research topics include religion online, religion and popular culture, interreligious studies, and Judaism. Dr. Epafras publications and full CV can be accessed at leonardchrysostomosepafras.academia.edu.

José-Luis Fernández-Fernández is director of the Iberdrola Chair in Economic and Business Ethics and professor at the Faculty of Economics and Business Administration (ICADE) at Universidad Pontificia Comillas. He is also a visiting professor at the faculty of social sciences at the Pontificia Università Gregoriana (Rome). He is a fellow of the Caux Round Table, chairman of the ethics and social responsibility subcommittee (CTN 165 SC2) of the Spanish Association for Standardization (UNE). He is also an advisory board member for several organisations, including ASCOM, Impact Bridge, and Sostenibilidad Ética.

Erin Green is an interdisciplinary researcher and digital tech advocate working in the area of AI, democracy, and disarmament. She holds a PhD from the University of St Michael's College where she developed a novel interdisciplinary approach to understanding and responding to the historical, ecological, and social impacts of AI and robots. Erin gives frequent lectures and interviews about the militarisation of AI, democracy, and how to respond to these technologies from a theological and ethical perspective. Erin also has over 15 years' experience working in communications in the NGO sector and is dedicated to ecological and social justice.

Erny Gillen, Luxembourg, Ethicist, is the founder and CEO of Moral Factory. He is an internationally experienced specialist in social ethics and works with private companies, governments as well as public and non-profit organisations willing to address their values and normative systems. For more information: moralfactory.com

Brad Huddleston is an international speaker, consultant, teacher, and author on important issues such as technology and culture. He has worked with universities, schools, churches, and law enforcement, and spoken to hundreds of thousands around the world on both the advantages of well-used technology tools and the dangers of the growing trend toward technology addiction. Brad has an ongoing collaboration with the Bureau of Market Research (BMR) and its Neuroscience Division at the University of South Africa. Brad has a degree in Computer Science and a Diploma in Biblical Studies and is a credentialed minister in the Acts 2 Alliance (A2A) movement in Australia. He's also a frequent guest on radio and television and author of Digital Cocaine: A Journey Toward iBalance and The Dark Side of Technology: Restoring Balance in the Digital Age.

R. W. Alexander Jesudasan is the former principal and secretary of Madras Christian College, which is one of the historic and premier Liberal Arts and Science Colleges in India. Dr Jesudasan is now associated with the Hindustan Institute of Technology and Science with his vast experience in Higher Education Administration. He has been an active researcher with many high-quality publications, guided research scholars, conducted funded research projects and held several responsibilities both at the national and international levels. His passion for new technologies with a concern for ethics and environment has been aptly demonstrated. He has authored many articles on higher education in a reputed National Daily.

Daan Kayser is project leader autonomous weapons at the Dutch peace organisation PAX. His work focuses on tracking developments in increasing autonomy in weapon systems. He also closely follows political developments in European countries.

Carina Lion holds a PhD in Education Sciences from the University of Buenos Aires. She is Professor of Education and Technologies as well as Communication and Education in the Department of Education Sciences at the University of Buenos Aires. She is the principal evaluator of national and international university degrees and an international consultant on technology and education issues. She is the executive director of Edutrama and holds three patents of ownership. Her recent publications include Learning and Technologies: Present skills, future projections (Novedades Educativas, Buenos Aires).

D. John Methuselah is an educational consultant who encourages disruptive thinking for ethical testing, evaluation and assessment in schools and colleges. He is experienced in Industry-Academia interface. He is also a published poet. Currently he teaches English Literature at Adikavi Nannayya University, Rajahmundry, Andhra Pradesh, India.

M.M. Ramya is currently a professor in the Centre for Automation and Robotics (ANRO) at the Hindustan Institute of Technology and Science. Her research activities focus on machine learning, with particular emphasis on image processing applications. She has published over 40 refereed papers and two chapters in books. She has guided over 15 PhDs and is a Life Member of Soft Computing Research Society, a member of Institution of Engineering and Technology, and Board Member of International Society for Stereology and Image Analysis.

Avani Singh is an independent legal consultant and a digital rights specialist. She is an attorney of the High Court of South Africa, as well as a certified mediator. She previously co-founded ALT Advisory and Power Singh Inc., and has also worked in the Dispute Resolution team at Webber Wentzel and the Constitutional Litigation Unit at the Legal Resources Centre. Further to this, she clerked at the Constitutional Court of South Africa and the International Criminal Court. Her work focuses primarily on research, policy and litigation in the fields of constitutional law, privacy and emergent technologies, with a particular interest in issues pertaining to artificial intelligence.

Divya Singh holds a Doctorate in Law and a second Masters in Tertiary Education Management. She is a certified ethics officer and the Executive Director of Globethics.net, Southern Africa. Divya is a professionally trained advocate and her academic career in higher education spans more than thirty years, including leadership roles in public and private higher education institutions. Divya is currently the Chief Academic Officer at STADIO Holdings Ltd, a private higher education investment company listed on the Johannesburg Stock Exchange. Her research profile includes extensive journal articles, chapters, and the editing of many publications in law, ethics, values-driven leadership, education innovation and online learning. She has served on boards, commissions of enquiry, and audit committees and has received acclaim and stakeholder recognition both domestically and internationally for her academic contributions and community engagement.

Laura Smith is a sociologist, teacher, and musician. She lost her sight at a young age and continues to live a happy and fulfilled life. She publishes, sometimes with Peter, on topics relating to disability, rock music and the UK radio show "The Archers", of which she is a passionate follower and listener. She is a mother of two children and lives in the North-East of the UK. She is a qualified social worker, teacher and a classically trained singing teacher.

Peter Smith is Emeritus Professor at the University of Sunderland, UK. He is paralysed from the neck down; however, he continues to teach students online, and research and write about a number of topics. He has recently published articles and books on topics related to disability, postgraduate education and rock music. He supports a number of students who are completing their Masters dissertations and PhD theses.

Ezekiel Kwetchi Takam is an assistant in theological ethics, as part of his PhD contract at the University of Geneva. His research explores, from a theological perspective, the ethical issues of artificial intelligence. More precisely, he proposes, in the light of the theology of justice, a critique of algorithmic injustice and data injustice. In parallel to his research, he is the founder of the Euro-African Observatory of Artificial Intelligence, a think tank that works for an ethical culture of artificial intelligence in Europe and Africa. It is within the framework of this project that he was awarded the Geneus-Fongit Prize: Prize for the Best Idea - Life Science, which is awarded by the Geneus incubator of the Geneva Foundation for Technological Innovation.

Globethics.net Publications

The list below is only a selection of our publications. To view the full collection, please visit our website.

All products are provided free of charge and can be downloaded in PDF form from the Globethics.net library and at www.globethics.net/publications. Bulk print copies can be ordered from *publictions@globethics.net* at special rates for those from the Global South.
Paid products not provided free of charge are indicated*.
The Editor of the different Series of Globethics.net Publications is Prof. Dr Obiora Ike, Executive Director of Globethics.net in Geneva and Professor of Ethics at the Godfrey Okoye University Enugu/Nigeria.

Contact for manuscripts and suggestions: *publications@globethics.net*

Global Series

Christoph Stückelberger / Jesse N.K. Mugambi (eds.), *Responsible Leadership. Global and Contextual Perspectives*, 2007, 376pp. ISBN: 978–2–8254–1516–0

Heidi Hadsell / Christoph Stückelberger (eds.), *Overcoming Fundamentalism. Ethical Responses from Five Continents*, 2009, 212pp.
ISBN: 978–2–940428–00–7

Ariane Hentsch Cisneros / Shanta Premawardhana (eds.), *Sharing Values. A Hermeneutics for Global Ethics*, 2010, 418pp.
ISBN: 978–2–940428–25–0.

Christoph Stückelberger, Walter Fust, Obiora Ike (eds.), *Global Ethics for Leadership. Values and Virtues for Life,* 2016, 444pp.
ISBN: 978–2–88931–123–1

Dietrich Werner / Elisabeth Jeglitzka (eds.), *Eco-Theology, Climate Justice and Food Security: Theological Education and Christian Leadership Development,* 316pp. 2016, ISBN 978–2–88931–145–3

Obiora Ike, Andrea Grieder and Ignace Haaz (Eds.), *Poetry and Ethics: Inventing Possibilities in Which We Are Moved to Action and How We Live Together,* 271pp. 2018, ISBN 978–2–88931–242–9

Christoph Stückelberger / Pavan Duggal (Eds.), *Cyber Ethics 4.0: Serving Humanity with Values,* 503pp. 2018, ISBN 978–2–88931-264-1

Texts Series

Principles on Sharing Values across Cultures and Religions, 2012, 20pp. Available in English, French, Spanish, German and Chinese. Other languages in preparation. ISBN: 978–2–940428–09–0

Ethics in Politics. Why it Matters More than Ever and How it Can Make a Difference. A Declaration, 8pp, 2012. Available in English and French. ISBN: 978–2–940428–35–9

Religions for Climate Justice: International Interfaith Statements 2008–2014, 2014, 45pp. Available in English. ISBN 978–2–88931–006–7

Ethics in the Information Society: The Nine 'P's. A Discussion Paper for the WSIS+10 Process 2013–2015, 2013, 32pp. ISBN: 978–2–940428–063–2

Principles on Equality and Inequality for a Sustainable Economy. Endorsed by the Global Ethics Forum 2014 with Results from Ben Africa Conference 2014, 2015, 41pp. ISBN: 978–2–88931–025–8

Water Ethics: Principles and Guidelines, 2019, 41pp. ISBN 978–2–88931-313-6, available in three languages.

Ethics in Higher Education. A Key Driver for Recovery in a World Living with COVID-19. A Globethics.net Discussion Paper, 2022, 44pp.. ISBN 978-2-88931-440-9

Praxis Series

Christoph Stückelberger, *Responsible Leadership Handbook : For Staff and Boards,* 2014, 116pp. ISBN :978-2-88931-019-7 (Available in Russian)

Oscar Brenifier, *Day After Day 365 Aphorisms,* 2019, 395pp. ISBN 978-2-88931-272-6

Christoph Stückelberger, *365 Way-Markers,* 2019, 416pp. ISBN: 978-2-88931-282-5 (available in English and German).

Benoît Girardin / Evelyne Fiechter-Widemann (Eds.), *Blue Ethics: Ethical Perspectives on Sustainable, Fair Water Resources Use and Management,* forthcoming 2019, 265pp. ISBN 978-2-88931-308-2

Didier Ostermann, *Le rôle de l'Église maronite dans la construction du Liban: 1500 ans d'histoire, du Ve au XXe siècle,* 2020, 122pp. ISBN: 978-2-88931-365-5

Elli Kansiime, *Theology of Work and Development,* 2020, 158pp. ISBN: 978-2-88931-373-0

Christoph Stückelberger (Ed.), *Corruption-free Religions are Possible: Integrity, Stewardship, Accountability,* 2021, 295pp. ISBN: 978-2-88931-422-5

Philosophy Series

Ignace Haaz, *Empathy and Indifference: Philosophical Reflections on Schizophrenia,* 2020, 154pp. ISBN 978-2-88931-345-7

Theses Series

Symphorien Ntibagirirwa, *Philosophical Premises for African Economic Development: Sen's Capability Approach,* 2014, 384pp.
ISBN: 978–2–88931–001–2

Jude Likori Omukaga, *Right to Food Ethics: Theological Approaches of Asbjørn Eide,* 2015, 609pp. ISBN: 978–2–88931–047–0

Jörg F. W. Bürgi, *Improving Sustainable Performance of SME's, The Dynamic Interplay of Morality and Management Systems,* 2014, 528pp.
ISBN: 978–2–88931–015–9

Jun Yan, *Local Culture and Early Parenting in China: A Case Study on Chinese Christian Mothers' Childrearing Experiences,* 2015, 190pp.
ISBN 978–2–88931–065–4

Frédéric-Paul Piguet, *Justice climatique et interdiction de nuire,* 2014, 559 pp.
ISBN 978–2–88931–005–0

Mulolwa Kashindi, *Appellations johanniques de Jésus dans l'Apocalypse: une lecture Bafuliiru des titres christologiques,* 2015, 577pp. ISBN 978–2–88931–040–1

Naupess K. Kibiswa, *Ethnonationalism and Conflict Resolution: The Armed Group Bany2 in DR Congo.* 2015, 528pp. ISBN: 978–2–88931–032–6

John Kasuku, *Intelligence Reform in the Post-Dictatorial Democratic Republic of Congo,* 2016, 355pp. ISBN 978–2–88931–121–7

Tibor Héjj, *Human Dignity in Managing Employees. A performative approach, based on the Catholic Social Teaching (CST),* 2019, 320pp. ISBN: 978-2-88931-280-1

Sabina Kavutha Mutisya, *The Experience of Being a Divorced or Separated Single Mother: A Phenomenological Study,* 2019, 168pp. ISBN: 978-2-88931-274-0

Florence Muia, *Sustainable Peacebuilding Strategies. Sustainable Peacebuilding Operations in Nakuru County, Kenya: Contribution to the Catholic Justice and Peace Commission (CJPC)*, 2020, 195pp. ISBN: 978-2-88931-331-0

Nestor Engone Elloué, *La justice climatique restaurative: Réparer les inégalités Nord/Sud*, 2020, 198pp. ISBN 978-2-88931-379-2

Hilary C. Ike, *Organizational Improvement of Nigerian Catholic Chaplaincy in Central Ohio*, 2021, 154pp. ISBN 978-2-88931-385-3

Paul K. Musolo W'Isuka, *Missional Encounter: Approach for Ministering to Invisible Peoples*, 2021, 462pp. ISBN: 978-2-88931-401-0

Education Ethics Series

Divya Singh / Christoph Stückelberger (Eds.), *Ethics in Higher Education Values-driven Leaders for the Future*, 2017, 367pp. ISBN: 978–2–88931–165–1

Obiora Ike / Chidiebere Onyia (Eds.) *Ethics in Higher Education, Foundation for Sustainable Development*, 2018, 645pp. IBSN: 978-2-88931-217-7

Obiora Ike / Chidiebere Onyia (Eds.) *Ethics in Higher Education, Religions and Traditions in Nigeria* 2018, 198pp. IBSN: 978-2-88931-219-1

Obiora F. Ike, Justus Mbae, Chidiebere Onyia (Eds.), *Mainstreaming Ethics in Higher Education: Research Ethics in Administration, Finance, Education, Environment and Law Vol. 1*, 2019, 779pp. ISBN 978-2-88931-300-6

Ikechukwu J. Ani/Obiora F. Ike (Eds.), *Higher Education in Crisis Sustaining Quality Assurance and Innovation in Research through Applied Ethics*, 2019, 214pp. ISBN 978-2-88931-323-5

Obiora Ike, Justus Mbae, Chidiebere Onyia, Herbert Makinda (Eds.), *Mainstreaming Ethics in Higher Education Vol. 2*, 2021, 420pp. ISBN: 978-2-88931-383-9

Christoph Stückelberger, Joseph Galgalo and Samuel Kobia (Eds.), *Leadership with Integrity: Higher Education from Vocation to Funding*, 2021, 280pp. ISBN: 978-2-88931-389-1

Jacinta M. Adhiambo and Florentina N. Ndeke (Eds.), *Educating Teachers for Tomorrow: on Ethics and quality in Pedagogical Formation*, 2021, 196pp. ISBN: 978-2-88931-407-2

Erin Green / Divya Singh / Roland Chia (Eds.), *AI Ethics and Higher Education Good Practice and Guidance for Educators, Learners, and Institutions*, 2022, 324pp. ISBN 978-2-88931-442-3

Co-publications & Other

Jose Nandhikkara (Ed.), *Environmental Interface: Literature, Law, Science, and Philosophy*, 2015, 42pp. ISBN: 978938496417-7

Patrice Meyer-Bisch, Stefania Gandolfi and Greta Balliu (Eds.), *Souveraineté et coopérations: Guide pour fonder toute governance démocratique sur l'interdépendance des droits de l'homme*, 2016, 101pp. ISBN: 978-2-88931-118-7 (Available in Italian)

Samuel Ngayihembako Mutahinga, *Le déclin des Baghole. Processus d'aliénation sociale des femmes en Afrique centrale*, 2018, 166pp. ISBN: 978-2-88931-262-7

Stefania Gandolfi (Ed.), *Diaspore y democrazie. Le diaspore sono portatrici di valori*, 2018, 207pp. ISBN: 978-2-88931-266-5

Patrice Meyer-Bisch, Stefania Gandolfi, Greta Balliu (Eds.), *L'interdépendance des droits de l'homme au principe de toute gouvernance démocratique. Commentaire de Souveraineté et coopération*, 2019, 324pp. ISBN: 978-2-88931-310-5

Obiora F. Ike, *Applied Ethics to Issues of Development Culture, Religion and Education*, 2020, 280pp. ISBN: 978-2-88931-335-8

Obiora F. Ike, *Moral and Ethical Leadership, Human Rights and Conflict Resolution – African and Global Contexts*, 2020, 191pp. ISBN: 978-2-88931-333-4

Kenneth R. Ross, *Mission Rediscovered: Transforming Disciples*, 2020, 138pp. ISBN 978-2-88931-369-3

Obiora Ike, Amélé Adamavi-Aho Ekué, Anja Andriamay, Lucy Howe López (Eds.), *Who Cares About Ethics? 2020*, 352pp. ISBN 978-2-88931-381-5

Obiora Ike, Amelé Adamavi-Aho Ekué, Anja Andriamasy and Lucy Howe López (Eds.), *Who Cares About Ethics?*, 2020, 352pp. ISBN: 978-2-88931-381-5

Fanny Iona Morel, *Whispers from the Land of Snows: Culture-based Violence in Tibet.* 2021, 218pp. ISBN: 978-2-88931-418-8

Ignace Haaz, Amélé Adamavi-Aho Ekué (Eds.), *Walking with the Earth, Intercultural Perspectives on Ethics of Ecological Caring*, 2022, 324pp. ISBN: 978-2-88931-434-8

This is only a selection of our latest publications, to view our full collection please visit:

www.globethics.net/publications